Enterprise Risk Management

Applied CQRM Book Series

Volume IV

Applying Monte Carlo Risk Simulation, Strategic Real
Options, Stochastic Forecasting, Portfolio Optimization,
Data and Decision Analytics

IIPER Press

IIPER
Press

Johnathan Mun, Ph.D.

California, USA

ROV Project Economics Analysis Tool

For Jayden, Emma, and Penny.

In a world where risk and uncertainty abound, you are the only constants in my life.

Dedicated in loving memory of my mom.

Delight yourself in the Lord and He will give you the desires of your heart.

Psalm 37:4

Printed in the United States of America

PREFACE

The Applied CQRM Book Series showcases how the advanced analytics covered in the Certified in Quantitative Risk Management (CQRM) certification program can be applied to real-life business problems. In Volume IV, we show how these analytics can be applied in the context of Enterprise Risk Management, using both qualitative risk registers and extending the results using quantitative analytical methods.

Pragmatic applications are emphasized in order to demystify the many elements inherent in risk analysis. A black box will remain a black box if no one can understand the concepts despite its power and applicability. It is only when the black box methods become transparent, so that researchers can understand, apply, and convince others of their results, value-add, and applicability, that the approaches will receive widespread attention. This transparency is achieved through step-by-step applications of quantitative modeling as well as presenting multiple cases and discussing real-life applications.

This book is targeted at those individuals who have completed the CQRM certification program but can also be used by anyone familiar with basic quantitative research methods—there is something for everyone. It is also applicable for use as a second-year MBA/MS-level or introductory PhD textbook. The examples in the book assume some prior knowledge of the subject matter.

Additional information on the CQRM program can be obtained at:

www.iiper.org

www.realoptionsvaluation.com

www.rovusa.com

Dr. Johnathan C. Mun is the founder, chairman, and CEO of Real Options Valuation, Inc. (ROV), a consulting, training, and software development firm specializing in strategic real options, financial valuation, Monte Carlo risk simulation, stochastic forecasting, optimization, decision analytics, business intelligence, healthcare analytics, enterprise risk management, project risk management, quantitative research methods, and risk analysis located in northern Silicon Valley, California. ROV has partners around the world including Argentina, Beijing, Chicago, China, Colombia, Ghana, Hong Kong, India, Italy, Japan, Malaysia, Mexico City, New York, Nigeria, Peru, Puerto Rico, Russia, Saudi Arabia, Shanghai, Singapore, Slovenia, South Africa, South Korea, Spain, United Kingdom, Venezuela, Zurich, and others. ROV also has a local office in Shanghai.

Dr. Mun is also the chairman of the International Institute of Professional Education and Research (IIPER), an accredited global organization staffed by professors from named universities from around the world that provides the Certified in Quantitative Risk Management (CQRM) and Certified in Risk Management (CRM) designations, among others. He is the creator of many powerful software tools including Risk Simulator, Real Options SLS Super Lattice Solver, Modeling Toolkit, Project Economics Analysis Tool (PEAT), Credit Market Operational Liquidity Risk (CMOL), Employee Stock Options Valuation, ROV BizStats, ROV Modeler Suite (Basel Credit Modeler, Risk Modeler, Optimizer, and Valuator), ROV Compiler, ROV Extractor and Evaluator, ROV Dashboard, ROV Quantitative Data Miner, and other software applications, as well as the risk-analysis training DVD. He holds public seminars on risk analysis and CQRM programs. He has over 21 registered patents and patents pending globally. He has authored over 23 books published by John Wiley & Sons, Elsevier Science, IIPER Press, and ROV Press, including multiple volumes of the Applied CQRM Series (IIPER Press, 2019-2020); *Modeling Risk: Applying Monte Carlo Simulation, Strategic Real Options, Stochastic Forecasting, Portfolio Optimization, Data Analytics, Business Intelligence, and Decision Modeling,* First Edition (Wiley, 2006), Second Edition (Wiley, 2010), and Third Edition

(ROV Press, 2015); *The Banker's Handbook on Credit Risk* (2008); *Advanced Analytical Models: 250 Applications from Basel II Accord to Wall Street and Beyond* (2008); *Real Options Analysis: Tools and Techniques,* First Edition (2003) and Second Edition (2005); *Real Options Analysis Course: Business Cases* (2003); *Applied Risk Analysis: Moving Beyond Uncertainty* (2003); and *Valuing Employee Stock Options* (2004). His books and software are being used at over 350 top universities around the world, including the Bern Institute in Germany, Chung-Ang University in South Korea, Georgetown University, ITESM in Mexico, Massachusetts Institute of Technology, U.S. Naval Postgraduate School, New York University, Stockholm University in Sweden, University of the Andes in Chile, University of Chile, University of Hull, University of Pennsylvania Wharton School, University of York in the United Kingdom, and Edinburgh University in Scotland, among others.

Currently a risk, finance, and economics professor, Dr. Mun has taught courses in financial management, investments, real options, economics, and statistics at the undergraduate and the graduate MS, MBA, and PhD levels. He teaches and has taught at universities all over the world, from the U.S. Naval Postgraduate School (Monterey, California) and University of Applied Sciences (Switzerland and Germany) as full professor, to Golden Gate University (California) and St. Mary's College (California), and has chaired many graduate research MBA thesis and PhD dissertation committees. He also teaches weeklong Risk Analysis, Real Options Analysis, and Risk Analysis for Managers public courses where participants can obtain the CRM and CQRM designations on completion. He is a senior fellow at the Magellan Center and sits on the board of standards at the American Academy of Financial Management.

He was formerly the Vice President of Analytics at Decisioneering, Inc., where he headed the development of options and financial analytics software products, analytical consulting, training, and technical support, and where he was the creator of the Real Options Analysis Toolkit software, the older and much less powerful predecessor of the Real Options Super Lattice software. Prior to joining Decisioneering, he was a Consulting Manager and Financial Economist in the Valuation Services and Global Financial Services practice of KPMG Consulting and a Manager with the Economic Consulting Services practice at KPMG LLP.

He has extensive experience in econometric modeling, financial analysis, real options, economic analysis, and statistics. During his tenure at Real Options Valuation, Inc., Decisioneering, and KPMG Consulting, he taught and consulted on a variety of real options, risk analysis, financial forecasting, project management, and financial valuation issues for more than 100 multinational firms (current and former clients include 3M, Airbus, Boeing, BP, Chevron Texaco, Financial Accounting Standards Board, Fujitsu, GE, Goodyear, Microsoft, Motorola, Northtrop Grumman, Pfizer, Timken, U.S. Department of Defense, U.S. Navy, Veritas, and many others). His experience prior to joining KPMG included being department head of financial planning and analysis at Viking Inc. of FedEx, performing financial forecasting, economic analysis, and market research. Prior to that, he did financial planning and freelance financial consulting work.

Dr. Mun received a PhD in finance and economics from Lehigh University, where his research and academic interests were in the areas of investment finance, econometric modeling, financial options, corporate finance, and microeconomic theory. He also has an MBA in business administration, an MS in management science, and a BS in biology and physics. He is Certified in Financial Risk Management, Certified in Financial Consulting, and Certified in Quantitative Risk Management. He is a member of the American Mensa, Phi Beta Kappa Honor Society, and Golden Key Honor Society as well as several other professional organizations, including the Eastern and Southern Finance Associations, American Economic Association, and Global Association of Risk Professionals.

In addition, he has written many academic articles published in the *Journal of Expert Systems with Applications; Defense Acquisition Research Journal; American Institute of Physics Proceedings; Acquisitions Research (U.S. Department of Defense); Journal of the Advances in Quantitative Accounting and Finance; Global Finance Journal; International Financial Review; Journal of Financial Analysis; Journal of Applied Financial Economics; Journal of International Financial Markets, Institutions and Money; Financial Engineering News;* and *Journal of the Society of Petroleum Engineers.* Finally, he has contributed chapters in dozens of books and written over a hundred technical whitepapers, newsletters, case studies, and research papers for Real Options Valuation, Inc.

JohnathanMun@cs.com

San Francisco, California

ACCOLADES FOR DR. MUN'S BOOKS

...powerful toolset for portfolio/program managers to make rational choices among alternatives...
> Rear Admiral James Greene (Ret.), Acquisitions Chair
> Naval Postgraduate School (USA)

...unavoidable for any professional...logical, concrete, and conclusive approach...
> Jean Louis Vaysse, Vice President, Airbus (France)

...proven, revolutionary approach to quantifying risks and opportunities in an uncertain world...
> Mike Twyman, President, Mission Solutions,
> Cubic Global Defense, Inc. (USA)

...must read for anyone running investment economics...best way to quantify risk and strategic options...
> Mubarak A. Alkhater, Executive Director, New Business,
> Saudi Electric Co. (Saudi Arabia)

... pragmatic powerful risk techniques, valuable theoretical insights and analytics useful in any industry...
> Dr. Robert S. Finocchiaro, Director,
> Corporate R&D Services, 3M (USA)

...most important risk tools in one volume, definitive source on risk management with vivid examples...
> Dr. Ricardo Valerdi, Engineering Systems,
> Massachusetts Institute of Technology (USA)

...step-by-step complex concepts with unmatched ease and clarity... a "must read" for all professionals...
> Dr. Hans Weber, Product Development Leader,
> Syngenta AG (Switzerland)

...clear step-by-step approach...latest technology in decision making for real-world business...
> Dr. Paul W. Finnegan, Vice President, Alexion Pharmaceuticals (USA)

...clear roadmap and breadth of topics to create dynamic risk-adjusted strategies and options...
> Jeffrey A. Clark, Vice President Strategic Planning,
> The Timken Company (USA)

...clearly organized and tool-supported exploration of real-life business risks, options, strategy...
> Robert Mack, Vice President, Distinguished Analyst,
> Gartner Group (USA)

...full range of methodologies for quantifying and mitigating risk for effective enterprise management...
> Raymond Heika, Director of Strategic Planning,
> Northrop Grumman Corporation (USA)

...a must-read for product portfolio managers...captures risk exposure of strategic investments...
> Rafael Gutierrez, Executive Director Strategic Marketing Planning,
> Seagate Technologies (USA)

...complex topics exceptionally explained...
can understand and practice...
> Agustín Velázquez, Senior Economist,
> Venezuela Central Bank (Venezuela)

...constant source of practical applications with risk management theory...simply excellent!
> Alfredo Roisenzvit, Executive Director/Professor,
> Risk-Business Latin America (Argentina)

...the best risk modeling book is now better...
required reading by all executives...
> David Mercier, Vice President Corporate Dev.,
> Bonanza Creek Energy [Oil & Gas] (USA)

...bridge of theory and practice, intuitive,
understandable interpretations...
> Luis Melo, Senior Econometrician,
> Colombia Central Bank (Colombia)

...valuable tools for corporations to deliver value to shareholders and society even in rough times...
> Dr. Markus Götz Junginger, Lead Partner,
> Gallup (Germany)

CONTENTS

ENTERPRISE RISK MANAGEMENT

Enterprise Risk Management (ERM) in an organization includes the business processes and methods used to identify and manage risks as well as seize upside opportunities to achieve its objectives. ERM, therefore, provides a specific methodological framework in risk management for identifying risky events or conditions relevant to the organization's objectives, risks, and opportunities, identifying and assessing these conditions in terms of *Likelihood* or frequency of occurrence as well as the risk condition's magnitude of *Impact*, determining risk mitigation and postrisk response strategy, and monitoring the progress of these risk controls. When organizations identify and proactively address risks and opportunities, they are able to protect and create value for their stakeholders (e.g., owners, employees, shareholders, executives, customers, regulators, nations, and society in general).

ERM is also commonly described as a risk-based approach for strategic planning as well as for managing an organization by integrating internal risk controls and external risk-compliance requirements (e.g., COSO, ISO 31000:2009, Basel III, and Sarbanes–Oxley Act). It applies to a broad spectrum of risks facing an organization to ensure that these risks are properly identified and managed. Investors, government regulators, banks, and debt rating agencies, among others, tend to scrutinize the risk-management processes of an organization as a key metric to its potential success.

In addition, the reasons for an organization to implement ERM should, at the very least, include the following areas of concern:

- Alignment of Risk Appetite and Strategy. Senior management typically considers the organization's risk appetite when strategic investment alternatives are being evaluated, as well as when setting objectives and developing mechanisms to manage risks. This tactic helps the organization to align its risk objectives with its business processes.

- Enhanced Risk-Response Decisions. ERM provides both the qualitative and quantitative rigor to identify and select from among alternative risk responses, including strategic real options and analysis of alternatives for risk avoidance, risk reduction, risk sharing, risk mitigation, and risk acceptance.

- Reduction in Operational Surprises and Losses. Organizations will gain enhanced capabilities to Identify, Assess, Prioritize, Value, Diversify, and Mitigate potential risk events' losses using advanced quantitative risk analytics. Instead of just qualitatively identifying risks, organizations can translate these qualitative elements into quantitative risk models where Monte Carlo Risk Simulations, Stochastic Modeling, Portfolio Optimization, Predictive Forecasting, Business Intelligence, and Capital Investment Valuation and Modeling can be performed.

- Identify and Manage Multiple Cross-Enterprise Correlated Risks within a Corporate Portfolio Environment. Every enterprise faces a myriad of risks affecting different parts of the organization. ERM facilitates effective response to these interrelated and correlated impacts and integrates responses to multiple risks. Financial risks and risks in capital investment projects can also be handled within the environment of a correlated portfolio of projects where risks are hedged and diversified.

- Seizing Opportunities. Risks imply uncertainties, and uncertainties carry with them downside risks as well as upside potential. By considering a full range of potential events and risks and creating strategic investment flexibility or strategic real options, management will be positioned to proactively realize upside opportunities, while at the same time mitigate downside risks.

- Improved Capital Deployment. Robust Quantitative Risk Metrics and Key Performance Indicators (KPI) generated through a comprehensive ERM process will allow management to effectively assess overall capital needs and enhance its capital allocation (e.g., creating an efficient investment portfolio subject to budgetary, schedule, strategic, and other constraints).

TRADITIONAL APPROACHES

Traditionally, the ERM process involves *qualitative* risk assessment and documentation. The following lists the standard approach and traditional ERM process, which of course, can be modified and adapted to fit the organization under analysis. Throughout the rest of the chapter, we will revisit some of these steps to incorporate Integrated Risk Management (IRM)® methods and overlay *quantitative* risk management techniques onto the process.

- Establish senior management buy-in and risk-management culture.

- Seek the board of directors' and senior management's involvement and oversight to discuss a risk-management framework and its benefits and to obtain agreement on high-level objectives and expectations with resources and target dates regarding risk management in line with the organization's strategic plan.

- Review existing ERM practices in the organization and identify the areas for improvement.

- Facilitate initial training and working sessions to ensure buy-in and establish risk-management culture with key personnel involved with ERM implementation.

- Conduct working group discussions with stakeholders and key personnel to identify sources of risks.

- Provide input for implementation in the strategic business planning process.

- Coordinate the development, implementation, and monitoring of identified risk metrics.

- Document risk inventories and mitigations within Risk Registers in the organization.

- Develop risk dashboards for presentation to senior decision makers and the board of directors.

- Assess exposure to the risk, assess adequacy of existing risk mitigation or monitoring, and identify opportunities to enhance mitigation or monitoring activities, then suggest and build best practices for enhanced risk-adjusted returns.

- Create reports that effectively and concisely supply the business intelligence based on risk measures that management needs to make cost-effective financial decisions.

- Put in place a reporting process for management and the board.

- Establish a management working group to support the resources identified and drive the risk-management effort across the organization.

RISK REGISTERS AND BASIC ENTERPRISE RISK MANAGEMENT

The typical traditional ERM method uses *Risk Registers*, which simply involves recording all risks present or anticipated. Each *Risk Element* (i.e., each risk item that is recorded in the Risk Register) may include information on the name of the risk; the category or type of the risk; who reported it; who is responsible or is assigned the risk; what, if any, risk mitigation or risk control is required; the contact person; documentation; and so forth. Sometimes additional information such as frequency, or *Likelihood,* and severity, or *Impact,* that risk may have on the organization is included. These Likelihood and Impact measures are usually qualitative estimates (high, medium, low) or can be assigned numerical values (1 to 5 or 1 to 10, where the higher the frequency or severity, the higher the value assigned). Alternate methods of using *Vulnerability* (or the inverse of amount of risk mitigation completed) with multiple risk controls are also supported.

Clearly the amount of information and detail required varies depending on the organization. One way to think of Risk Registers is akin to a check register. For example, if you have a checking account, you can write a check to pay a specific bill; on that single check, you write the recipient's name, date, and amount. You can, of course, write multiple checks to different recipients. And every time a check is written, you would record said checks in a check register (whether electronically in an accounting software or manually in a physical check register). Continuing with this analogy, each check represents a different risk element, and multiple risk elements make up the Risk Register. You may also own multiple bank accounts, each with its own check register, or, in other words, an organization may have multiple Risk Registers set up, one for each division or business unit or project, and so forth.

However, the use of only Risk Registers by themselves often leads to ritualistic decision making, an illusion of control, and the fallacy of misplaced concreteness and reliance on purely qualitative risk assessments. While the use of Risk Registers is a good starting point, Integrated Risk Management takes this qualitative assessment to the next level with more powerful quantitative risk management approaches.

CASE EXAMPLE: HOSPITAL RISK MANAGEMENT

A simple example of a Risk Register in a hospital is shown in Figure 1.1, where certain types of risk events (e.g., wrong dosage given, equipment failure, etc.) that have occurred within specific departments (e.g., surgery, intensive care) and the number of events that happened within a specific time period are recorded, as well as other qualitative notes and associated details. Reports are then typically generated. Figure 1.2 shows a sample periodic (e.g., monthly) report of another organization showing the number of risk events that occurred in the past.

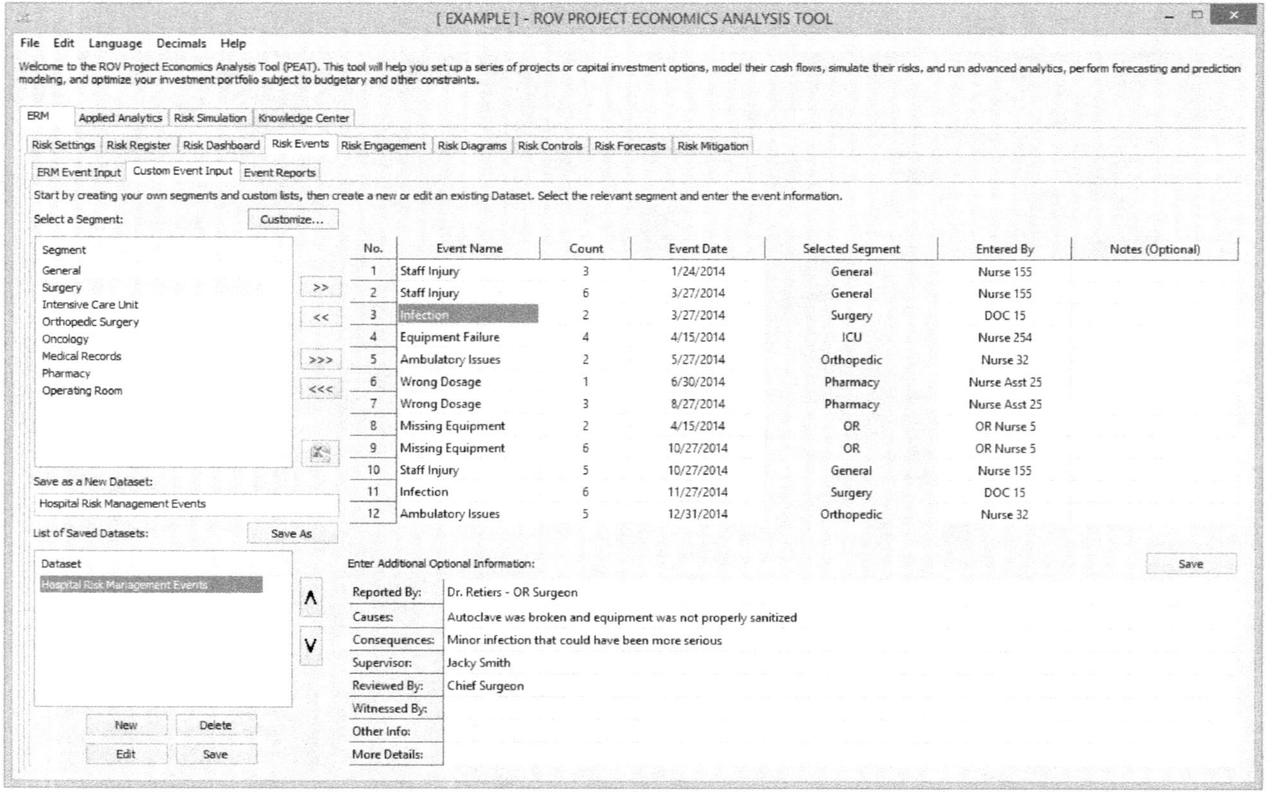

[EXAMPLE] - ROV PROJECT ECONOMICS ANALYSIS TOOL

File   Edit   Language   Decimals   Help

Welcome to the ROV Project Economics Analysis Tool (PEAT). This tool will help you set up a series of projects or capital investment options, model their cash flows, simulate their risks, and run advanced analytics, perform forecasting and prediction modeling, and optimize your investment portfolio subject to budgetary and other constraints.

ERM   Applied Analytics   Risk Simulation   Knowledge Center

Risk Settings   Risk Register   Risk Dashboard   Risk Events   Risk Engagement   Risk Controls   Risk Diagrams   Risk Forecasts   Risk Mitigation

ERM Event Input   Custom Event Input   Event Reports

Start by creating your own segments and custom lists, then create a new or edit an existing Dataset. Select the relevant segment and enter the event information.

Select a Segment: Customize...

Segment
General
Surgery
Intensive Care Unit
Orthopedic Surgery
Oncology
Medical Records
Pharmacy
Operating Room

>   >>
<<   >>>
<<<
🔍

No.	Event Name	Count	Event Date	Selected Segment	Entered By	Notes (Optional)
1	Staff Injury	3	1/24/2014	General	Nurse 155	
2	Staff Injury	6	3/27/2014	General	Nurse 155	
3	Infection	2	3/27/2014	Surgery	DOC 15	
4	Equipment Failure	4	4/15/2014	ICU	Nurse 254	
5	Ambulatory Issues	2	5/27/2014	Orthopedic	Nurse 32	
6	Wrong Dosage	1	6/30/2014	Pharmacy	Nurse Asst 25	
7	Wrong Dosage	3	8/27/2014	Pharmacy	Nurse Asst 25	
8	Missing Equipment	2	4/15/2014	OR	OR Nurse 5	
9	Missing Equipment	6	10/27/2014	OR	OR Nurse 5	
10	Staff Injury	5	10/27/2014	General	Nurse 155	
11	Infection	6	11/27/2014	Surgery	DOC 15	
12	Ambulatory Issues	5	12/31/2014	Orthopedic	Nurse 32	

Enter Additional Optional Information:

Reported By: Dr. Reiters - OR Surgeon
Causes: Autoclave was broken and equipment was not properly sanitized
Consequences: Minor infection that could have been more serious
Supervisor: Jacky Smith
Reviewed By: Chief Surgeon
Witnessed By:
Other Info:
More Details:

Save

Save as a New Dataset: Save As

Hospital Risk Management Events

List of Saved Datasets:

Dataset
Hospital Risk Management Events

<   >

New   Delete
Edit   Save

Figure 1.1: Example Risk Events in a Hospital

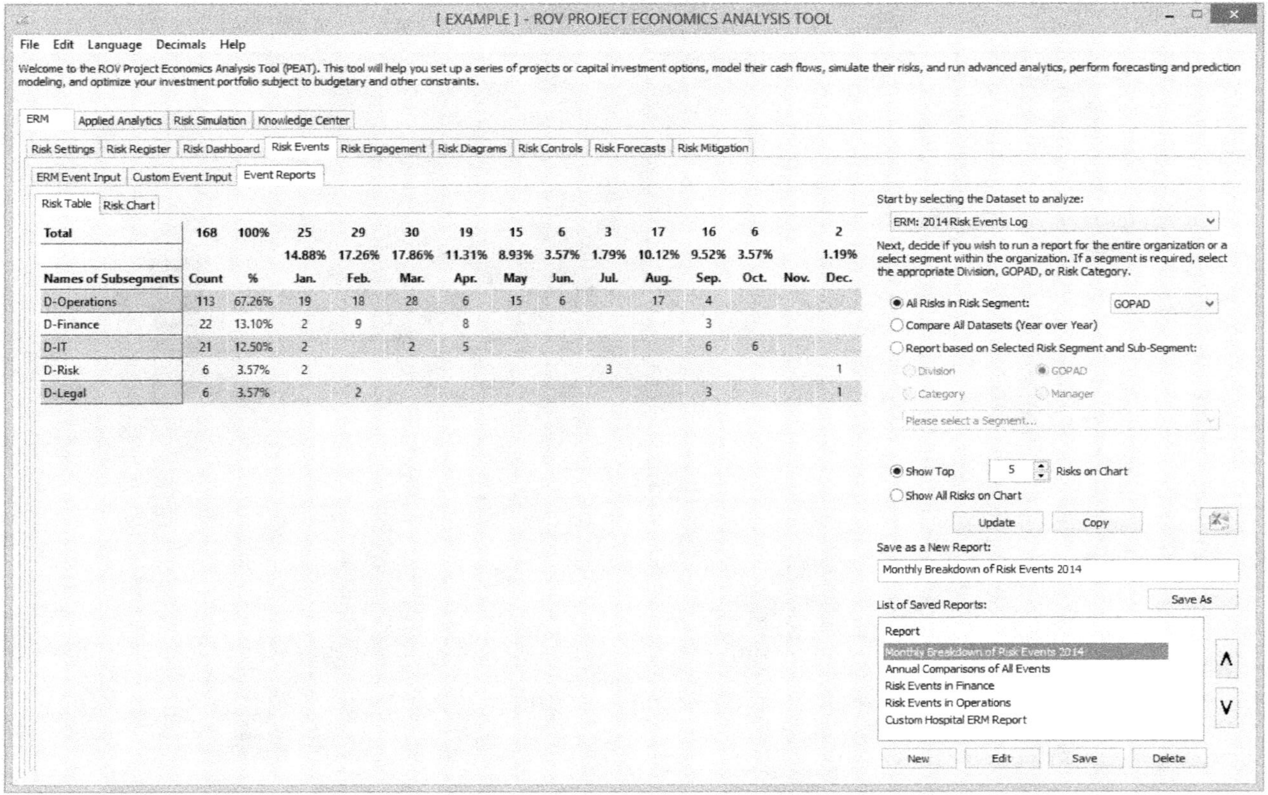

[EXAMPLE 1 - ROV PROJECT ECONOMICS ANALYSIS TOOL

File   Edit   Language   Decimals   Help

Welcome to the ROV Project Economics Analysis Tool (PEAT). This tool will help you set up a series of projects or capital investment options, model their cash flows, simulate their risks, and run advanced analytics, perform forecasting and prediction modeling, and optimize your investment portfolio subject to budgetary and other constraints.

ERM | Applied Analytics | Risk Simulation | Knowledge Center

Risk Settings | Risk Register | Risk Dashboard | Risk Events | Risk Engagement | Risk Diagrams | Risk Controls | Risk Forecasts | Risk Mitigation

ERM Event Input | Custom Event Input | Event Reports

Risk Table | Risk Chart

| Total | 168 | 100% | 25 | 29 | 30 | 19 | 15 | 6 | 3 | 17 | 16 | 6 | | 2 |
| | | | 14.88% | 17.26% | 17.86% | 11.31% | 8.93% | 3.57% | 1.79% | 10.12% | 9.52% | 3.57% | | 1.19% |
Names of Subsegments	Count	%	Jan.	Feb.	Mar.	Apr.	May	Jun.	Jul.	Aug.	Sep.	Oct.	Nov.	Dec.
D-Operations	113	67.26%	19	18	28	6	15	6		17	4			
D-Finance	22	13.10%	2	9		8			3					
D-IT	21	12.50%	2		2	5				6	6			
D-Risk	6	3.57%							3		3			1
D-Legal	6	3.57%		2							3			1

Start by selecting the Dataset to analyze:

ERM: 2014 Risk Events Log ⌄

Next, decide if you wish to run a report for the entire organization or a select segment within the organization. If a segment is required, select the appropriate Division, GOPAD, or Risk Category.

○ All Risks in Risk Segment: GOPAD ⌄

○ Compare All Datasets (Year over Year)

○ Report based on Selected Risk Segment and Sub-Segment:

  ○ Division   ● GOPAD
  ○ Category   ○ Manager

  Please select a Segment... ⌄

● Show Top [5 ⇕] Risks on Chart
○ Show All Risks on Chart

[Update]   [Copy]

Save as a New Report:
Monthly Breakdown of Risk Events 2014

List of Saved Reports:

Report
Monthly Breakdown of Risk Events 2014
Annual Comparisons of All Events
Risk Events in Finance
Risk Events in Operations
Custom Hospital ERM Report

[Save As]
< >

[New]   [Edit]   [Save]   [Delete]

Figure 1.2: Example Risk Event Reports

RISK MATRIXES

In other types of Risk Registers, *Likelihood* (*L*) and *Impact* (*I*) values can be used and entered for each risk element, and the product of these two variables is termed the *Key Risk Indicator* (*KRI*), where $KRI = L \times I$. These KRI values can be color coded into various regions based on their respective values. For instance, Figure 1.3 shows a 10 $\times$ 10 matrix where the columns going from left to right represent the Likelihood from 1 to 10 (low to high), and the rows from bottom to top represent the Impact from 1 to 10 (low to high). The values inside each of the cells represent the KRI, and the color coding depends on the computed KRI (typically, lower KRI values are green, medium KRI values are yellow, and high KRI values are red). In a later section, we showcase examples of how these KRI values can be incorporated into the ERM Risk Register. As will be seen later, the color coding, matrix size, and category labels can be customized as required.

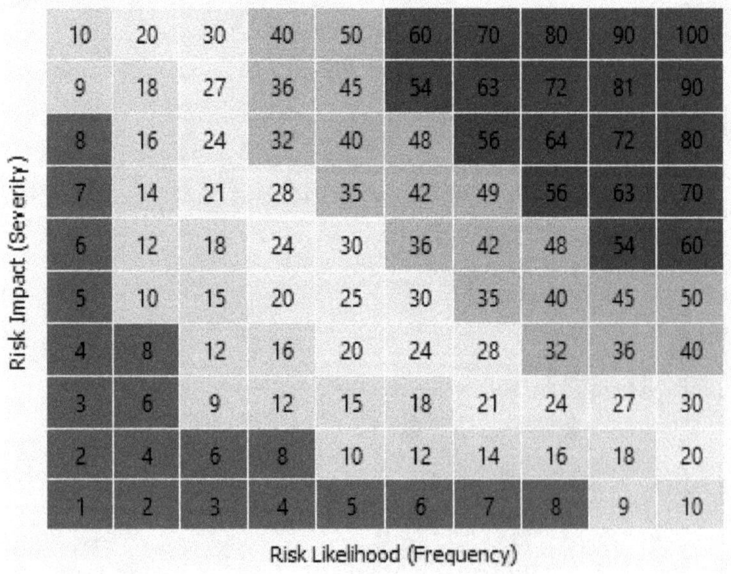

Risk Impact (Severity)									
10	20	30	40	50	60	70	80	90	100
9	18	27	36	45	54	63	72	81	90
8	16	24	32	40	48	56	64	72	80
7	14	21	28	35	42	49	56	63	70
6	12	18	24	30	36	42	48	54	60
5	10	15	20	25	30	35	40	45	50
4	8	12	16	20	24	28	32	36	40
3	6	9	12	15	18	21	24	27	30
2	4	6	8	10	12	14	16	18	20
1	2	3	4	5	6	7	8	9	10

Risk Likelihood (Frequency)

Figure 1.3: Risk Matrix

In some organizations with potential public risk exposures—such as nuclear power plants, airline companies, oil and gas exploration and drilling firms, banks, and government or public institutions—additional risk documentation is also recommended. These documentations are also part of the traditional ERM process. As an example, the following are typical procedures and documentation arising from operational risk planning, and they can be customized to an organization's unique needs.

- **Business Continuity Plan (BCP)** focuses on sustaining business functions during and after a disruption (e.g., business functions may include an organization's payroll process or consumer information process). A BCP may be written for a specific business process or it may address all key business processes. IT systems are considered in the BCP in terms of their support to the business processes. A Disaster Recovery Plan, Business Resumption Plan, and Occupant Emergency Plan may be appended to the BCP as required.

- **Business Recovery Plan (BRP)** or **Business Resumption Plan** addresses the restoration of business processes after an emergency. Development of the BRP will be coordinated with the Disaster Recovery Plan and BCP.

- **Continuity of Operations Plan (COOP)** focuses on restoring an organization's main essential functions at an alternate site and performing those functions for up to 4 weeks before returning to normal operations. A COOP addresses headquarters-level issues; it is developed and executed independently from the BCP. The document can include Delegation of Authority, Orders of Succession, and Procedures for Vital Records and Databases.

- **Continuity of Support Plan** and **IT Contingency Plan (Recovery Strategy)** include the development and maintenance of continuity of support plans for general support systems and contingency plans for major applications.

- **Cyber Incident Response Plan (CIRP)** establishes procedures to address cyber-attacks against an organization's IT system. A CIRP is designed to enable security personnel to identify, mitigate, and recover from malicious computer incidents, such as unauthorized access to a system or data, denial of service, or unauthorized changes to system hardware, software, or data (e.g., malicious logic, such as a virus, worm, or Trojan horse).

- **Disaster Recovery Plan (DRP)** becomes applicable after catastrophic events that deny access to the normal facility for an extended period. Depending on the organization's needs, several DRPs may be appended to the BCP.

- **Crisis Management Plan (CMP)** and **Crisis Communications Plan (CCP)** detail how organizations prepare their internal and external procedures prior to and during a disaster. A crisis communications plan is often developed by the organization that is responsible for public outreach. Plan procedures are included as an appendix to the BCP. The communications plan includes designation of specific individuals as the only authority for answering questions from the public regarding disaster response.

COMPREHENSIVE ERM WITH QUANTITATIVE RISK MANAGEMENT

A true next-generation comprehensive ERM process should include, at a minimum, the qualitative methods and steps previously outlined plus quantitative IRM methodologies. Instead of continuing the chapter by outlining additional items and bullet lists of methods and steps, we illustrate the quantitative ERM methods through the use of the PEAT (Project Economics Analysis Tool) software's ERM Module, which is showcased in the next chapter.

The Project Economics Analysis Tool (PEAT) software was developed to perform a comprehensive Integrated Risk Management analysis on capital investments, discounted cash flow, cost and schedule risk project management, oil and gas applications, healthcare analytics, and Enterprise Risk Management. This tool will help you to set up a series of projects or capital investment options, model their cash flows, simulate their risks, run advanced risk simulations, perform business intelligence analytics, run forecasting and prediction modeling, optimize your investment portfolio subject to budgetary and other resource and qualitative constraints, and generate automated reports and charts, all within a single easy-to-use integrated software suite. The following modules are available in PEAT, and Chapter 2 focuses on the ERM module in particular.

- Enterprise Risk Management (ERM)
- Corporate Investments (Dynamic Discounted Cash Flow)
- Corporate Investments (Lease versus Buy)
- Goals Analytics (Sales Force Automation)
- Healthcare Economics (HEAT and REJ)
- Oil and Gas (Oil Field Reserves, Oil Recovery Analysis, Well-Type Curves)
- Project Management (Cost and Schedule Risk)
- Public Sector Analysis (Knowledge Value Added)
- ROV Compiled Models
- Customized company-specific modules and applications

ROV's PEAT incorporates all of the advanced risk and decision analytical methodologies covered in this book into a simple-to-use and step-by-step integrated software application suite. It simplifies the risk-based decision analysis process and empowers the decision maker with insights from powerful analytics. If you already perform discounted cash flow modeling or Enterprise Risk Management in Excel, why do you still need PEAT? Because PEAT's integrated advanced analytical techniques extend the analysis you have already performed and do so in a simple-to-use, simple-to-understand, and automated format, thus generating valuable insights that would be impossible without such advanced methods. PEAT allows you to scale and replicate your analysis, archive and encrypt your models and data, create automated reports, and customize your own PEAT modules.

- *Enterprise Risk Management (ERM)*: Perform traditional qualitative ERM with Risk Registers but also enhance the analysis with more quantitative analysis. This ERM module comes with an online Web version as well as a module within PEAT, where you can enter and save multiple Risk Registers to generate Key Risk Indicators (KRI) by Risk Divisions and Risk Taxonomy (Geographic, Operations, Products, Activity or Process, and Department); assign risk items to different Risk Managers by performing Risk Mapping of Risk Categories to different Risk Divisions; create

Risk Dashboards of the results; enter Risk Elements within multiple customizable Risk Engagements; draw Risk Diagrams; perform and run Risk Controls on KRIs to see if certain risks are within control or out of control; perform Risk Forecasts; check if certain Risk Mitigation projects do, indeed, work or are statistically ineffective; perform Risk Sensitivity on KRIs; perform Risk Scenarios on quantitative risk metrics; run Risk Simulations on risk metrics; generate Risk Reports; and encrypt your data and files for the purposes of Risk Security. (See Chapter 4's case study on Eletrobrás in Brazil on how the PEAT ERM was employed at this multinational company.)

- *Corporate Investments (Dynamic Discounted Cash Flow)*: With a few simple assumptions, you can auto-generate cash flow statements of multiple projects; obtain key performance indicators and financial metrics (NPV, IRR, MIRR, PP, DPP, ROI); run risk simulations on uncertainty inputs; generate static tornado sensitivity analysis; run dynamic sensitivities; simultaneously compare multiple projects within a portfolio; perform forecasts of future revenues and cash flow; draw multiple strategic investment pathways and options, and model and value these strategic paths; compute and optimize the best projects within a portfolio subject to multiple constraints and restrictions; view results in management dashboards; encrypt your model and data; and auto-generate analysis reports.

- *Corporate Investments (Lease versus Buy)*: Run a lease versus buy analysis; compare capital and operating leases with interest payments and tax advantages; value the lease contract from the point of view of the lessee and lessor; and generate the complete cash flow analysis to obtain the net advantage to leasing.

- *Goals Analytics (Sales Force Automation)*: Develop and maintain corporate sales goals. A Web-based SaaS and desktop-based PEAT module, it focuses on the creation and use of goals that help make goal-setting more accurate and sustainable by any company seeking to improve its sales performance (sales goal forecasting, probability of hitting corporate revenues, sales pipeline analysis, and other sales-based metrics analysis).

- *Healthcare Economics (HEAT and REJ)*: Run the economics of various options available under the U.S. Affordable Care Act (Obamacare) for corporations providing employer-sponsored healthcare by loading employee-census data (healthcare economics analysis tool, HEAT), or perform rapid economic justification (REJ) of each option by simulating its high-level inputs.

- *Oil and Gas (Oil Field Reserves, Oil Recovery, and Well-Type Curves)*: Perform oil and gas industry models on analyzing the economics of oil field reserves and available oil recovery based on uncertainty and risks, as well as generate oil-well–specific type curves and economics.

- *Project Management (Cost and Schedule Risk)*: Draw your own project pathways (simple linear project tasks versus complex parallel and recombining projects), then click a button to auto-generate the model. Enter the cost and schedule estimates as well as their spreads, then run a risk simulation on the model to determine the probability of cost-schedule overruns, cost-schedule buffers at various probabilities of completion, critical path identification, and sensitivity analysis.

- *Public Sector Analysis (Knowledge Value Added)*: Model government and nonprofit organizations' value, value to society, or intangible value via Knowledge Value Added utilizing market comparables to identify and monetize such projects and assets.

- *ROV Compiled Models*: With the compiler software, users can compile their existing Excel models into license-controlled executable EXE files. ROV's patented methods can be used to encrypt and lock up the intellectual property and mathematical algorithms of the model, and issue hardware-controlled and timed licenses to the purchaser's own users or customers.

HANDS-ON PROJECT MANAGEMENT IN PEAT

PEAT ERM is both a desktop software and an online Web-based application, with over 20 related U.S. and worldwide patents and patents pending. The desktop PEAT version is for internal risk department personnel to manage the results and dataset, keep the data encrypted and safe, and run analyses such as simulations, scenarios, tornado analysis, and so forth. Not everyone needs these advanced analytics. Therefore, in a large corporation, there can be multiple end users who should have the ability to enter data, and a few local administrators with access to control everything from granting access to and creating end users, to setting up the risk profile of the company. End users (e.g., plant managers, supervisors, secretaries, etc.) can only enter in data and information. These end users have limited access and limited knowledge, making training simple, and they enter in values only pertaining to their areas of responsibilities. Local administrators then have a database that rolls up to the corporate level and they can see results, generate reports, perform more advanced quantitative risk analytics, and so on.

The best way to get started with PEAT's ERM module is to start PEAT, select the *Enterprise Risk Management* module (the second radio selection on the main list in Figure 2.1), and click on *Load Example*. This will start the ERM module as well as load an example dataset. The rest of this chapter provides an overview of each section of the software.

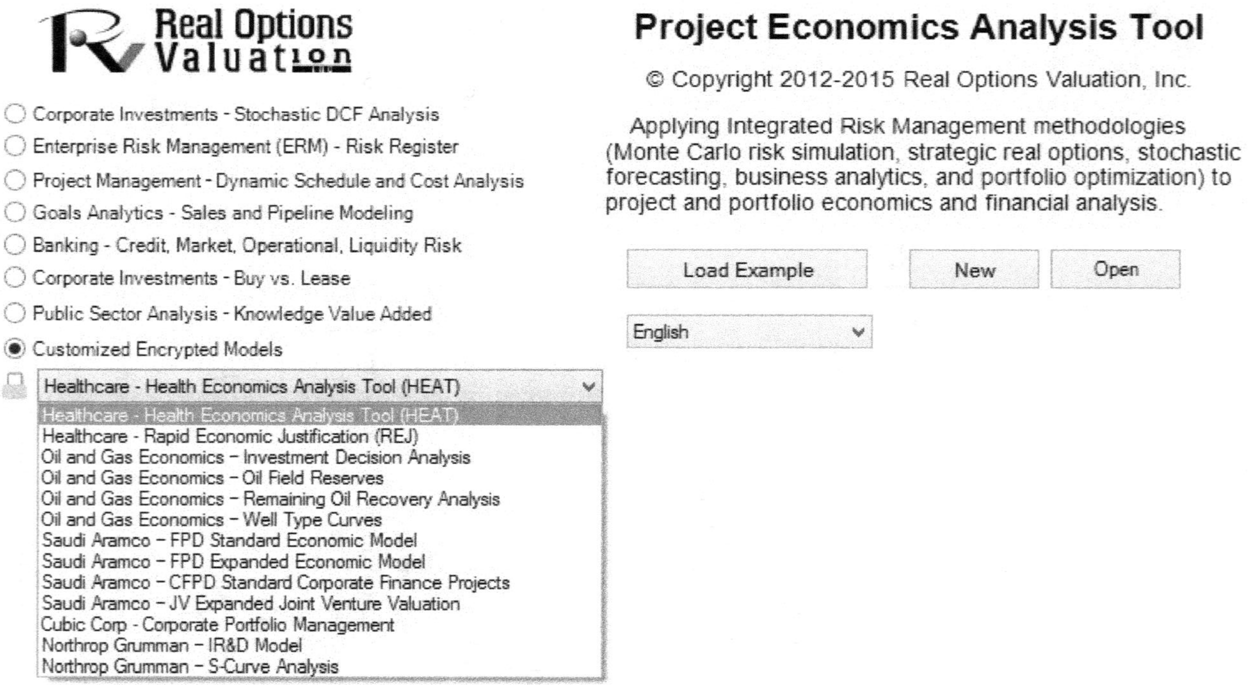

Real Options Valuation

Project Economics Analysis Tool

© Copyright 2012-2015 Real Options Valuation, Inc.

Applying Integrated Risk Management methodologies (Monte Carlo risk simulation, strategic real options, stochastic forecasting, business analytics, and portfolio optimization) to project and portfolio economics and financial analysis.

Load Example	New	Open

English

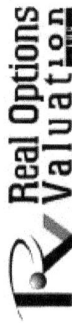

○ Corporate Investments - Stochastic DCF Analysis
○ Enterprise Risk Management (ERM) - Risk Register
○ Project Management - Dynamic Schedule and Cost Analysis
○ Goals Analytics - Sales and Pipeline Modeling
○ Banking - Credit, Market, Operational, Liquidity Risk
○ Corporate Investments - Buy vs. Lease
○ Public Sector Analysis - Knowledge Value Added
● Customized Encrypted Models

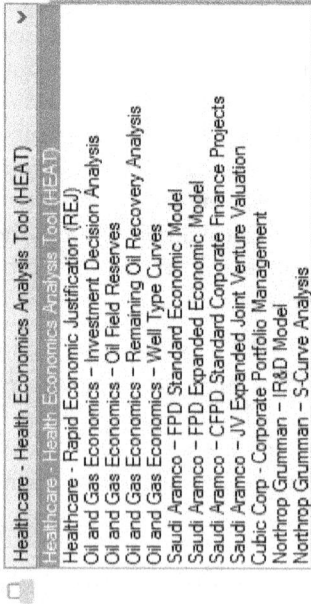

Healthcare - Health Economics Analysis Tool (HEAT)
Healthcare - Health Economics Analysis Tool (HEAT)
Healthcare - Rapid Economic Justification (REJ)
Oil and Gas Economics – Investment Decision Analysis
Oil and Gas Economics – Oil Field Reserves
Oil and Gas Economics – Remaining Oil Recovery Analysis
Oil and Gas Economics – Well Type Curves
Saudi Aramco – FPD Standard Economic Model
Saudi Aramco – FPD Expanded Economic Model
Saudi Aramco – CFPD Standard Corporate Finance Projects
Saudi Aramco – JV Expanded Joint Venture Valuation
Cubic Corp - Corporate Portfolio Management
Northrop Grumman – IR&D Model
Northrop Grumman – S-Curve Analysis

Figure 2.1: Project Economics Analysis Tool (PEAT) by ROV

When the module starts, you will begin in the **Global Settings** section. Start with steps 1–3 by first establishing the *Date Settings* (MM/DD/YYYY or DD/MM/YYYY) as well as *Key Risk Indicators* (KRI). The *KRI Matrix* is a color-coded $n \times n$ matrix made up of *Risk Likelihood or Frequency* and *Risk Impact or Severity* levels, which can be set as 1–5 or 1–10 (from low to high), with customizable color codes (Figure 2.2). Note that the KRI is computed as *Risk Likelihood × Risk Impact*. For instance, a risk item that has a likelihood frequency category of 5 and a risk impact severity category of 6 would yield a KRI of 30. The higher the likelihood or impact, the higher the KRI, indicating a higher risk condition. The default setting is 10 categories for likelihood and impact with 5 different colors. The color scheme goes from dark green (very low risk) to red (very high risk), and the labels on the horizontal and vertical axes have some predefined values such as average or above average risk, and so on. These can all be changed by clicking on the *Customize* button. In other words, the entire KRI matrix can be customized as needed, from the color codes to the category names.

Step 4 provides an option for *Risk Controls*. These are typically % weights and is selected by default. These weights are used later on in the *Risk Register* section. Alternatively, integer weights (discussed later) can be used. Step 5 provides the ability to customize the variables measured, that is, risk impact or severity versus risk likelihood or frequency. Some companies may wish to measure other elements such as risk of business losses, human resource impact, impact to the environment, and so forth. Any such modifications can be made here. Typically, most ERM performed in corporations tends to use the standard risk impact or severity versus risk likelihood or frequency matrix (the default setting in PEAT ERM).

Step 6 provides the ability to use global units or unique units for risk registers. For instance, if a firm is only concerned with the risk of financial impacts, it might use $ or £ for all its risk elements. This may be globally applied, which means for all risks, the selected unit will be used. In contrast, a multinational with businesses running in various currencies may require unique currency settings for each risk register. Finally, the droplist allows the use of other nonstandard units such as hours, joules, megawatt hours, and so forth, for firms interested in measuring their manufacturing and output capacity risks in these units.

Risk Groups (Risk Segmentation and Risk Taxonomy)

Typically, ERM implementation also requires the ability to create various divisions, departments, risk categories, and other segmentations within an organization. Such segmentations are required because data entered for the risk registers later can be sliced and diced every which way, as well as being in compliance with COSO Integrated Risk Framework.

Figure 2.3 shows the PEAT ERM software's **Risk Groups** section. A multitude of *Risk Divisions, Risk G.O.P.A.D., Risk Category,* and *Risk Managers* can be set up here. Cumulatively, these categories represent the Risk Taxonomy of the ERM system.

For example, multiple business or operational divisions within a company can be created, such that the company can manage multiple risk profiles for each division. Users can also create and assign various G.O.P.A.D. (geographic, operations, products, activity or process, and department) categories such that a company's risk profile can be analyzed from multiple points of view.

Start by creating one or more divisions, then the G.O.P.A.D. categories, then the risk categories, and, finally, risk managers or people in charge of certain aspects of the company. When creating risk categories, PEAT's default library of predefined risk categories can also be called up to assist, via the *Load Risk Inventory Library* button. Once categories are created, these will be displayed in the data grid at the bottom. Click on the *Edit* pencil icon to edit a particular item.

Click on the *Report* button to generate an Excel report of the created categories. This report can serve as an archive or as a template to import additional or new categories. For instance, by generating a report from this current default example model, you can then clear the report, enter any new categories into the Excel worksheets, and subsequently *Import* them into the software. Importing data will allow a large number of categories to be entered quickly. Manual inputs are optimal when only a few categories are needed. Regardless of the approach, it is highly recommended that category names be brief but descriptive. For example, the finance department can be named D-Finance or oil and gas products can be named P-Oil. Brief category names tend to generate more visually pleasing reports.

Based on previously created *Risk Groups* and their risk taxonomy, the next step is to map and link these hierarchies on one or more dimensions. This process will allow putting various projects with related risks into the various groups and segments for analysis and the ability to view how a certain risk permeates through the organization as well as how a specific risk element may touch mul-tiple departments, divisions, processes, and so forth.

The previously completed segments can then be mapped in the **Risk Mapping** section, as shown in Figure 2.4. For example, a *Risk Category* can be mapped to one or multiple *G.O.P.A.D.* categories, which can then be mapped to one or more *Divisions*. Note that all divisions roll up to the corporation. This way, when a risk element is entered in the Risk Register later on, a risk category can be selected, and the remaining connection routes will be automatically determined. Using these mapped connections, the software can slice and dice and look at different Divisions or G.O.P.A.D. categories and see the risk profile from various points of view.

While it is tempting to connect a single risk category to multiple G.O.P.A.D. or Divisions, it is recommended that the connections be set as one to one. This one-to-one correspondence allows any risk values and KRI to be attributed correctly to the relevant risk categories or divisions and prevents any accidental double counting.

Created connections can be seen in the data grid at the bottom. Connections can be edited by clicking on the *Edit* pencil icons, and changes can then be saved after any modifications. A report can also be created, indicating all the connections.

As a reminder, setting up these three sections, *Global Settings*, *Risk Groups*, and *Risk Mapping*, should be done with great care, as the settings here will flow throughout the entire ERM software. All subsequent reports and analysis will be based on these settings. Sometimes preliminary planning and strategizing is critical to create a good ERM model.

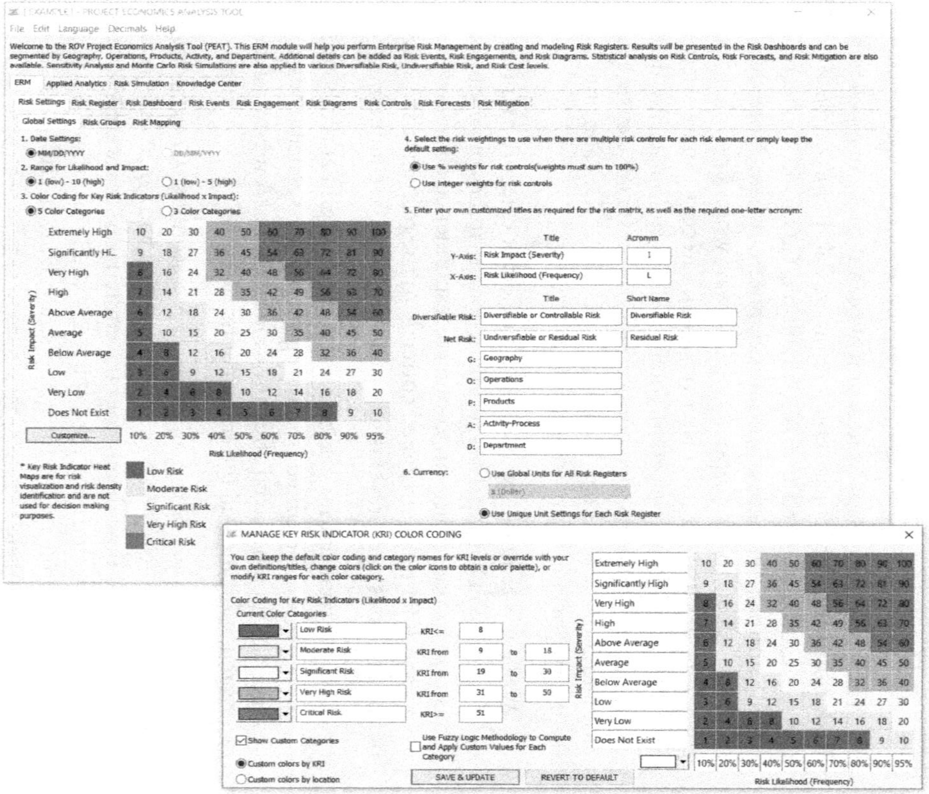

Figure 2.2: Risk Settings

File   Edit   Language   Decimals   Help

Welcome to the ROV Project Economics Analysis Tool (PEAT). This ERM module will help you perform Enterprise Risk Management by creating and modeling Risk Registers. Results will be presented in the Risk Dashboards and can be segmented by Geography, Operations, Products, Activity, and Department. Additional details can be added as Risk Events, Risk Engagements, and Risk Diagrams. Statistical analysis on Risk Controls, Risk Forecasts, and Risk Mitigation are also available. Sensitivity Analysis and Monte Carlo Risk Simulations are also applied to various Diversifiable Risk, Undiversifiable Risk, and Risk Cost levels.

ERM   Applied Analytics   Risk Simulation   Knowledge Center

Risk Settings   Risk Register   Risk Dashboard   Risk Events   Risk Engagement   Risk Diagrams   Risk Controls   Risk Forecasts   Risk Mitigation

Global Settings   Risk Groups   Risk Mapping

Choose the risk level/hierarchy you would like to either manually add and edit individual items or copy/paste multiple entries at once in the data grid below. You should start by adding Divisions followed by G.O.P.A.D., then Risk Category and Risk Manager. Select the risk level to manage, then add a new or edit/search for an existing entry.

○ DIVISION

Division Name:
Acronym:
Location:
Notes:

◉ G.O.P.A.D.

Type: Products
Item Name:
Acronym:
Location:
Notes:

Geography
Operations
Products
Activity-Process
Department
London, U.K.

Development of 225 retail units by the end of 2017

○ RISK CATEGORY

Risk Category Name:
Acronym:
Status: Active
Notes:

Local Risk Inventory Library

○ RISK MANAGER

Risk Manager Name:
Acronym:
Title/Position:
Department:
Direct Dial:
E-mail:
Location:
Notes:

Report   Import   Save As New   Save Edits   Delete

Edit	Type	Name	Acronym	Location	Notes	Create Date
⁄	Products	BRG 225 Retail Development in Croydon	P-Croydon	London, U.K.	Development of 225 retail units by the end of...	3/13/2014
⁄	Products	LLS 550 Housing Development in Dublin	P-Dublin	Northern California, U.S.A.	Development of 550 condominium units by L...	3/13/2014
⁄	Products	SXI 101 Parking Structure in Saudi Arabia	P-Saudi	Dammam, Saudi Arabia, KSA	Development of a 10-floor state of the art pa...	3/13/2014
⁄	Department	Risk Management Department	D-Risk	Silicon Valley, CA, U.S.A.		3/13/2014
⁄	Department	Finance Department	D-Finance	Silicon Valley, CA, U.S.A.		3/13/2014
⁄	Department	Operations Department	D-Operations	Silicon Valley, CA, U.S.A.		3/13/2014
⁄	Department	IT Department	D-IT	Silicon Valley, CA, U.S.A.		3/13/2014
⁄	Department	Legal Department	D-Legal	Silicon Valley, CA, U.S.A.		3/13/2014

Figure 2.3: Risk Groupings in an Organization

![[EXAMPLE] - PROJECT ECONOMICS ANALYSIS TOOL   — □ ✕

File   Edit   Language   Decimals   Help

Welcome to the ROV Project Economics Analysis Tool (PEAT). This ERM module will help you perform Enterprise Risk Management by creating and modeling Risk Registers. Results will be presented in the Risk Dashboards and can be segmented by Geography, Operations, Products, Activity, and Department. Additional details can be added as Risk Events, Risk Engagements, and Risk Diagrams. Statistical analysis on Risk Controls, Risk Forecasts, and Risk Mitigation are also available. Sensitivity Analysis and Monte Carlo Risk Simulations are also applied to various Diversifiable Risk, Undiversifiable Risk, and Risk Cost levels.

ERM   Applied Analytics   Risk Simulation   Knowledge Center

Risk Settings   Risk Register   Risk Dashboard   Risk Events   Risk Engagement   Risk Diagrams   Risk Controls   Risk Forecasts   Risk Mitigation

Global Settings   Risk Groups   Risk Mapping

Based on previously created Risk Categories, G.O.P.A.D., and Divisions, you can now map and link these hierarchies. Each Risk Category can be mapped to one or more G.O.P.A.D. and Divisions. Hold down CTRL key to select multiple items.

Select One or More:

Category
☑ Client Risk
☑ Competitive Risk
☐ Compliance Risk
☐ Concentration Risk
☐ Cost Risk
☐ Credit Risk
☐ Cultural Risk
☐ Economic Risk
☐ Financial Risk
☐ Foreign Exchange Risk
☐ Human Resource Risk

Select One or More:

GOPAD
☐ P-Croydon
☑ P-Dublin
☐ P-Saudi
☐ D-Risk
☐ D-Finance
☐ D-Operations
☐ D-IT
☐ D-Legal

Select One or More:

Division
☐ Europe
☐ ME
☑ USA

Add New Connection   Save Edited Changes   Delete Connection

Report

Edit	Risk Category	GOPAD Assignment	Division Assignment	Status
✓	Client Risk	P-Croydon	Europe	Active
✓	Competitive Risk	P-Dublin	USA	Active
✓	Cost Risk	D-Finance	USA	Active
✓	Cost Risk	D-Risk	USA	Active
✓	Cost Risk	P-Dublin	USA	Active
✓	Economic Risk	P-Saudi	ME	Active
✓	Financial Risk	D-Finance	USA	Active
✓	Human Resource Risk	P-Saudi	ME	Active
✓	Inflation Rate Risk	P-Saudi	ME	Active
✓	IT Risk	D-IT	USA	Active
✓	Legal Risk	P-Croydon	Europe	Active

Figure 2.4: Risk Mapping or Grouped Relationships

Risk Register

The **Risk Register** section represents the center of the ERM world, and in the PEAT software, multiple *Risk Registers* can be created in a single file. That is, users are able to create multiple Risk Registers as seen in Figure 2.5, where we see three example registers: Project DGS728, CEO Presentation to the Board, and Project MMS5528. Each of these Risk Registers has multiple *Risk Elements*. These Risk Elements are shown at the bottom grid of the software. In Figure 2.5, the first four Risk Elements can be seen. Each Risk Element consists of a Risk Element Name, Acronym or Short Name, Causes of Risk, Consequences of Risk, Risk Mitigation Response, Action Plan, Active Status, Risk Manager Assignments, Risk Category, Risk Likelihood, Risk Impact, Key Risk Indicators, Risk Dates (Creation, Edit, and Due Dates), Diversifiable or Controllable Risk ($), Undiversifiable or Residual Risk ($), Mitigation Cost ($), Multiple Risk Controls (Control Names, Weights, and % Mitigation), and so forth, as illustrated in Figure 2.5.

A simple analogy for a Risk Register and its Risk Elements would be a checkbook. In a family (corporation), there might be several individuals each with their own checkbooks (Risk Register). In each checkbook, there will be a stack of checks. Each check can be seen as a Risk Element, where the recipient's name, amount, date, and notes, can be entered (risk element name, causes, consequences, risk mitigation response, etc.). All Risk Elements roll up into a checkbook or Risk Register. A company can have one or more Risk Registers and each one can be created based on different projects, business units, investment initiatives, plants, facilities, and so on. So, each Risk Register contains multiple Risk Elements (e.g., the individual risks such as fire, fraud, IT downtime, human errors, accidents, and so forth, within each project, business unit, initiative, facility, etc.), shown as rows in the data grid (Figure 2.5).

Risk Category is also a required input and is based on the Risk Mapping previously performed, whereby selecting a specific Risk Category will automatically insert the inputted risk into all mapped relationships, as will be used later in the Risk Dashboards and risk reports.

Multiple Risk Registers can be created and saved here. However, the ERM file needs to be saved as well, using the *File | Save* menu. A single saved **.rovprojecon* file can hold multiple Risk Registers, each with multiple Risk Elements.

To get started creating a new Risk Register, click on the *New* button in the Risk Register list window (top right corner of the software). Then, proceed to enter at least some sample data such as Risk Element Name and Acronym, select the *Status, Risk Manager, Risk Category*, and enter the *Risk Likelihood* and *Risk Impact* values. All other inputs are optional. Then, click on the *Create New* button to create a new Risk Element based on the information that was just entered. Once there is at least one Risk Element, you can now enter a name for the Risk Register. Type in a name and then click *Save As* to create and save the Risk Register. You can stop at this point or continue. To continue adding more Risk Elements, click on the name of the new Risk Register or any other Risk Register of choice, then click *Edit* to edit the Risk Register. Then, proceed to add more Risk Element information and click *Create New* to create each new Risk Element. When done adding Risk Elements, click on *Save Edited* and the Risk Register will be saved. When all data entry is done, do not forget to save the file using the menu *File | Save* or *File | Save As*, depending on what is required.

If data exists, clicking on *Report* will generate a report of all the Risk Registers. Each Excel worksheet will be its own Risk Register. A second report will also be generated, for all the Risk Controls. These reports can also be used as data input templates to *Import* into the software. Using the same files, replace the data with new data to import, save the Excel file and then, in the PEAT ERM software, click on the *Import* button to upload the Risk Registers.

Risk Element General Information

At a minimum, the required information for a Risk Element would be its name, acronym, likelihood and impact values, as well as the droplists for risk management assignment, and risk category. All other inputs are optional.

Risk Element Name should be descriptive, but its corresponding acronym or short name should be brief. The *Acronym or Short Name* should ideally fit into the data grid (8 characters or fewer).

Causes, Consequences, and *Risk Mitigation Response* are open-ended text input. These can be any length but would ideally be the length that can fit in the data grid, for the purposes of data clarity (around 80 characters or fewer).

A more detailed *Action Plan* such as an external document can be linked to a Risk Element by using the *Browse* button. The *Notes* icon beside the browse button can also be used to enter additional notes as required. This item is optional.

The three droplists need to be selected as these are considered required inputs. The *Status* droplist is defaulted to *Active*. Risk Elements that are subsequently deemed no longer applicable can either be *Deleted* or set as *Inactive* using this droplist. Making an item inactive will still keep it in the Risk Register for archiving purposes but its effects will not be computed in the Risk Dashboard later. The *Assigned To* droplist is where the relevant Risk Manager is selected. The list of Risk Managers was previously created in the *Risk Settings | Risk Groups* section. The same goes for the *Risk Category* droplist.

Risk Likelihood, Risk Impact, Risk Controls, Diversifiable Risk, Undiversifiable Risk, and Risk Mitigation

As previously mentioned, the Risk Element entries require a two-dimensional input of *Risk Likelihood* (L) or frequency of a risk event occurring and a *Risk Impact* (I) or the severity in terms of financial, economic, and non-economic effects of the risk. These likelihood and impact concepts are industry standard and used even in regulatory environments such as the Basel IV Accords (initiated by the Bank of International Settlements in Switzerland and accepted by most Central Banks around the world as regulatory reporting standards for operational risks). Alternate measures such as Vulnerability (V), Velocity (υ), and others can be used as well. (The case study in Chapter 4 on applying PEAT ERM at Eletrobrás in Brazil showcases one example of how Vulnerability measures are used.)

The uncertainties of repetitive events observed in enterprises' operations over long periods of time can become predictable but usually not with absolute certainty. Such observances can be associated with mathematical functions that reflect the statistical properties of something likely to occur at a future time. The risk of an event occurring is connected to two parameters: The Risk Impact caused by an uncertain event and the probability, or Risk Likelihood, of an event occurring. Given some known probability of a risk event occurring, the higher the impact, the greater the risk. If the impact is zero, the risk will be zero even though the event has a high probability of occurring. The reverse argument is also true. If the probability of a risk event occurring is equal to zero, then the risk is zero (this is an environment of pure certainty), regardless of the magnitude of the impact.

Risks are also segregated into *Diversifiable* (risks that can be hedged, reduced, mitigated, or even completely eliminated) and *Undiversifiable* (these are residual or leftover risks that cannot be reduced any further). A simple example would be that of a fire risk. A manufacturing facility that has total assets of $1M may be able to hedge its fire risk by purchasing fire insurance and installing a state-of-the-art sprinkler system. These are two *Risk Controls* that may cost, say, $25,000 and $15,000 respectively. However, the total risk of $1M may not be completely reduced because if a fire does break out and the entire facility goes down in flames, the insurance may only cover 90% of the asset, as there is a $100,000 deductible. This $100,000 deductible is the undiversified risk, and the $900,000 would be the diversified risk.

So, the required inputs of *Risk Likelihood* and *Risk Impact* are also divided into *Diversifiable Risk* and *Undiversifiable Risk*. By construction, the diversifiable amount is greater than or equal to the undiversifiable amount. The data input in the four boxes are integers and are based on the range previously selected in the *Risk Settings | Global Settings* section where either 1–5 or 1–10 is selected. Figure 2.5 shows an example Risk Element with a 4 and 3 in terms of Risk Likelihood (based on a 1–10 range), then a 5 and 3 in terms of Risk Impact. Hence, the KRI would be $4 \times 5 = 20$ for the diversifiable risk and $3 \times 3 = 9$ for the undiversifiable risk. These KRIs are computed in the data grid and color coded based on the color scheme previously selected in the *Global Settings* section.

The *Date Created* and *Date Updated* are automatically set, whereas the *Due Date* can be set up as required, indicating by when a certain risk issue needs to be updated or resolved.

The optional section of Risk Controls can be entered if required. Using the examples above, Risk Control 1 can be fire insurance and the sprinkler system can be Risk Control 2. The *% Weight* can be entered such that the total equals 100%, indicating how much of a certain risk can be reduced with each control. The *% Mitigation* is between 0% and 100% indicating how much of that control has been implemented. For instance, if only one quarter of the facility has sprinkler controls, then this would be entered as 25%. Additional rows of Risk Controls can be added or removed by clicking on the

+ and − icons. The total weight is also computed and by definition, must be 100%.

Diversifiable or Controllable Risk, Undiversifiable or Residual Risk, and *Mitigation Cost* are the optional monetary inputs in each Risk Element. Each one requires a *Minimum, Most Likely,* and *Maximum* input. Clearly, minimum needs to be less than or equal to most likely, which is then less than or equal to the maximum value. Entering these ranges of values will allow Monte Carlo Risk Simulation to be run. For instance, the risks of a counterparty violating an existing contract may have financial impacts, where the minimal impact might be, say, $0 if the contract is still in force through the end of its term, to a most likely impact of $100,000 in anticipated delays and cost over-runs by the counterparty, to a maximum of $300,000 if the counterparty becomes insolvent, resulting in lost business opportunities due to nonperformance of the counterparty.

The *Mitigation Cost* is the amount of money used to reduce the risk exposure of the specific Risk Element, for instance, the cost of obtaining a secondary subcontractor with prenegotiated terms whose contract becomes live only if the original contractor is not performing. Such risk mitigation methods tend to have a financial cost.

Finally, the computed *Risk Exposure* columns in the data grid deserve some added explanations. For example, in Figure 2.5, there are three Risk Controls with the following weights: 60%, 30%, and 10%, which add to 100%. The percent mitigation completed for these three controls are 100%, 0%, and 0%. This means the expected value of controls would be $(60\% \times 100\%) + (30\% \times 0\%) + (10\% \times 0\%) = 60\%$. This 60% completion value is automatically calculated and shown in the *% OK* column in the data grid. Also in the example, we see that the most likely diversifiable risk is $155,000 and undiversifiable risk is $65,000. Since only 60% of the controllable diversifiable risk is executed, we have $65,000 + $155,000(1 − 60\%) = $127,000 remaining, or the *Current Risk* level. As another example, if there are no controls or all controls have 0% Mitigation, it means there have been no risk controls, so, the current risk in this case would be $65,000 + $155,000 = $220,000. Alternatively, if all mitigations were 100%, all diversifiable risks have been controlled and all that is left is the undiversifiable risks or $65,000 + $155,000(1 − 100\%) = $65,000 where current risk equals the undiversifiable residual risk.

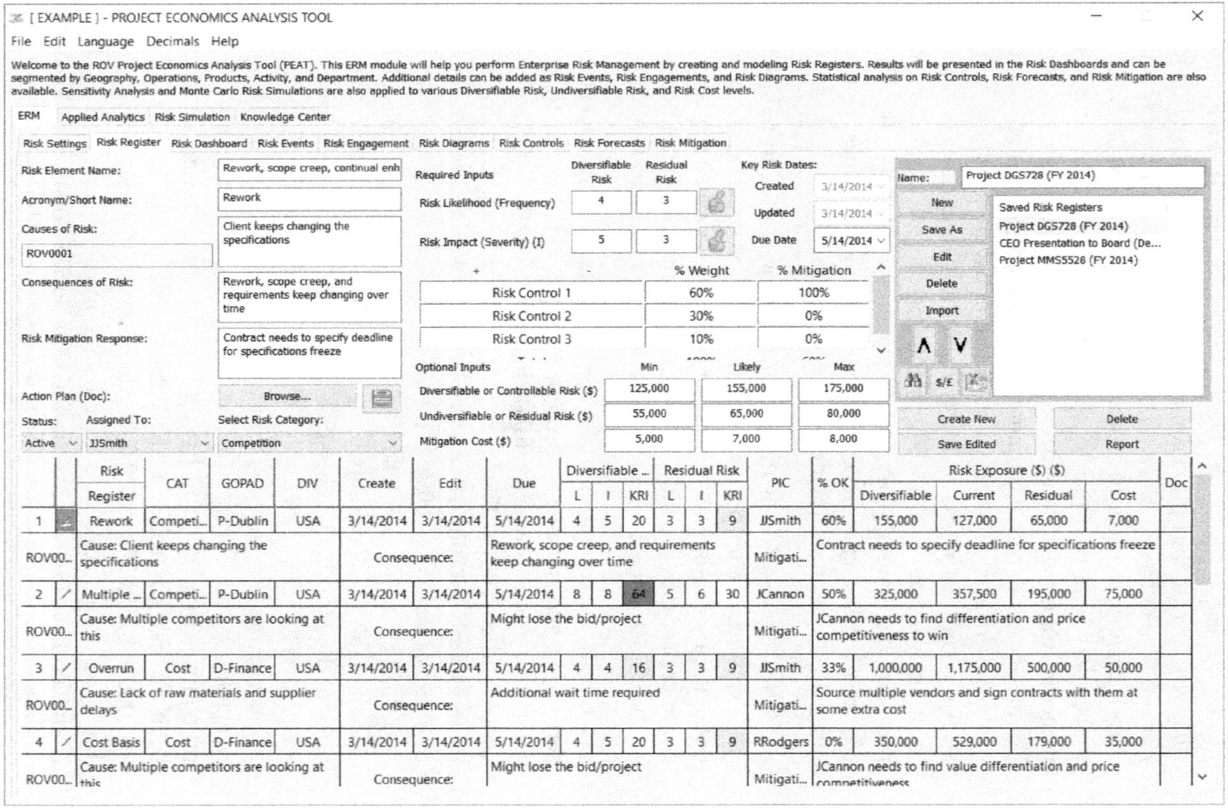

File Edit Language Decimals Help

Welcome to the ROV Project Economics Analysis Tool (PEAT). This ERM module will help you perform Enterprise Risk Management by creating and modeling Risk Registers. Results will be presented in the Risk Dashboards and can be segmented by Geography, Operations, Products, Activity, and Department. Additional details can be added as Risk Events, Risk Engagements, and Risk Diagrams. Statistical analysis on Risk Controls, Risk Forecasts, and Risk Mitigation are also available. Sensitivity Analysis and Monte Carlo Risk Simulations are also applied to various Diversifiable Risk, Undiversifiable Risk, and Risk Cost levels.

ERM   Applied Analytics   Risk Simulation   Knowledge Center

Risk Settings   Risk Register   Risk Dashboard   Risk Events   Risk Engagement   Risk Diagrams   Risk Controls   Risk Forecasts   Risk Mitigation

Risk Element Name: Rework, scope creep, continual enh

Acronym/Short Name: Rework

Causes of Risk: Client keeps changing the specifications

ROV0001

Consequences of Risk: Rework, scope creep, and requirements keep changing over time

Risk Mitigation Response: Contract needs to specify deadline for specifications freeze

Required Inputs

	Diversifiable Risk	Residual Risk
Risk Likelihood (Frequency)	4	3
Risk Impact (Severity) (I)	5	3

	% Weight
Risk Control 1	60%
Risk Control 2	30%
Risk Control 3	10%

	% Mitigation
	100%
	0%
	0%

Optional Inputs

	Min	Likely	Max
Diversifiable or Controllable Risk ($)	125,000	155,000	175,000
Undiversifiable or Residual Risk ($)	55,000	65,000	80,000
Mitigation Cost ($)	5,000	7,000	8,000

Key Risk Dates:
Created 3/14/2014
Updated 3/14/2014
Due Date 5/14/2014

Name: Project DGS728 (FY 2014)

Saved Risk Registers
Project DGS728 (FY 2014)
CEO Presentation to Board (De....
Project MMS5528 (FY 2014)

New   Save As   Edit   Delete   Import
Create New   Save Edited
Delete   Report

Action Plan (Doc): Browse...
Status: Select Risk Category:
Active   JISmith   Competition
Assigned To: JISmith

	Register	Risk	CAT	GOPAD	DIV	Create	Edit	Due	L	I	KRI	L	I	KRI	PIC	% OK	Diversifiable	Current	Residual	Cost	Doc
1	ROV00...	Rework	Competi...	P-Dublin	USA	3/14/2014	3/14/2014	5/14/2014	4	5	20	3	3	9	JISmith	60%	155,000	127,000	65,000	7,000	
		Cause: Client keeps changing the specifications				Consequence:		Rework, scope creep, and requirements keep changing over time							Mitigati...	Contract needs to specify deadline for specifications freeze					
2	ROV00...	Multiple ...	Competi...	P-Dublin	USA	3/14/2014	3/14/2014	5/14/2014	8	8	64	5	6	30	JCannon	50%	325,000	357,500	195,000	75,000	
		Cause: Multiple competitors are looking at this				Consequence:		Might lose the bid/project							Mitigati...	JCannon needs to find differentiation and price competitiveness to win					
3	ROV00...	Overrun	Cost	D-Finance	USA	3/14/2014	3/14/2014	5/14/2014	4	4	16	3	3	9	JISmith	33%	1,000,000	1,175,000	500,000	50,000	
		Cause: Lack of raw materials and supplier delays				Consequence:		Additional wait time required							Mitigati...	Source multiple vendors and sign contracts with them at some extra cost					
4	ROV00...	Cost Basis	Cost	D-Finance	USA	3/14/2014	3/14/2014	5/14/2014	4	5	20	3	3	9	RRodgers	0%	350,000	529,000	179,000	35,000	
		Cause: Multiple competitors are looking at this				Consequence:		Might lose the bid/project							Mitigati...	JCannon needs to find value differentiation and price competitiveness					

Diversifiable... Residual Risk

Risk Exposure ($) ($)

Figure 2.5: Risk Register

Risk Dashboard

In the **Risk Dashboard** section, multiple customized chart views complete with reports, data grids, charts, and visuals based on specific G.O.P.A.D. category, Division, Risk Category, or Risk Dates can be created. The Risk Dashboard is used to slice and dice the Risk Register elements into various drill-down views. Following are descriptions of some dashboards. Note that the dashboard will show results of the active Risk Register only. To activate a Risk Register, go back to the *Risk Register* section and double-click on a saved Risk Register. Make sure it has Risk Element data in the data grid, so that the dashboard will be able to show the results.

Risk Dashboard – Risk Elements

In the **Risk Elements** section, KRI scores can be viewed across different selected segments, divisions, or G.O.P.A.D. category of the organization over a specified time span, as shown in Figure 2.6. Simply select or change the relevant settings such as whether to *Show All Risks* or risks within a specified *Risk Category, G.O.P.A.D., Division,* or *Risk Manager.* Then, either show all dates or specify a date range as well as only active risks or all risks, both active and inactive, need to be included. The *Risk Elements View* allows users to see the color-coded KRI for each risk element and a pie chart showcasing the percentage allocation of each KRI color code. The *Pareto Chart View* shows the same results using a Pareto chart where the KRIs are ranked from the highest to the lowest and the cumulative contributions to variance are computed (e.g., we can determine that the top 5 risk elements contribute to 80% of the risk portfolio).

Risk Dashboard – Risk Heat Maps

The **Risk Maps** section shows KRI counts with relevant customizable risk-based color codes across various risk categories, divisions, and segments over specified time periods (Figure 2.7). Each value in the matrix's cells represents the total number of Risk Elements falling within that specific cross-section of Likelihood and Impact levels. The color settings (green to red), number of color categories (3 colors or 5 colors), and the granularity of the risk matrix (5 × 5 or 10 × 10) are based on the inputs in the *Risk Settings* tab. The axis labels are also customizable in the *Risk Settings* tab (Risk Likelihood, Risk Impact, and the category labels).

The **Risk Groups** section shows the risk accumulation by G.O.P.A.D. category or other risk groups can be shown as bar charts indicating the Risk Element counts within these selected groups (Figure 2.8). The ability to slice and dice the data to generate customized reports comes from the previously set up various G.O.P.A.D. components and their mapped relationships to risk types and risk categories. In the example shown in Figure 2.8, the x-axis shows the 5 risk levels aggregated by Risk Groups. The y-axis of the bar charts can be set as the total KRI for each Risk Group or by Risk Element counts.

The **Risk Exposure** section shows the results of the selected segment as risk dials and charts and is compared against the entire Company (Figure 2.9). These dials and charts represent the Diversifiable and Undiversifiable Risk Exposure for the selected category and time period by summing all the relevant Risk Elements' dollar or monetary exposures in the active Risk Register. The default terms of Diversifiable and Undiversifiable Residual Risk can all be user-defined in the Risk Settings tab as described previously.

This report provides top-down (drill-down) visual representation of the structure of the corporation and its risk associations or **Risk Taxonomy**, as well as a bottom-up view of how a specific risk permeates throughout the corporation (Figure 2.10).

Customized risk profiles and risk reports by Division, G.O.P.A.D. category, Risk Category, Risk Dates, and so forth can be easily set up to query the active Risk Register for all the relevant Risk Elements that fall within the search parameters and return a **Risk Inventory** of all the risks identified (Figure 2.11). This report allows for the Risk Monitoring of project management, tasks, completion, and assignments. It also provides for Risk Governance; provides a Risk Effectiveness Summary, Risk Audit Trail, and Compliance; and complies with International Standards Organization (ISO) Standards.

See Chapter 3 on how PEAT and ROV technology is in compliance with multiple global risk standards such as COSO, BASEL III/IV, NIST, ISO 31000:2009, and others.

Risk Dashboard – Risk Probability

This **Risk Probability** section provides users the ability to compute the probability density function (PDF) and cumulative distribution function (CDF) of a discrete risk event occurring or continuous risk amounts using historical experience. The analysis is similar to that in Risk Simulator's Distributional Analysis tool, where after a probability distribution is selected and its required input parameters are entered, the PDF and CDF values are returned as a probability table.

Figure 2.12 shows an example situation where a discrete Poisson distribution is selected and the Lambda (mean) value entered is 1.5 (e.g., data was collected for 3 months on the number of errors in bank check deposits per work week at a specific branch of a national bank, and the data shows that there are, on average, 1.5 errors per work week). By setting some starting and ending range and step size, the computed table shows the PDF probability and CDF cumulative probability of a specific risk category's number of events per work week (check deposit errors). The probability that within any work week there will be no check deposit errors is 22.31%, exactly one error is 33.47%, exactly two errors is 25.10%, and so forth. Cumulatively, we can also state that we are 93.44% sure that within any work week, there will be three or fewer risk event errors of the same risk category, assuming history is the best indicator of future performance.

[EXAMPLE] - PROJECT ECONOMICS ANALYSIS TOOL

File Edit Language Decimals Help

Welcome to the ROV Project Economics Analysis Tool (PEAT). This ERM module will help you perform Enterprise Risk Management by creating and modeling Risk Registers. Results will be presented in the Risk Dashboards and can be segmented by Geography, Operations, Products, Activity, and Department. Additional details can be added as Risk Events, Risk Engagements, and Risk Diagrams. Statistical analysis on Risk Controls, Risk Forecasts, and Risk Mitigation are also available. Sensitivity Analysis and Monte Carlo Risk Simulations are also applied to various Diversifiable Risk, Undiversifiable Risk, and Risk Cost levels.

ERM Applied Analytics Risk Simulation Knowledge Center

Risk Settings Risk Register Risk Dashboard Risk Events Risk Engagement Risk Diagrams Risk Controls Risk Forecasts Risk Mitigation

Select what risk categories to show and then click on each of the subtabs below to view different dashboards.

View By: ● Show All   ○ Risk Category: ○ G.O.P.A.D.:   ○ Division: Date Selection:
                                                                                            ● Show All
          Based on Diversifiable or Controllable Risk ∨   Select Category: Select GOPAD: Select Division: ○ Custom:
          ☑ Show Active Risks Only   ☑ Ignore Duplicates   ○ Manager: Select Manager:
                                                                                            Period:
Risk Elements Risk Map Risk Groups Risk Exposure Risk Taxonomy Risk Inventory Risk Probability   1/ 2/2019   to   1/ 2/2019
● Risk Elements View   ○ Pareto Chart View   Report

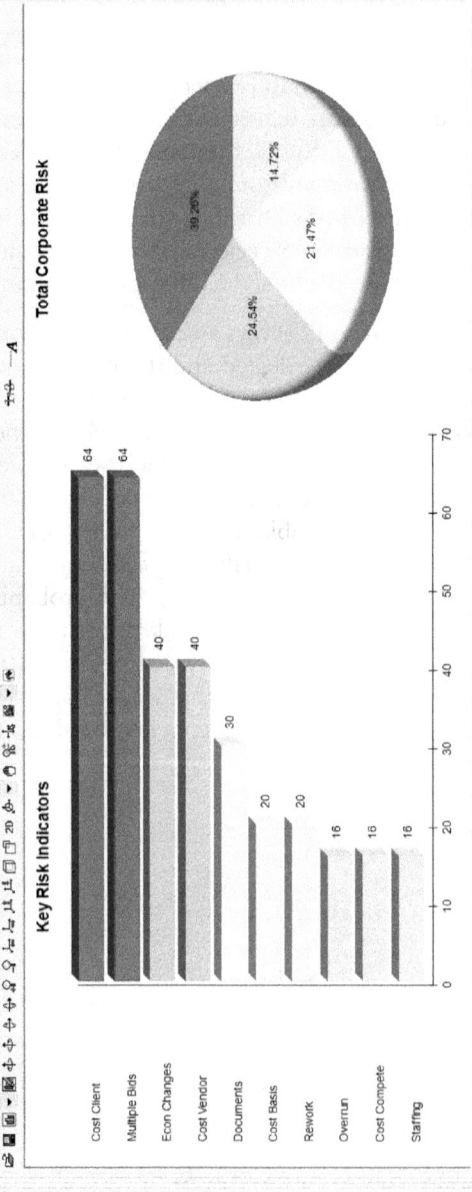

                                                                                            Based on Create Date
                                                                                            Current Year

Key Risk Indicators

Cost Client — 64
Multiple Bids — 64
Econ Changes — 40
Cost Vendor — 40
Documents — 30
Cost Basis — 20
Rework — 20
Overrun — 16
Cost Compete — 16
Staffing — 16

(axis: 0 10 20 30 40 50 60 70)

Total Corporate Risk

39.26%
14.72%
21.47%
24.54%

Figure 2.6: Risk Dashboard's Risk Elements

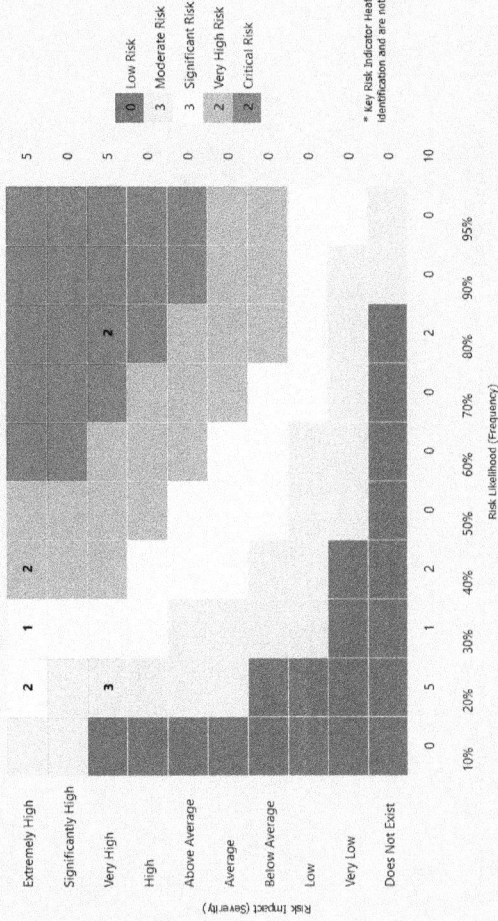

Figure 2.7: Risk Dashboard's Risk Heat Map

[EXAMPLE] - PROJECT ECONOMICS ANALYSIS TOOL

File Edit Language Decimals Help

Welcome to the ROV Project Economics Analysis Tool (PEAT). This ERM module will help you perform Enterprise Risk Management by creating and modeling Risk Registers. Results will be presented in the Risk Dashboards and can be segmented by Geography, Operations, Products, Activity, and Department. Additional details can be added as Risk Events, Risk Engagements, and Risk Diagrams. Statistical analysis on Risk Controls, Risk Forecasts, and Risk Mitigation are also available. Sensitivity Analysis and Monte Carlo Risk Simulations are also applied to various Diversifiable Risk, Undiversifiable Risk, and Risk Cost levels.

ERM Applied Analytics Risk Simulation Knowledge Center

Risk Settings Risk Register Risk Dashboard Risk Events Risk Engagement Risk Diagrams Risk Controls Risk Forecasts Risk Mitigation

Select what risk categories to show and then click on each of the subtabs below to view different dashboards.

View By:
○ Show All
○ Based on Diversifiable or Controllable Risk
☑ Show Active Risks Only   ☑ Ignore Duplicates

○ Risk Category: Select Category
○ G.O.P.A.D.: Select GOPAD
○ Division: Select Division
○ Manager: Select Manager

Date Selection:
● Show All
○ Custom: 1/ 2/2019 to 1/ 2/2019
○ Period: 1/ 2/2019

Based on Create Date
Current Year

Report

Risk Elements Risk Map Risk Groups Risk Exposure Risk Taxonomy Risk Inventory Risk Probability

Key Risk Indicators (KRI) Count: Heat Map

Risk Impact (Severity)	10%	20%	30%	40%	50%	60%	70%	80%	90%	95%	
Extremely High	0	2	1	2							5
Significantly High											0
Very High	0	3						2			5
High											0
Above Average											0
Average											0
Below Average											0
Low											0
Very Low											0
Does Not Exist	0	0	1	2	0	0	0	0	0	0	0
	10%	20%	30%	40%	50%	60%	70%	80%	90%	95%	10

Risk Likelihood (Frequency)

0	Low Risk
3	Moderate Risk
3	Significant Risk
2	Very High Risk
2	Critical Risk

* Key Risk Indicator Heat Maps are for risk visualization and risk density identification and are not used for decision making purposes.

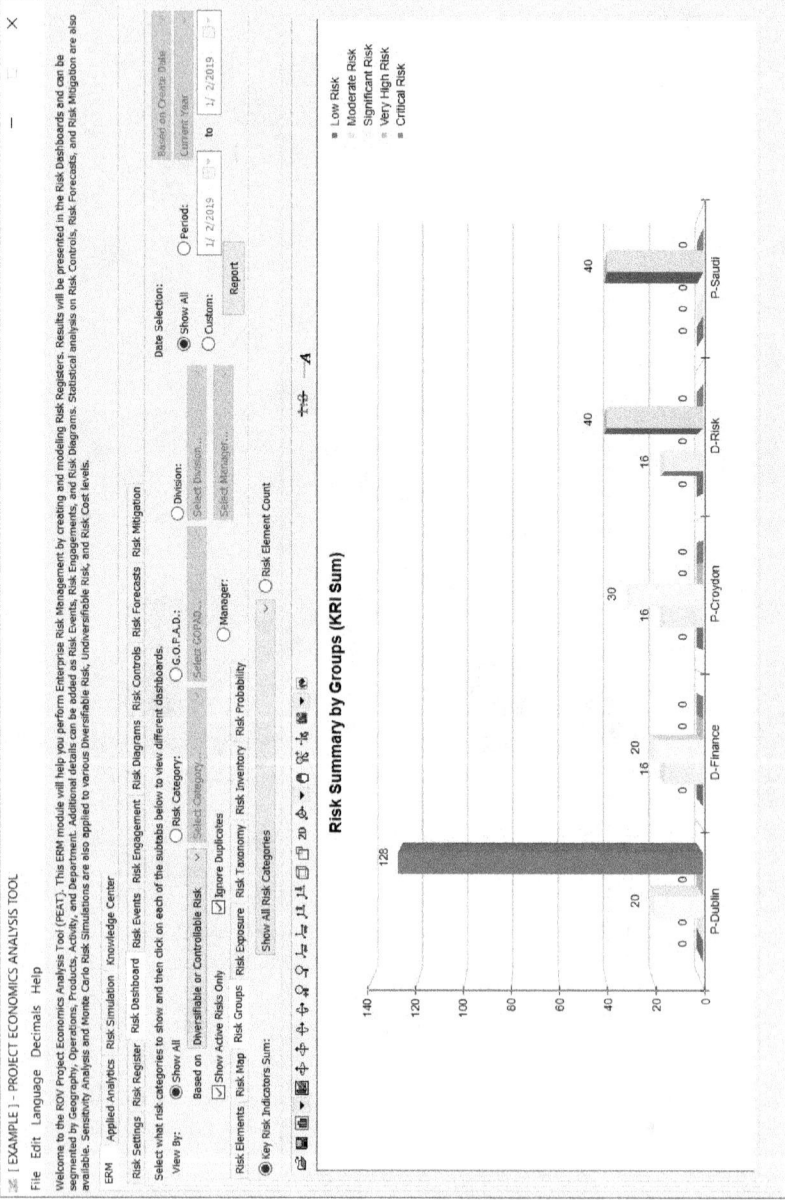

Figure 2.8: Risk Dashboard's Risk Groups (Element Count by Division)

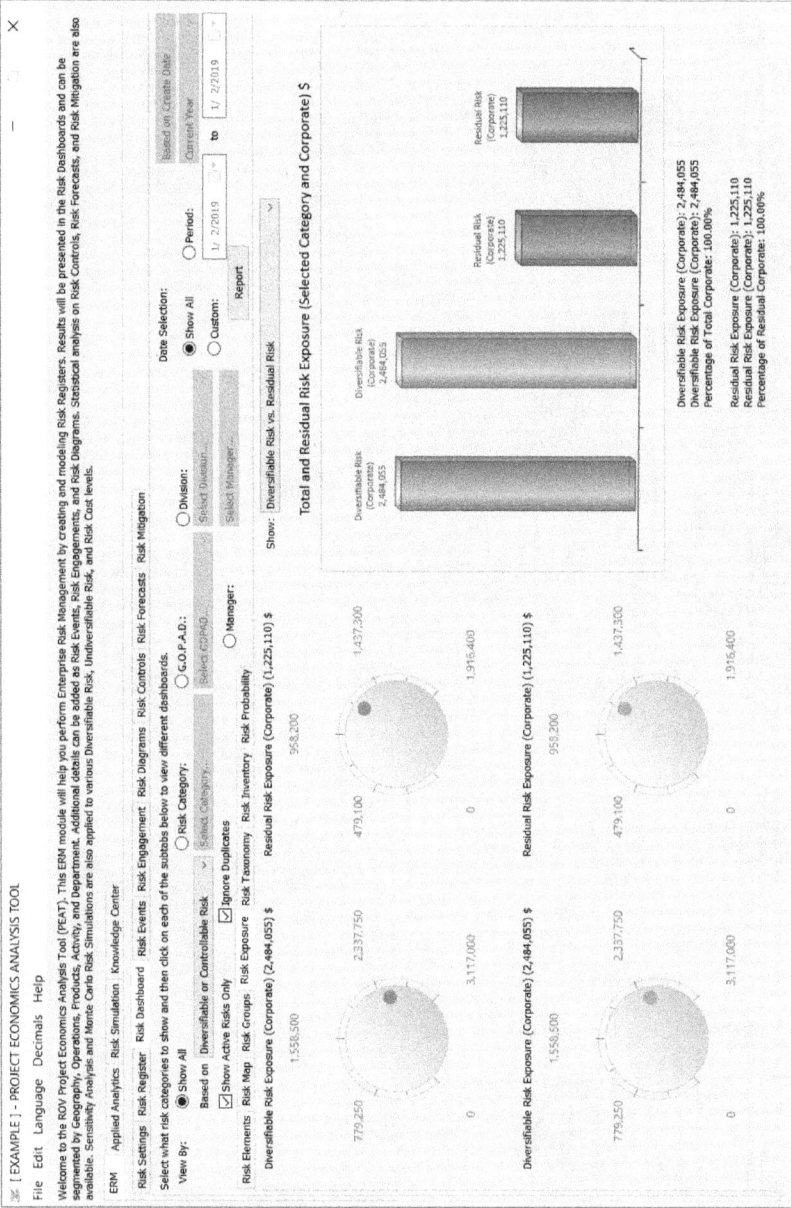

Figure 2.9: Risk Dashboard's Risk Exposure Levels (by G.O.P.A.D. and Corporate)

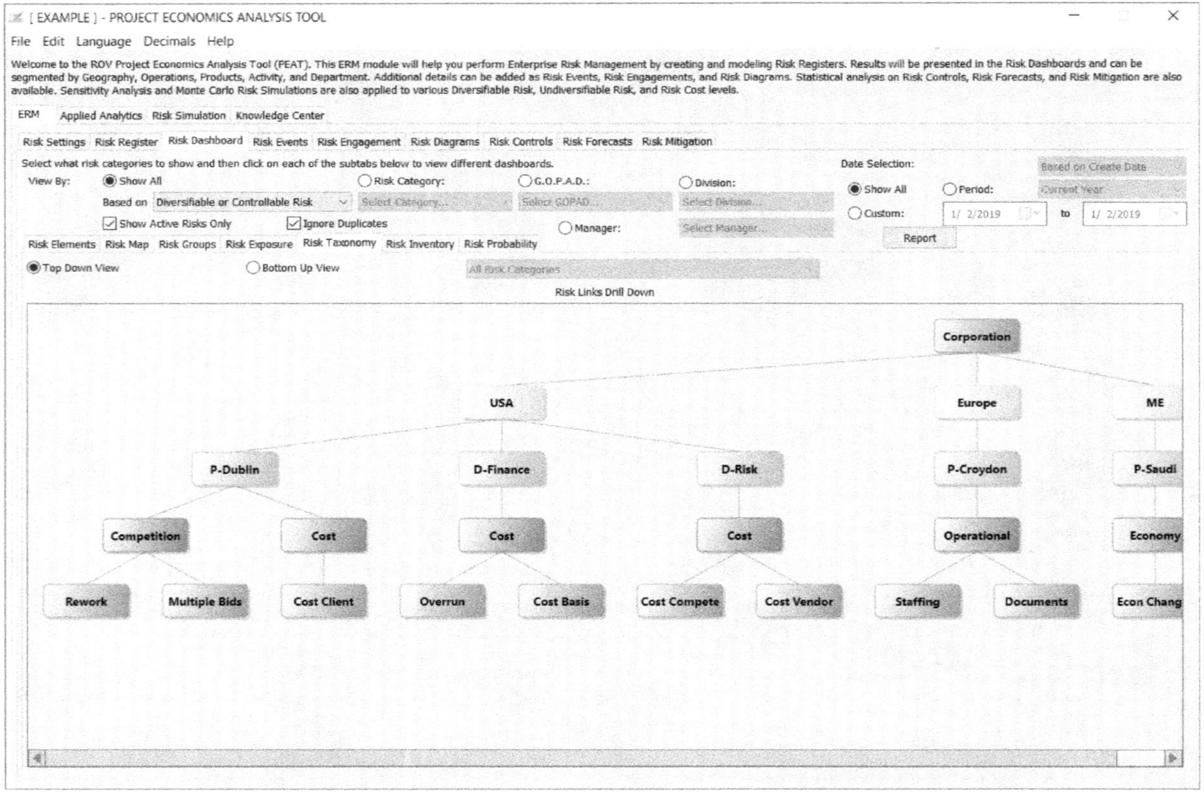

Figure 2.10: Risk Dashboard's Risk Taxonomy (Top-Down View)

File   Edit   Language   Decimals   Help

Welcome to the ROV Project Economics Analysis Tool (PEAT). This ERM module will help you perform Enterprise Risk Management by creating and modeling Risk Registers. Results will be presented in the Risk Dashboards and can be segmented by Geography, Operations, Products, Activity, and Department. Additional details can be added as Risk Events, Risk Engagements, and Risk Diagrams. Statistical analysis on Risk Controls, Risk Forecasts, and Risk Mitigation are also available. Sensitivity Analysis and Monte Carlo Risk Simulations are also applied to various Diversifiable Risk, Undiversifiable Risk, and Risk Cost levels.

ERM   Applied Analytics   Risk Simulation   Knowledge Center

Risk Settings   Risk Register   Risk Dashboard   Risk Events   Risk Engagement   Risk Diagrams   Risk Controls   Risk Forecasts   Risk Mitigation

Select what risk categories to show and then click on each of the subtabs below to view different dashboards.

View By: ● Show All
Based on Diversifiable or Controllable Risk
☑ Show Active Risks Only

○ Risk Category: Select Category
☑ Ignore Duplicates

○ G.O.P.A.D.: Select GOPAD
○ Division: Select Division
○ Manager: Select Manager

Date Selection: ● Show All   ○ Custom   ○ Period: 1/ 2/2019   to   1/ 2/2019
Report

Risk Elements   Risk Map   Risk Groups   Risk Exposure   Risk Taxonomy   Risk Inventory   Risk Probability

	Risk Register	CAT	GOPAD	DIV	Create	Edit	Due	Diversifiable L	I	KRI	Residual Risk L	I	KRI	PIC	% OK	Risk Exposure ($) Diversifiable	Current	Residual	Cost	Doc
1	Rework	Competi...	P-Dublin	USA	3/14/2014	3/14/2014	5/14/2014	4	5	20	3	3	9	JJSmith	60%	155,000	127,000	65,000	7,000	
ROV00...	Cause: Client keeps changing the specifications				Consequence:		Rework, scope creep, and requirements keep changing over time							Mitigati...	Contract needs to specify deadline for specifications freeze					
2	Multiple...	Competi...	P-Dublin	USA	3/14/2014	3/14/2014	5/14/2014	8	8	64	5	6	30	JCannon	50%	325,000	357,500	195,000	75,000	
ROV00...	Cause: Multiple competitors are looking at this				Consequence:		Might lose the bid/project							Mitigati...	JCannon needs to find differentiation and price competitiveness to win					
3	Overrun	Cost	D-Finance	USA	3/14/2014	3/14/2014	5/14/2014	4	4	16	3	3	9	JJSmith	33%	1,000,000	1,175,000	500,000	50,000	
ROV00...	Cause: Lack of raw materials and supplier delays				Consequence:		Additional wait time required							Mitigati...	Source multiple vendors and sign contracts with them at some extra cost					
4	Cost Basis	Cost	D-Finance	USA	3/14/2014	3/14/2014	5/14/2014	4	5	20	3	3	9	RRodgers	0%	350,000	529,000	179,000	35,000	
ROV00...	Cause: Multiple competitors are looking at this				Consequence:		Might lose the bid/project							Mitigati...	JCannon needs to find value differentiation and price competitiveness					
5	Staffing	Operati...	P-Croyd...	Europe	3/14/2014	3/14/2014		4	4	16	3	3	9	SMinh	0%	89,000	118,000	29,000	2,500	
ROV00...	Cause:				Consequence:									Mitigati...						
6	Cost Co...	Cost	D-Risk	USA	3/14/2014	3/14/2014	5/14/2014	4	4	16	3	3	9	SMinh	0%	85,555	121,110	35,555	6,500	
ROV00...	Cause: Multiple competitors are looking at this				Consequence:		Might lose the bid/project							Mitigati...	JCannon needs to create price competitiveness to win					
7	Cost Ven...	Cost	D-Risk	USA	4/8/2014	4/8/2014	6/8/2014	8	5	40	4	4	16	JCannon	0%	174,500	244,000	69,500	29,000	

Figure 2.11: Risk Dashboard's Risk Inventory

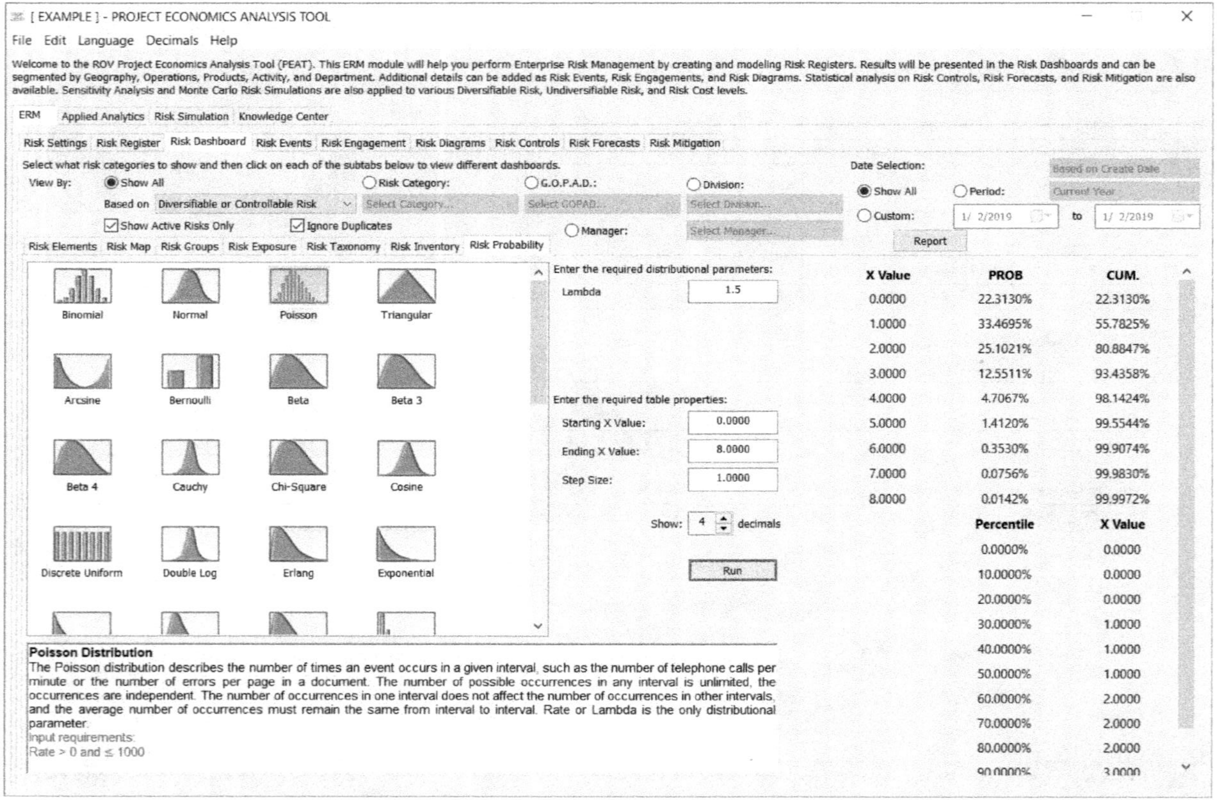

☰ [EXAMPLE] - PROJECT ECONOMICS ANALYSIS TOOL — □ ×

File   Edit   Language   Decimals   Help

Welcome to the ROV Project Economics Analysis Tool (PEAT). This ERM module will help you perform Enterprise Risk Management by creating and modeling Risk Registers. Results will be presented in the Risk Dashboards and can be segmented by Geography, Operations, Products, Activity, and Department. Additional details can be added as Risk Events, Risk Engagements, and Risk Diagrams. Statistical analysis on Risk Controls, Risk Forecasts, and Risk Mitigation are also available. Sensitivity Analysis and Monte Carlo Risk Simulations are also applied to various Diversifiable Risk, Undiversifiable Risk, and Risk Cost levels.

ERM   Applied Analytics   Risk Simulation   Knowledge Center

Risk Settings   Risk Register   Risk Dashboard   Risk Events   Risk Engagement   Risk Diagrams   Risk Controls   Risk Forecasts   Risk Mitigation

Select what risk categories to show and then click on each of the subtabs below to view different dashboards.

View By:	○ Show All		Date Selection:	
Based on	Risk Category:	○ Division:	● Show All	
☑ Show Active Risks Only	Select Category... ▼	Select Division...	○ Custom:	○ Period:
☑ Show Diversifiable or Controllable Risk	○ G.O.P.A.D.:		1/ 2/2019 ▼ to 1/ 2/2019 ▼	
☑ Ignore Duplicates	Select GOPAD...	○ Manager:		
		Select Manager...		Based on Create Date
				Current Year

Risk Elements   Risk Map   Risk Groups   Risk Exposure   Risk Taxonomy   Risk Inventory   Risk Probability

Binomial   Normal   Poisson   Triangular

Arcsine   Bernoulli   Beta   Beta 3

Beta 4   Cauchy   Chi-Square   Cosine

Discrete Uniform   Double Log   Erlang   Exponential

Enter the required distributional parameters:

Lambda	1.5

Enter the required table properties:

Starting X Value:	0.0000
Ending X Value:	8.0000
Step Size:	1.0000

Show: 4 ⬍ decimals

Report   Run

X Value	PROB	CUM.
0.0000	22.3130%	22.3130%
1.0000	33.4695%	55.7825%
2.0000	25.1021%	80.8847%
3.0000	12.5511%	93.4358%
4.0000	4.7067%	98.1424%
5.0000	1.4120%	99.5544%
6.0000	0.3530%	99.9074%
7.0000	0.0756%	99.9830%
8.0000	0.0142%	99.9972%

Percentile	X Value
0.0000%	0.0000
10.0000%	0.0000
20.0000%	0.0000
30.0000%	1.0000
40.0000%	1.0000
50.0000%	1.0000
60.0000%	2.0000
70.0000%	2.0000
80.0000%	2.0000
90.0000%	3.0000

Poisson Distribution
The Poisson distribution describes the number of times an event occurs in a given interval, such as the number of telephone calls per minute or the number of errors per page in a document. The number of possible occurrences in any interval is unlimited, the occurrences are independent. The number of occurrences in one interval does not affect the number of occurrences in other intervals, and the average number of occurrences must remain the same from interval to interval. Rate or Lambda is the only distributional parameter.

Input requirements:
Rate > 0 and ≤ 1000

Figure 2.12: Risk Dashboard's Exact Probability Analysis (CDF and PDF)

Risk Diagrams

In the **Risk Diagrams** section, ready-made templates on Bowtie Hazard Diagrams, Cause and Effect Ishikawa Fishbone Diagrams, Drill-Down Diagrams, Influence Diagrams, Mind Maps, and Node Diagrams can be used to create customized diagrams. Sometimes, customized risk diagrams such as those shown in Figure 2.13 can be used to better illustrate the risk process, risk mitigation, risk cause and effect, and risk impact of the Risk Register. Right-click on the *Risk Diagram 1* tab to add additional diagrams, to delete, or to rename existing diagrams. In addition, various pre-configured diagram templates are available in the droplist to help users get started in generating their own risk diagrams.

Risk Controls

The PEAT ERM system also allows for the creation of **Risk Control** charts and KRI trends over time (Figure 2.14), and statistical process controls can be applied. Control charts help to visually and statistically determine if a specific risk event is in-control or out-of-control. For instance, if the number of risk events, such as a plant accident, spikes within a certain time period, was that set of events considered expected under statistically normal circumstances or was it an outlier requiring more detailed analysis?

Start by typing in or pasting into the grid some historical data, select the type of chart to show, and type in the variable to test (e.g., VAR7), and hit *Run*. Multiple charts can be saved for future retrieval by adding in a name and clicking *Save As*.

The charts' statistical control limits are computed based on the actual data collected (e.g., the number of risks on a manufacturing factory floor). The number of risk events is taken over time and the upper control limit (UCL) and lower control limit (LCL) are computed, as are the central line (CL) and other sigma levels. The resulting chart is called a control chart, and if the process if out-of-control, the actual defect line will be outside of the UCL and LCL lines. Typically, when the LCL is a negative value, we set the floor as zero. The ERM software presents several control chart types, and each type is used under different circumstances.

- *X*-chart: used when the variable has raw data values and there are multiple measurements in a sample experiment, multiple experiments are run, and the average of the collected data is of interest.

- *R*-chart: used when the variable has raw data values and there are multiple measurements in a sample experiment, multiple experiments are run, and the range of the collected data is of interest.

- *XmR*-chart: used when the variable has raw data values and is a single measurement taken in each sample experiment, multiple experiments are run, and the actual value of the collected data is of interest.

- *P*-chart: used when the variable of interest is an attribute (e.g., defective or nondefective) and the data collected are in proportions of defects (or number of defects in a specific sample) and there are multiple measurements in a sample experiment, multiple experiments are run, and the average proportion of defects of the collected data is of interest; and the number of samples collected in each experiment differs.

- *NP*-chart: used when the variable of interest is an attribute (e.g., defective or nondefective) and the data collected are in proportions of defects (or number of defects in a specific sample) and there are multiple measurements in a sample experiment, multiple experiments are run, and the average proportion of defects of the collected data is of interest; also, the number of samples collected in each experiment is constant for all experiments.

- *C*-chart: used when the variable of interest is an attribute (e.g., defective or nondefective) and the data collected are in total number of defects (actual count in units) and there are multiple measurements in a sample experiment, multiple experiments are run, and the average number of defects of the collected data is of interest; also, the number of samples collected in each experiment are the same.

- *U*-chart: used when the variable of interest is an attribute (e.g., defective or nondefective) and the data collected are in total number of defects (actual count in units) and there are multiple measurements in a sample experiment, multiple experiments are run, and the average number of defects of the collected data is of interest; also, the number of samples collected in each experiment differs.

Risk Forecast

Historical risk data can be used to apply predictive modeling to forecast future states of risk, as well as Risk Tracking, Time-Series Risk Forecasts, PDF/CDF Likelihood of Occurrence, and Snapshots per period and over time (Figure 2.15). In the **Risk Forecast** section, using either historical data or subject matter estimates, you can run forecast models on time-series or cross-sectional data by applying advanced forecast analytics such as ARIMA, Auto ARIMA, Auto Econometrics, Basic Econometrics, Cubic Splines, Fuzzy Logic, GARCH (8 variations), Exponential J-Curves, Logistic S-Curves, Markov Chains, Generalized Linear Models (Logit, Probit, and Tobit), Multivariate Regressions (Linear and Nonlinear), Neural Network, Stochastic Processes (Brownian Motion, Mean-Reversion, Jump-Diffusion), Time-Series Analysis, and Trendlines.

Risk Mitigation

The **Risk Mitigation** section in PEAT's ERM helps determine if a specific risk mitigation strategy or technique is working, at least statistically speaking (Figure 2.16). Risk managers can collect data from *before* and *after* a risk mitigation strategy is implemented and determine if there is a statistically significant difference between the two. The utility allows for the valuation and statistical computation of the effectiveness of risk mitigation programs through various hypothesis testing methods. For example, in the risk event of check deposit errors, the bank could potentially invest in high-resolution check scanners with smart optical character recognition software with embedded algorithms to check for any potential human errors. If the number of check errors is tracked before the new scanner system was implemented and compared with after the implementation, risk analysts can determine the efficacy and effectiveness of said scanner, if it was worth the money invested, and if additional scanners should be implemented across other bank branches.

Risk Knowledge

Any good ERM system should always include quick getting started guides and training videos. The **Knowledge Center** in PEAT's ERM module has slides, training materials, and videos that are all fully customizable for an organization (Figure 2.17).

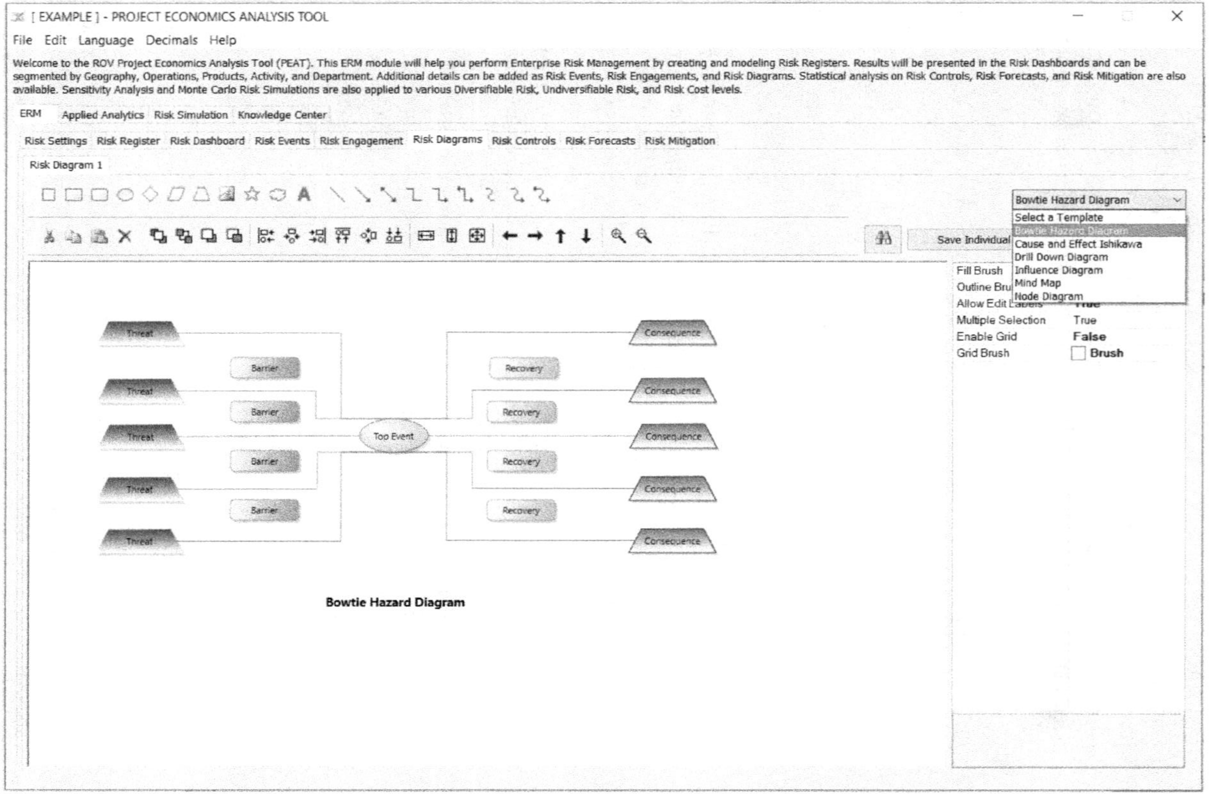

Figure 2.13: Risk Diagrams

ERM [EXAMPLE] - PROJECT ECONOMICS ANALYSIS TOOL

File   Edit   Language   Decimals   Help

Welcome to the ROV Project Economics Analysis Tool (PEAT). This ERM module will help you perform Enterprise Risk Management by creating and modeling Risk Registers. Results will be presented in the Risk Dashboards and can be segmented by Geography, Operations, Products, Activity, and Department. Additional details can be added as Risk Events, Risk Engagements, and Risk Diagrams. Statistical analysis on Risk Controls, Risk Forecasts, and Risk Mitigation are also available. Sensitivity Analysis and Monte Carlo Risk Simulations are also applied to various Diversifiable Risk, Undiversifiable Risk, and Risk Cost levels.

ERM   Applied Analytics   Risk Simulation   Knowledge Center

Risk Settings   Risk Register   Risk Dashboard   Risk Events   Risk Engagement   Risk Diagrams   Risk Controls   Risk Forecasts   Risk Mitigation

| Name | VAR1 | VAR2 | VAR3 | VAR4 | VAR5 |
	M1	M2	X2	X4	Y
1	138.9000	286.7000	185.0000	79.6000	521.0000
2	139.4000	287.8000	600.0000	1.0000	367.000
3	139.7000	289.1000	372.0000	32.3000	443.000
4	139.7000	290.1000	142.0000	45.1000	365.000
5	140.7000	292.3000	432.0000	190.8000	614.000
6	140.7000	293.9000	290.0000	31.8000	385.000
7	141.7000	295.3000	346.0000	678.4000	286.000
8	141.9000	296.4000	328.0000	340.8000	397.000
9	141.0000	296.5000	354.0000	239.6000	764.000
10	140.5000	296.6000	266.0000	111.9000	427.000
11	140.4000	297.2000	320.0000	172.5000	153.000
12	140.0000	297.8000	197.0000	12.2000	231.000
13	140.0000	298.3000	266.0000	205.6000	524.000
14	139.9000	298.5000	173.0000	154.6000	328.000
15	139.8000	299.2000	190.0000	49.7000	240.000
16	139.6000	300.1000	239.0000	30.3000	286.000
17	139.6000	301.0000	190.0000	92.8000	285.000
18	139.6000	302.2000	241.0000	96.9000	569.000
19	140.2000	304.2000	189.0000	39.8000	96.000C
20	141.3000	306.8000	358.0000	489.2000	498.000
21	141.2000	308.2000	315.0000	767.6000	481.000
22	140.9000	309.6000	303.0000	163.6000	468.000

Analysis
Control Chart: C
Control Chart: NP
Control Chart: P
Control Chart: R
Control Chart: U
Control Chart: X
Control Chart: XMR
Charts: 2D Area
Charts: 2D Bar
Charts: 2D Line
Charts: 2D Pareto

Load Example   Clear Data

Data:
> Var1

Name: Control Chart C

Save As
Save
Edit
Delete

Run   Grid   Copy Chart

Model
Chart 2D Area
Chart 2D Bar
Chart 2D Line
Chart 2D Pareto
Chart 2D Point
Chart 2D Scatter
Chart 3D Area
Chart 3D Bar
Chart 3D Line

— Defect Units — LCL — CL — UCL — 1 Sigma + — 2 Sigma + — 1 Sigma — — 2 Sigma -

Value

Itm

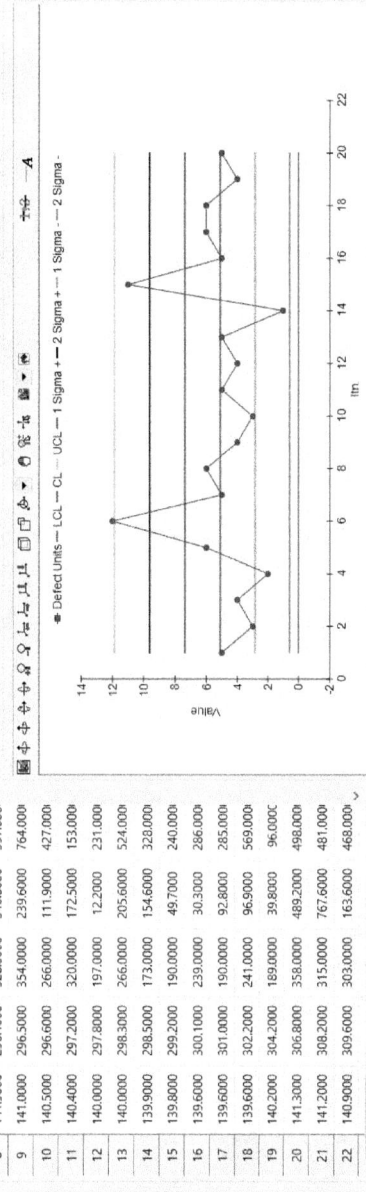

Figure 2.14: Risk Controls Charts (Sample C-Chart)

File   Edit   Language   Decimals   Help

Welcome to the ROV Project Economics Analysis Tool (PEAT). This ERM module will help you perform Enterprise Risk Management by creating and modeling Risk Registers. Results will be presented in the Risk Dashboards and can be segmented by Geography, Operations, Products, Activity, and Department. Additional details can be added as Risk Events, Risk Engagements, and Risk Diagrams. Statistical analysis on Risk Controls, Risk Forecasts, and Risk Mitigation are also available. Sensitivity Analysis and Monte Carlo Risk Simulations are also applied to various Diversifiable Risk, Undiversifiable Risk, and Risk Cost levels.

ERM   Applied Analytics   Risk Simulation   Knowledge Center

Risk Settings   Risk Register   Risk Dashboard   Risk Events   Risk Engagement   Risk Diagrams   Risk Controls   Risk Forecasts   Risk Mitigation

Name	VAR1	VAR2	VAR3	VAR4	VAR5
	Historical	Y	X1	X2	X3
1	684.2000	521.0000	18,308.00...	185.0000	4.0410
2	584.1000	367.0000	1,148.0000	600.0000	0.5500
3	765.4000	443.0000	18,068.00...	372.0000	3.6650
4	892.3000	365.0000	7,729.0000	142.0000	2.3510
5	885.4000	614.0000	100,484.0...	432.0000	29.760C
6	677.0000	385.0000	16,728.00...	290.0000	3.2940
7	1,006.6000	286.0000	14,630.00...	346.0000	3.2870
8	1,122.1000	397.0000	4,008.0000	328.0000	0.6660
9	1,163.4000	764.0000	38,927.00...	354.0000	12.938C
10	993.2000	427.0000	22,322.00...	266.0000	6.4780
11	1,312.5000	153.0000	3,711.0000	320.0000	1.1080
12	1,545.3000	231.0000	3,136.0000	197.0000	1.0070
13	1,596.2000	524.0000	50,508.00...	266.0000	11.431C
14	1,260.4000	328.0000	28,886.00...	173.0000	5.5440
15	1,735.2000	240.0000	16,996.00...	190.0000	2.7770
16	2,029.7000	286.0000	13,035.00...	239.0000	2.4780
17	2,107.8000	285.0000	12,973.00...	190.0000	3.6850
18	1,650.3000	569.0000	16,309.00...	241.0000	4.2200
19	2,304.4000	96.0000	5,227.0000	189.0000	1.2280
20	2,639.4000	498.0000	19,235.00...	358.0000	4.7810
21		481.0000	44,487.00...	315.0000	6.0160
22		468.0000	44,213.00...	303.0000	9.2950

Forecast
- Stepwise Regression (Backward)
- Stepwise Regression (Correlation)
- Stepwise Regression (Forward)
- Stepwise Regression (Forward-Backward)
- Multiple Regression (Linear)
- Multiple Regression (Nonlinear)
- Time-Series Analysis (Auto)
- Time-Series Analysis (Double Exponential...
- Time-Series Analysis (Double Moving Ave...
- Time-Series Analysis (Double Moving Ave...
- Time-Series Analysis (Holt-Winter's Additi...
- Time-Series Analysis (Holt-Winter's Multi...
- Time-Series Analysis (Seasonal Additive)
- Time-Series Analysis (Seasonal Multiplica...
- Time-Series Analysis (Single Exponential)
- Time-Series Analysis (Single Moving Aver...

Load Example   Clear Data

Chart   Statistics

Var1
4
8

Data,
Seasonality(Periods/Cycle),
Forecast Periods,
Alpha(Optional):0-1 else optimized),
Beta(Optional):0-1 else optimized),
Gamma(Optional:0-1 else optimized)):
- Var1
- 4
- 3
- 2.57
- 10.3
- 9.26

Name: TS Analysis HWM

Model
- TS Analysis Auto
- TS Analysis DES
- TS Analysis DMA
- TS Analysis DMA Lag
- TS Analysis HWA
- TS Analysis HWM
- TS Analysis SA
- TS Analysis SM
- TS Analysis SES
- TS Analysis SMA
- Trend Line Diff Detrended
- Trend Line Exp Detrended
- Trend Line Exp

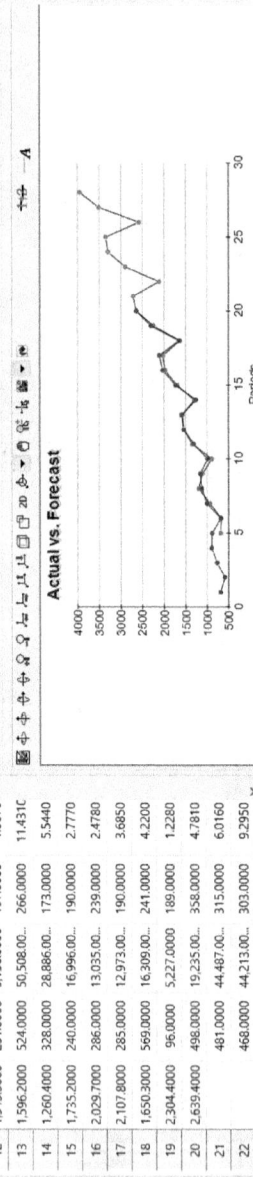

Save As   Save   Edit   Delete   ∧   ∨   Run   Grid   Copy Chart

Actual vs. Forecast

Figure 2.15: Risk Forecast

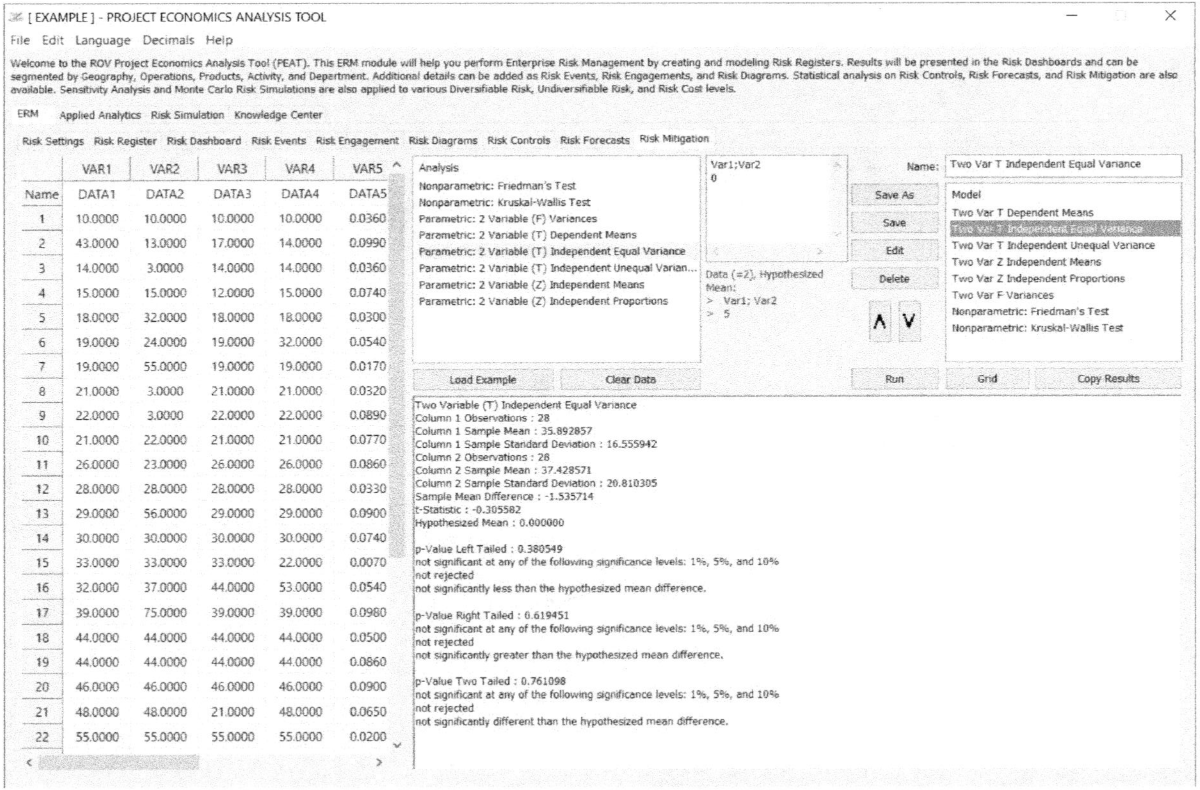

≡ [EXAMPLE] - PROJECT ECONOMICS ANALYSIS TOOL — ☐ ✕

File Edit Language Decimals Help

Welcome to the ROV Project Economics Analysis Tool (PEAT). This ERM module will help you perform Enterprise Risk Management by creating and modeling Risk Registers. Results will be presented in the Risk Dashboards and can be segmented by Geography, Operations, Products, Activity, and Department. Additional details can be added as Risk Events, Risk Engagements, and Risk Diagrams. Statistical analysis on Risk Controls, Risk Forecasts, and Risk Mitigation are also available. Sensitivity Analysis and Monte Carlo Risk Simulations are also applied to various Diversifiable Risk, Undiversifiable Risk, and Risk Cost levels.

ERM Applied Analytics Risk Simulation Knowledge Center

Risk Settings Risk Register Risk Dashboard Risk Events Risk Engagement Risk Diagrams Risk Controls Risk Forecasts Risk Mitigation

Name	VAR1	VAR2	VAR3	VAR4	VAR5
	DATA1	DATA2	DATA3	DATA4	DATA5
1	10.0000	10.0000	10.0000	10.0000	0.0360
2	43.0000	13.0000	17.0000	14.0000	0.0990
3	14.0000	3.0000	14.0000	14.0000	0.0360
4	15.0000	15.0000	12.0000	15.0000	0.0740
5	18.0000	32.0000	18.0000	18.0000	0.0300
6	19.0000	24.0000	19.0000	32.0000	0.0540
7	19.0000	55.0000	19.0000	19.0000	0.0170
8	21.0000	3.0000	21.0000	21.0000	0.0320
9	22.0000	3.0000	22.0000	22.0000	0.0890
10	21.0000	22.0000	21.0000	21.0000	0.0770
11	26.0000	23.0000	26.0000	26.0000	0.0860
12	28.0000	28.0000	28.0000	28.0000	0.0330
13	29.0000	56.0000	29.0000	29.0000	0.0900
14	30.0000	30.0000	30.0000	30.0000	0.0740
15	33.0000	33.0000	33.0000	22.0000	0.0070
16	32.0000	37.0000	44.0000	53.0000	0.0540
17	39.0000	75.0000	39.0000	39.0000	0.0980
18	44.0000	44.0000	44.0000	44.0000	0.0500
19	44.0000	44.0000	44.0000	44.0000	0.0860
20	46.0000	46.0000	46.0000	46.0000	0.0900
21	48.0000	48.0000	21.0000	48.0000	0.0650
22	55.0000	55.0000	55.0000	55.0000	0.0200

Analysis

Nonparametric: Friedman's Test
Nonparametric: Kruskal-Wallis Test
Parametric: 2 Variable (F) Variances
Parametric: 2 Variable (T) Dependent Means
Parametric: 2 Variable (T) Independent Equal Variance
Parametric: 2 Variable (T) Independent Unequal Variance
Parametric: 2 Variable (Z) Independent Means
Parametric: 2 Variable (Z) Independent Proportions

Load Example   Clear Data

Two Variable (T) Independent Equal Variance
Column 1 Observations : 28
Column 1 Sample Mean : 35.892857
Column 1 Sample Standard Deviation : 16.555942
Column 2 Observations : 28
Column 2 Sample Mean : 37.428571
Column 2 Sample Standard Deviation : 20.810305
Sample Mean Difference : -1.535714
t-Statistic : -0.305582
Hypothesized Mean : 0.000000

p-Value Left Tailed : 0.380549
not significant at any of the following significance levels: 1%, 5%, and 10%
not rejected
not significantly less than the hypothesized mean difference.

p-Value Right Tailed : 0.619451
not significant at any of the following significance levels: 1%, 5%, and 10%
not rejected
not significantly greater than the hypothesized mean difference.

p-Value Two Tailed : 0.761098
not significant at any of the following significance levels: 1%, 5%, and 10%
not rejected
not significantly different than the hypothesized mean difference.

Var1:Var2
0

Data (-z), Hypothesized
Mean:
> Var1 : Var2
> 5

Name: Two Var T Independent Equal Variance

Model
Two Var T Dependent Means
Two Var T Independent Equal Variance
Two Var T Independent Unequal Variance
Two Var Z Independent Means
Two Var Z Independent Proportions
Two Var F Variances
Nonparametric: Friedman's Test
Nonparametric: Kruskal-Wallis Test

Save As
Save
Edit
Delete
∧ ∨
< >
Run   Grid   Copy Results

Figure 2.16: Risk Mitigation

[EXAMPLE] - PROJECT ECONOMICS ANALYSIS TOOL

— □ ×

File   Edit   Language   Decimals   Help

Welcome to the ROV Project Economics Analysis Tool (PEAT). This ERM module will help you perform Enterprise Risk Management by creating and modeling Risk Registers. Results will be presented in the Risk Dashboards and can be segmented by Geography, Operations, Products, Activity, and Department. Additional details can be added as Risk Events, Risk Engagements, and Risk Diagrams. Statistical analysis on Risk Controls, Risk Forecasts, and Risk Mitigation are also available. Sensitivity Analysis and Monte Carlo Risk Simulations are also applied to various Diversifiable Risk, Undiversifiable Risk, and Risk Cost levels.

ERM   Applied Analytics   Risk Simulation   Knowledge Center

Step-by-Step Procedures   Practical Applications   Getting Started Videos

<< Prev   Step 09 of 28   Next >>

You can change the default sensitivity settings of each input assumption to test and decide how many input assumption variables to chart (large models with many inputs may generate unsightly and less useful charts, whereas showing just the top variables reveals more information through a more elegant chart). You can also choose to run the input assumptions as unique inputs, group them as a line item (all individual inputs on a single line item are assumed to be one variable), or run them as variable groups (e.g., all line items under Revenue will be assumed to be a single variable). Remember to click COMPUTE to update the analysis if you make any changes to any of the settings. The sensitivity results are also shown as a table grid at the bottom of the screen (e.g., the initial base value of the chosen output variable, the input assumption changes, and the resulting output variable's sensitivity results). Finally, you can COPY CHART or COPY GRID results into the Windows clipboard for pasting into another software application.

Project 1...Net Present Value (NPV)

Sensitivity +/-   10   %
Show the top   10   variables
Show results with   2   decimals

Reset

Select the granularity of the sensitivity analysis:
○ Individual Unique Inputs
○ Line Items
⦿ Variable Groups

Update | Excel | Copy Chart

The Tornado run has been completed.

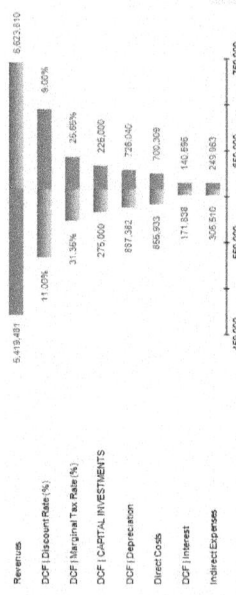

Project 1...Net Present Value (NPV)

Chart	% Up	% Down	Inputs	Base Value: Output Downside	Output Upside	Effective Range	Input Changes Input Downside	Input Upside	Base Case Value
					608,388.29				
✓	10.00%	10.00%	Revenues	471,501.67	745,274.91	273,773.24	5,419,480.60	6,623,809.62	6,021,645.11
✓	10.00%	10.00%	DCF	Discount Rate (%)	694,674.44	533,487.06	161,187.38	9.00%	11.00%	10.00%
✓	10.00%	10.00%	DCF	Marginal Tax Rate (%)	642,603.76	574,172.81	68,430.95	25.65%	31.35%	28.50%
✓	10.00%	10.00%	DCF	CAPITAL INVESTMENTS	633,388.29	583,388.29	50,000.00	225,000.00	275,000.00	250,000.00
✓	10.00%	10.00%	DCF	Depreciation	629,216.89	587,559.68	41,657.22	726,039.90	887,382.10	806,711.00

Figure 2.17: Risk Knowledge Center

Risk Events

Sometimes Risk Registers can be simplified to not require any Likelihood, Impact, Risk Exposure amounts, Mitigation Costs, or Residual Risk Exposure amounts. That is, only qualitative information and details are required by the organization. In such situations, you can bypass parts of the *Risk Settings* section and completely bypass the *Risk Register* section. Instead, proceed directly to the **Risk Events** and **Risk Engagement** sections.

Figure 2.18 shows an illustration of a simplified Risk Register of items in the PEAT ERM system using the **Risk Events | Event Input** section. The risk maps can still be used but only simple risk event counts, event names, and dates are used and captured. Select a *Division, G.O.P.A.D.*, or *Risk Category* and select the relevant *Risk Manager* and enter an *Event Name*, the *Count*, and *Event Date*. The entire grid dataset can be saved, and additional datasets can be added as needed.

If the more rigid *Event Input* needs more customization, proceed to the **Custom Event Input** section instead. Once here, click on the *Customize* button to add new segments and create your own custom inputs for the bottom grid (Figure 2.19). As usual, multiple datasets can be saved here.

Once either the *Event Input* or *Custom Event Input* sections have been filled, proceed to the **Event Reports** section to view the reports and charts. In **Risk Table**, start by selecting the dataset to analyze, and identify the risk segments to display and click on the *Update* button (Figure 2.20). A table of counts will be displayed. The results can also be displayed as a bar chart in the **Risk Chart** (Figure 2.21) section.

Risk Engagement

Sometimes, just qualitative risk event information needs to be saved and archived, without the need to create any divisions or segmentation, thereby bypassing the *Risk Settings* and *Risk Register* completely. This is where the PEAT ERM's **Risk Engagement** section comes in handy. Multiple Risk Engagements can be created in a single file where each of the following subsections has multiple Risk Elements: Pre-Engagement Risks, Engagement Risks, Lessons Learned, and Custom Risk Register as seen in Figures 2.22–2.25. By archiving these qualitative risk aspects, a Risk Library can be generated and historical risks can be analyzed over time.

In each of these four sections, the top sections are identical. For instance, each section can be *Customized* in terms of the column and category headers. Multiple rows of qualitative data can be entered or pasted into the data grid and saved as a dataset. Multiple datasets can be created and saved. *Reports* can also be generated for the active dataset. Finally, right-clicking on the tab names provides the ability to *Rename*, *Add a New Tab*, or *Duplicate* the existing tab. For instance, the default tab name of *Pre-Engagement* can be changed to something more appropriate if required.

The following provides a quick compare and contrast of the four sections.

- **Pre-Engagement**. Qualitative notes and comments can be entered, with three levels of *Risk Criteria* (Figure 2.22). This subsection allows up to three levels of risk elements to be identified and categorized.

- **Engagement**. Qualitative notes and comments can be similarly entered, but this subsection also allows the ability to enter a numerical value for *Likelihood* (L) and *Impact* (I), and the KRI is automatically computed (Figure 2.23).

- **Lessons Learned**. Qualitative notes and comments can be entered in a free-flowing format, without the need for any risk criteria levels or likelihood and impact inputs (Figure 2.24).

- **Custom Risk Register**. This subsection can be a mix of the traditional Risk Register and a more customized free-flowing dataset (Figure 2.25). Its *Custom Category* button can be used to add the traditional items such as *Risk Item*, which will automatically update the *Category* and *Division* columns.

Figure 2.18: Risk Events Data Entry and Archive

[EXAMPLE] - PROJECT ECONOMICS ANALYSIS TOOL — □ ×

File   Edit   Language   Decimals   Help

Welcome to the ROV Project Economics Analysis Tool (PEAT). This ERM module will help you perform Enterprise Risk Management by creating and modeling Risk Registers. Results will be presented in the Risk Dashboards and can be segmented by Geography, Operations, Products, Activity, and Department. Additional details can be added as Risk Events, Risk Engagements, and Risk Diagrams. Statistical analysis on Risk Controls, Risk Forecasts, and Risk Mitigation are also available. Sensitivity Analysis and Monte Carlo Risk Simulations are also applied to various Diversifiable Risk, Undiversifiable Risk, and Risk Cost levels.

ERM   Applied Analytics   Risk Simulation   Knowledge Center

Risk Settings   Risk Register   Risk Dashboard   Risk Events   Risk Engagement   Risk Diagrams   Risk Controls   Risk Forecasts   Risk Mitigation

ERM Event Input   Custom Event Input   Event Reports

Start by creating a new or editing an existing Dataset, then select a Division, GOPAD or Risk Category. Select a Risk Manager and enter the event information.

Select a Division:

Division
☑ Europe
☐ ME
☐ USA

OR

Select a GOPAD:

GOPAD
☐ P-Croydon
☐ P-Dublin
☐ P-Saudi
☐ D-Risk
☐ D-Finance
☐ D-Operations
☐ D-IT
☐ D-Legal

OR

Select a Risk Category:

Category
☐ Client
☐ Competition
☐ Compliance
☐ Concentration
☐ Cost
☐ Credit
☐ Cultural
☐ Economy
☐ Financial

AND

Risk Manager/Reporter

Manager
☑ JJSmith
☐ JCannon
☐ RCarter
☐ SMinh
☐ RRodgers

Add Event   Delete Event

Notes (Optional)

We recommend creating new saved datasets for each year or each physical location so that the risk events reporting can be compared later.

Save as a New Dataset:
2014 Risk Events Log   Save As

List of Saved Datasets:

Dataset
2014 Risk Events Log
2013 Risk Events Log

New   Delete
Edit   Save

< >

The total Count of Events is 168, the number of entry rows is 28, with the last event date entered of 12/15/2014

No.	Event Name	Count	Event Date	Selected Segment	Entered By
1	Missing Records	2	1/27/2014	D-Finance	JJSmith
2	Possible Fraud	3	2/20/2014	D-Finance	JCannon
3	Employee Injury	4	1/25/2014	D-Operations	SMinh
4	Employee Injury	6	3/15/2014	D-Operations	SMinh
5	Possible Fraud	4	4/27/2014	D-Finance	JCannon
6	Employee Injury	6	4/30/2014	D-Operations	SMinh
7	Late Payments	6	2/28/2014	D-Finance	JCannon
8	Late Payments	4	4/27/2014	D-Finance	JCannon
9	Customer Complaints	15	1/31/2014	D-Operations	RCarter
10	Customer Complaints	18	2/28/2014	D-Operations	RCarter
11	Customer Complaints	22	3/28/2014	D-Operations	RCarter
12	Employee Injury	6	6/30/2014	D-Operations	JCannon
13	Employee Injury	4	8/31/2014	D-Operations	JCannon

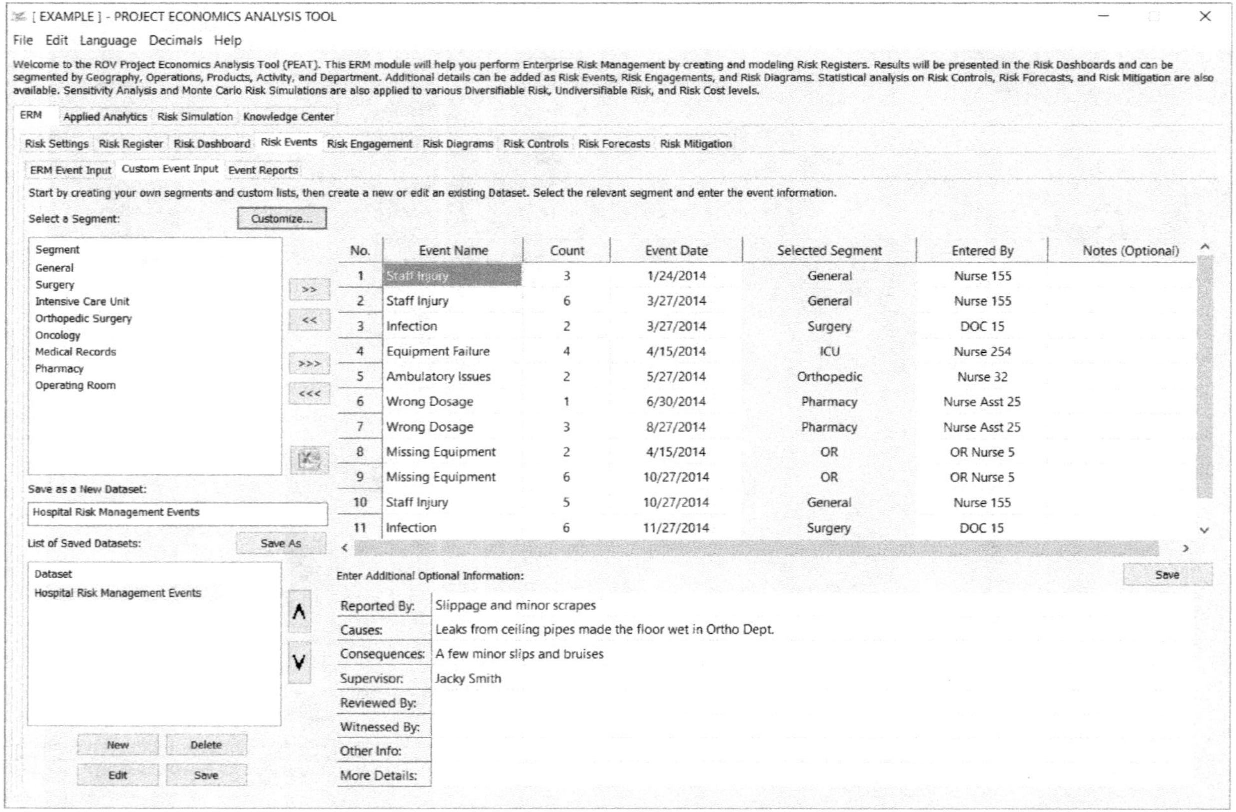
[EXAMPLE] - PROJECT ECONOMICS ANALYSIS TOOL
File Edit Language Decimals Help
Welcome to the ROV Project Economics Analysis Tool (PEAT). This ERM module will help you perform Enterprise Risk Management by creating and modeling Risk Registers. Results will be presented in the Risk Dashboards and can be segmented by Geography, Operations, Products, Activity, and Department. Additional details can be added as Risk Events, Risk Engagements, and Risk Diagrams. Statistical analysis on Risk Controls, Risk Forecasts, and Risk Mitigation are also available. Sensitivity Analysis and Monte Carlo Risk Simulations are also applied to various Diversifiable Risk, Undiversifiable Risk, and Risk Cost levels.
ERM Applied Analytics Risk Simulation Knowledge Center
Risk Settings Risk Register Risk Dashboard Risk Events Risk Engagement Risk Diagrams Risk Controls Risk Forecasts Risk Mitigation
ERM Event Input Custom Event Input Event Reports
Start by creating your own segments and custom lists, then create a new or edit an existing Dataset. Select the relevant segment and enter the event information.
Select a Segment:
Customize...
Segment
General
Surgery
Intensive Care Unit
Orthopedic Surgery
Oncology
Medical Records
Pharmacy
Operating Room
Save as a New Dataset:
Hospital Risk Management Events
List of Saved Datasets:
Save As
Dataset
Hospital Risk Management Events
New
Delete
Edit
Save
No. Event Name Count Event Date Selected Segment Entered By Notes (Optional)
1 Staff Injury 3 1/24/2014 General Nurse 155
2 Staff Injury 6 3/27/2014 General Nurse 155
3 Infection 2 3/27/2014 Surgery DOC 15
4 Equipment Failure 4 4/15/2014 ICU Nurse 254
5 Ambulatory Issues 2 5/27/2014 Orthopedic Nurse 32
6 Wrong Dosage 1 6/30/2014 Pharmacy Nurse Asst 25
7 Wrong Dosage 3 8/27/2014 Pharmacy Nurse Asst 25
8 Missing Equipment 2 4/15/2014 OR OR Nurse 5
9 Missing Equipment 6 10/27/2014 OR OR Nurse 5
10 Staff Injury 5 10/27/2014 General Nurse 155
11 Infection 6 11/27/2014 Surgery DOC 15
Enter Additional Optional Information:
Save
Reported By: Slippage and minor scrapes
Causes: Leaks from ceiling pipes made the floor wet in Ortho Dept.
Consequences: A few minor slips and bruises
Supervisor: Jacky Smith
Reviewed By:
Witnessed By:
Other Info:
More Details:

Figure 2.19: Risk Events Custom Event Input

File   Edit   Language   Decimals   Help

Welcome to the ROV Project Economics Analysis Tool (PEAT). This ERM module will help you perform Enterprise Risk Management by creating and modeling Risk Registers. Results will be presented in the Risk Dashboards and can be segmented by Geography, Operations, Products, Activity, and Department. Additional details can be added as Risk Events, Risk Engagements, and Risk Diagrams. Statistical analysis on Risk Controls, Risk Forecasts, and Risk Mitigation are also available. Sensitivity Analysis and Monte Carlo Risk Simulations are also applied to various Diversifiable Risk, Undiversifiable Risk, and Risk Cost levels.

ERM   Applied Analytics   Risk Simulation   Knowledge Center

Risk Settings   Risk Register   Risk Dashboard   Risk Events   Risk Engagement   Risk Diagrams   Risk Controls   Risk Forecasts   Risk Mitigation

ERM Event Input   Custom Event Input   Event Reports

Risk Table   Risk Chart

| Total | 168 | 100% | 14.88% | 17.26% | 17.86% | 11.31% | 8.93% | 3.57% | 1.79% | 10.12% | 9.52% | 3.57% | | 1.19% |

Names of Subsegments	Count	%	Jan.	Feb.	Mar.	Apr.	May	Jun.	Jul.	Aug.	Sep.	Oct.	Nov.	Dec.
	168	100%	25	29	30	19	15	6	3	17	16	6		2
D-Operations	113	67.26%	19	18	28	6	15	6		17	4			
D-Finance	22	13.10%		9	2	8					3			
D-IT	21	12.50%	2	2		5					6	6		
D-Risk	6	3.57%	2						3					1
D-Legal	6	3.57%	2								3			1

Start by selecting the Dataset to analyze:

[ERM: 2014 Risk Events Log ▾]

Next, decide if you wish to run a report for the entire organization or a select segment within the organization. If a segment is required, select the appropriate Division, GOPAD, or Risk Category.

(•) All Risks in Risk Segment: [GOPAD ▾]

( ) Compare All Datasets (Year over Year)

( ) Report based on Selected Risk Segment and Sub-Segment:
  ( ) Division   (•) GOPAD
  ( ) Category   ( ) Manager
  [Please select a Segment...]

(•) Show Top [5 ▲▼] Risks on Chart
( ) Show All Risks on Chart

[Update]   [Copy]

Save as a New Report:

Monthly Breakdown of Risk Events 2014   [Save As]

List of Saved Reports:

Report
Monthly Breakdown of Risk Events 2014
Annual Comparisons of All Events
Risk Events in Finance
Risk Events in Operations
Custom Hospital ERM Report

[<]   [>]

[New]   [Edit]   [Save]   [Delete]

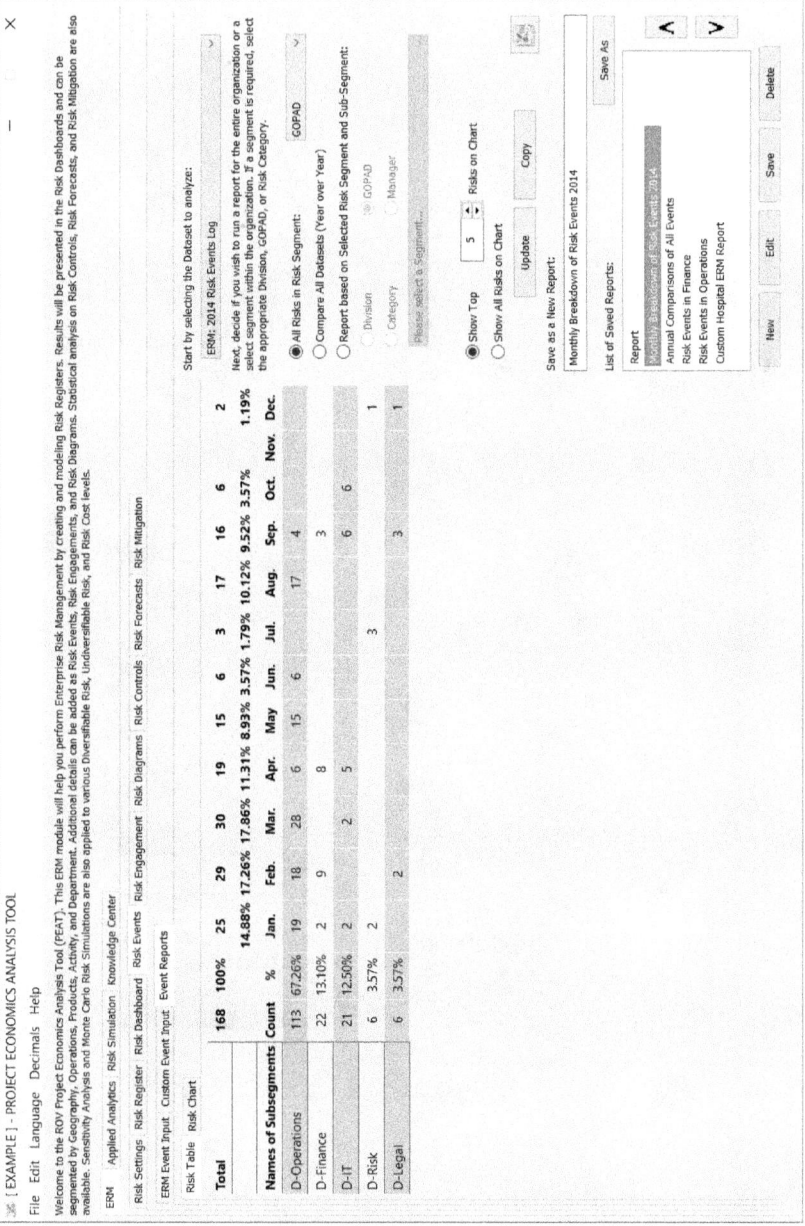

Figure 2.20: Risk Events Data Table

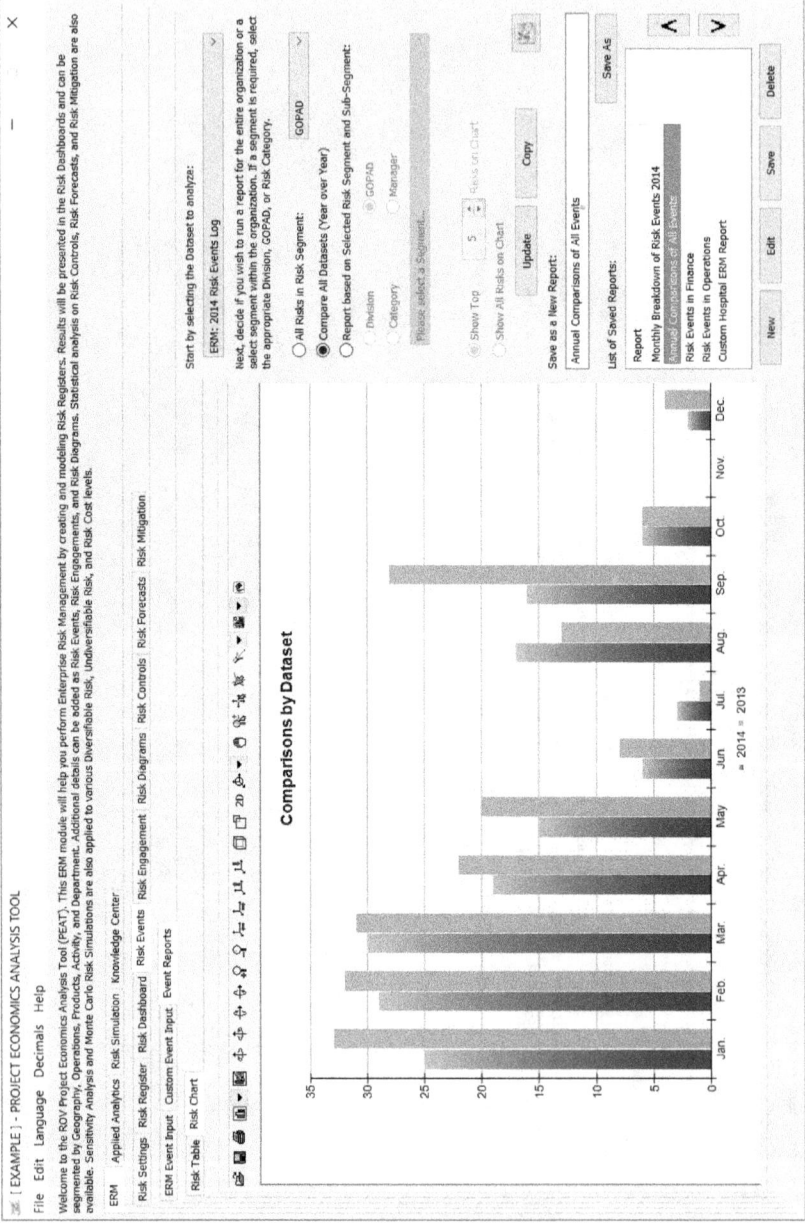

Figure 2.21: Risk Events Charts

[EXAMPLE] - PROJECT ECONOMICS ANALYSIS TOOL — □ ×

File   Edit   Language   Decimals   Help

Welcome to the ROV Project Economics Analysis Tool (PEAT). This ERM module will help you perform Enterprise Risk Management by creating and modeling Risk Registers. Results will be presented in the Risk Dashboards and can be segmented by Geography, Operations, Products, Activity, and Department. Additional details can be added as Risk Events, Risk Engagements, and Risk Diagrams. Statistical analysis on Risk Controls, Risk Forecasts, and Risk Mitigation are also available. Sensitivity Analysis and Monte Carlo Risk Simulations are also applied to various Diversifiable Risk, Undiversifiable Risk, and Risk Cost levels.

ERM   Applied Analytics   Risk Simulation   Knowledge Center

Risk Settings   Risk Register   Risk Dashboard   Risk Events   Risk Engagement   Risk Diagrams   Risk Controls   Risk Forecasts   Risk Mitigation

Pre-Engagement or Pre-Bid   Engagement or Bid Assessment   Lessons Learned   Custom Risk Register

Project Name: Project Saturn: Residential Housing Developr   Name: John Smith   Save As   Engagement
Project ID #: RH-563162   Notes: Development of 1000 residential units in the   Save   John Smith
Updated: 3/11/2014   Copy   Report   Edit
☐ Auto Fit   Custom Categories   Show: 30 ⊕ rows   Show: 3 ⊕ rows text   New   Risk Library   ∧ ∨   Delete

| ITEM/PILLAR | CATEGORIES | EXPLANATIONS & DE... | DATA SOURCE | RISK CRITERIA | | | NOTES |
				Low Risk	Significant Risk	Critical Risk	
Client Profile	Experience dealing with the client (integrity, ontime payment, frequent	We have dealt with the client before in the past and they are very picky	Past Experience		Manageable risk if our contracts are air tight on scope creeps		
Partnerships	Potential partners and subcontractors available to reduce project risk	We can mitigate any technical risks with our pool of partners		We have a pool of existing partners			
Project Profile	Insufficient information on bid order, RFP has limited details, future	RFP has some technical issues missing such as who will implement the	RFP		We can state this in the contract that client's responsibility		
Competitors	Key competitors for the project	HHSC and RMBH are two main competitors in the bid that we	Competitive Database	We can significantly outprice them			
Financial Profitability	Potential for financial losses if resource, cost, and schedule risks are	Lowered pricing will cause profits to shrink and if overrun happens,	Pricing Model			Pricing is a significant risk	
Internal Capabilities	Potential lack of expertise and experience in executing						
Contractual Obligations	Potential complex contract negotiations and loopholes						
Cost Risk	Potential for cost and						

Figure 2.22: Risk Engagement: Pre-Engagement, Engagement Assessment, and Lessons Learned

[EXAMPLE] - PROJECT ECONOMICS ANALYSIS TOOL — □ ×

File   Edit   Language   Decimals   Help

Welcome to the ROV Project Economics Analysis Tool (PEAT). This ERM module will help you perform Enterprise Risk Management by creating and modeling Risk Registers. Results will be presented in the Risk Dashboards and can be segmented by Geography, Operations, Products, Activity, and Department. Additional details can be added as Risk Events, Risk Engagements, and Risk Diagrams. Statistical analysis on Risk Controls, Risk Forecasts, and Risk Mitigation are also available. Sensitivity Analysis and Monte Carlo Risk Simulations are also applied to various Diversifiable Risk, Undiversifiable Risk, and Risk Cost levels.

ERM   Applied Analytics   Risk Simulation   Knowledge Center

Risk Settings   Risk Register   Risk Dashboard   Risk Events   Risk Engagement   Risk Diagrams   Risk Controls   Risk Forecasts   Risk Mitigation

Pre-Engagement or Pre-Bid   Engagement or Bid Assessment   Lessons Learned   Custom Risk Register

Project Name: | Project Mars: Residential Housing Developmen | Name: | Jaddyn Turner |

Project ID #: | RH-613356 | Notes: | Development of 2500 residential units in the |

Updated: | 3/11/2014 |

Custom Categories   ☐ Auto Fit   Show: | 20 ⬍ | rows   Copy   Report   Show: | 3 ⬍ | rows text   New

Save As
Save
Edit
Delete

Engagement
Jaddyn Turner

< [   ] >

⋀ ⋁

ITEM/PILLAR	RISK ISSUES, EVENTS, CONCERNS	POTENTIAL IMPACT DETAILS	RELEVANT?	RISK CRITERIA			PROPOSED ACTIONS
				L	I	KRI	
Business Development	Increase of strong competitors in the area	Aggressive pricing impacts and lowering our opportunity for a viable financial strategy	YES	3	5	15	
Technical Work	Insufficient technical knowledge	Need to hire three additional technical draftsmen to determine the final specifications (RFP items XI-XIV)	YES	3	2	6	

Figure 2.23: Risk Engagement: Engagement Assessment

File   Edit   Language   Decimals   Help

Welcome to the ROV Project Economics Analysis Tool (PEAT). This ERM module will help you perform Enterprise Risk Management by creating and modeling Risk Registers. Results will be presented in the Risk Dashboards and can be segmented by Geography, Operations, Products, Activity, and Department. Additional details can be added as Risk Events, Risk Engagements, and Risk Diagrams. Statistical analysis on Risk Controls, Risk Forecasts, and Risk Mitigation are also available. Sensitivity Analysis and Monte Carlo Risk Simulations are also applied to various Diversifiable Risk, Undiversifiable Risk, and Risk Cost levels.

ERM   Applied Analytics   Risk Simulation   Knowledge Center

Risk Settings   Risk Register   Risk Dashboard   Risk Events   Risk Engagement   Risk Diagrams   Risk Controls   Risk Forecasts   Risk Mitigation

Pre-Engagement or Pre-Bid   Engagement or Bid Assessment   Lessons Learned   Custom Risk Register

Project Name: Project Mars: Residential Housing Developm Name: Jacklyn Turner

Project ID #: RH-613356   Notes: Development of 2500 residential units in the

Updated: 3/11/2014

Engagement: Jacklyn Turner

[ ] Auto Fit   Show: 20 rows   Copy   Report   Show: 3 rows text   New   ∧ ∨   Save As   Save   Edit   Delete

Custom Categories

ITEM/PILLAR	CATEGORIES	RISK EVENT/ISSUE	CAUSE/DETAILS	IMPACT (RISK FACTORS)	ACTIONS TAKEN & RECOMMENDATIONS	IMPACT OF RISK	NOTES
Project Management	Technical staff required	Need project managers who are more technical or have a technical	Schedule overruns was in part due to bad project management	Cost and budget overruns causing losses	Hire and train better PMs	Operations and PM	
Cost Analysis	Cost analysts required	Cost calculations are high level estimates and were highly inaccurate	Cost overruns was in part due to bad forecasting of costs	Cost and budget overruns causing losses	Risk Simulation with Monte Carlo cost risk models are required	PM and Cost Analysis	
Schedule Modeling	Senior management oversight	Schedule on bid was too optimistic	Schedule overruns was in part due to bad project management	Cost and budget overruns causing losses		PM and Cost Analysis	
Schedule Modeling	Technical training required	Schedule calculations are high level estimates and were highly	Schedule delays were in part due to bad forecasting of time to	Cost and budget overruns causing losses	Risk Simulation with Monte Carlo schedule risk models are required	PM and Cost Analysis	

Figure 2.24: Risk Engagement: Lessons Learned

[EXAMPLE] - PROJECT ECONOMICS ANALYSIS TOOL

File   Edit   Language   Decimals   Help

Welcome to the ROV Project Economics Analysis Tool (PEAT). This ERM module will help you perform Enterprise Risk Management by creating and modeling Risk Registers. Results will be presented in the Risk Dashboards and can be segmented by Geography, Operations, Products, Activity, and Department. Additional details can be added as Risk Events, Risk Engagements, and Risk Diagrams. Statistical analysis on Risk Controls, Risk Forecasts, and Risk Mitigation are also available. Sensitivity Analysis and Monte Carlo Risk Simulations are also applied to various Diversifiable Risk, Undiversifiable Risk, and Risk Cost levels.

ERM   Applied Analytics   Risk Simulation   Knowledge Center

Risk Settings   Risk Register   Risk Dashboard   Risk Events   Risk Engagement   Lessons Learned   Custom Risk Register

Pre-Engagement or Pre-Bid   Engagement or Bid Assessment   Risk Diagrams   Risk Controls   Risk Forecasts   Risk Mitigation

Project Name: Report for CEO (Combined Elements)   Name: Jack Reacher
Project ID #: 14255-54A   Notes:
Updated: 2/14/2018

☐ Auto Fit   Show: 20 ⬍ grid rows   Copy   Report   Show: 3 ⬍ rows text

Custom Categories   New   ∧ ∨

Register
Jack Reacher

Save As
Save
Edit
Delete

RISK ID	RISK ITEM	CAT	DIV	CAUSE	CONSEQUENCE	MITIGATION	Custom 1	Custom 2	Custom 3
ROV0001	Rework	Client	Europe	Client keeps changing the specifications	Rework, scope creep, and requirements keep changing over time	Contract needs to specify deadline for specifications freeze			
ROV0003	Overrun	Cost	USA	Lack of raw materials and supplier delays	Additional wait time required	Source multiple vendors and sign contracts with them at			
ROV0011	Rework	Client	Europe	Client keeps changing the specifications	Rework, scope creep, and requirements keep changing over time	Contract needs to specify deadline for specifications freeze			

Figure 2.25: Risk Engagement: Custom Risk Register

ERM historically has been a qualitative risk management technique. However, in this chapter, Integrated Risk Management (IRM) methods have been applied and interjected into this traditional ERM process. For instance, Likelihood and Impact measures, Total Risk Levels, Residual Risk Levels, and Mitigation Costs are all numerical values. These variables are applicable to each Risk Element in the Risk Register and are Risk Mapped throughout various Risk Segments in the organization. By doing this, we are now able to apply quantitative IRM risk analytics to these values such as tornado analysis, Monte Carlo Risk simulations, scenario analysis, heat maps, and other analytics.

For more details, please see Dr. Johnathan Mun's book, *Modeling Risk,* Third Edition (Thomson–Shore). The book delves into these quantitative analytics that are beyond the scope of this current text.

Applied Analytics: Static Tornado Analysis

The **Static Tornado** section helps identify the critical success factors or which risk element contributes the most to the bottom-line risk profile of the company (or risk segment) by statically perturbing each of the risk element's financial risk levels (Figure 2.26).

Applied Analytics: Scenario Analysis

The **Scenario Analysis** section helps create multiple risk scenarios of your current or total risk amounts of individual risk elements to determine the impact on the corporate risk profile and to create scenario heat maps. Figure 2.27 shows the scenario settings and Figure 2.28 shows the scenario results.

Risk Simulations

The PEAT ERM system also allows for the creation of **Risk Simulations** of the user's risk register element input assumptions via ranges (e.g., minimum, most likely, maximum, average, standard deviation, location, scale, range, percentiles) and returns probabilistic distributions of the individual risk elements or rolled-up risks by categories (output metrics include risk element count, KRI sum, sum and count of risk register elements within a risk category, total risk dollars, total risk mitigation cost, etc.). These probability distributions are automatically generated based on the user's total and residual risk inputs and can be modified and updated as required in the **Set Input Assumptions** section (Figure 2.29). The **Simulation Results** show the simulation statistics and distribution of the result (Figure 2.30). Additional analysis such as distributional **Overlay Results** (Figure 2.31), **Analysis of Alternatives** (Figure 2.32), and dynamic **Risk Sensitivities** (Figure 2.33) are also available.

[EXAMPLE] - PROJECT ECONOMICS ANALYSIS TOOL

File   Edit   Language   Decimals   Help

Welcome to the ROV Project Economics Analysis Tool (PEAT). This ERM module will help you perform Enterprise Risk Management by creating and modeling Risk Registers. Results will be presented in the Risk Dashboards and can be segmented by Geography, Operations, Products, Activity, and Department. Additional details can be added on Risk Events, Risk Engagements, and Risk Diagrams. Statistical analysis on Risk Controls, Risk Forecasts, and Risk Mitigation are also available. Sensitivity Analysis and Monte Carlo Risk Simulations are also applied to various Diversifiable Risk, Undiversifiable Risk, and Risk Cost levels.

ERM   Applied Analytics   Risk Simulation   Knowledge Center

Static Tornado   Scenario Analysis

Tornado or static sensitivity analysis is performed by perturbing the inputs a preset amount one at a time to determine the impact on the output variable. Start by selecting the Option and Output Variable to test, then set the sensitivity levels and click Compute to run.

Select the Option and Output Variable to run:

Total Diversifiable Risk   All Categories

Sensitivity +/-   10   %
Show the top   10   variables
Show results with   2   decimals

Please note that Tornado Analysis only runs the current or active Risk Register elements. To run Tornado Analysis on another saved Risk Register, please go back to ERM | Risk Register and open or edit another saved Risk Register.

Reset

Update   Excel   Copy Chart

The Tornado run has been completed.

All Categories: Total Diversifiable Risk

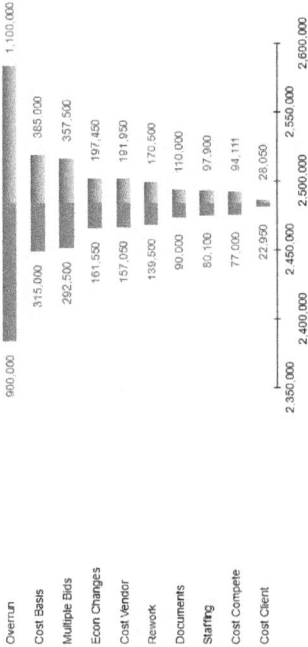

Base Value: 2,484,055.00

Show results with   2   decimals

All Categories: Total Diversifiable Risk

Chart	% Up	% Down	Inputs	Output Do...	Output Up	Range	Input Do...	Input Up	Base Case
✓	10.00%	10.00%	Overrun	2,384,055.00	2,584,055.00	200,000.00	900,000.00	1,100,000...	1,000,000...
✓	10.00%	10.00%	Cost Basis	2,449,055.00	2,519,055.00	70,000.00	315,000.00	385,000.00	350,000.00
✓	10.00%	10.00%	Multiple Bids	2,451,555.00	2,516,555.00	65,000.00	292,500.00	357,500.00	325,000.00
✓	10.00%	10.00%	Econ Changes	2,466,105.00	2,502,005.00	35,900.00	161,550.00	197,450.00	179,500.00
✓	10.00%	10.00%	Cost Vendor	2,466,605.00	2,501,505.00	34,900.00	157,050.00	191,950.00	174,500.00

Changes

All Categories: Total Diversifiable Risk

Overrun   900,000   1,100,000
Cost Basis   315,000   385,000
Multiple Bids   292,500   357,500
Econ Changes   161,550   197,450
Cost Vendor   157,050   191,950
Rework   139,500   170,500
Documents   90,000   110,000
Staffing   80,100   97,900
Cost Compete   77,000   94,111
Cost Client   22,950   28,050

2,350,000   2,400,000   2,450,000   2,500,000   2,550,000   2,600,000

Name: Diversifiable Risk All Categories

Model
Diversifiable Risk All Categories
Mitigation Cost USA

New   Save As   Edit   Save   Delete

Abc...

Figure 2.26: Tornado Analysis on ERM Risk Register Elements

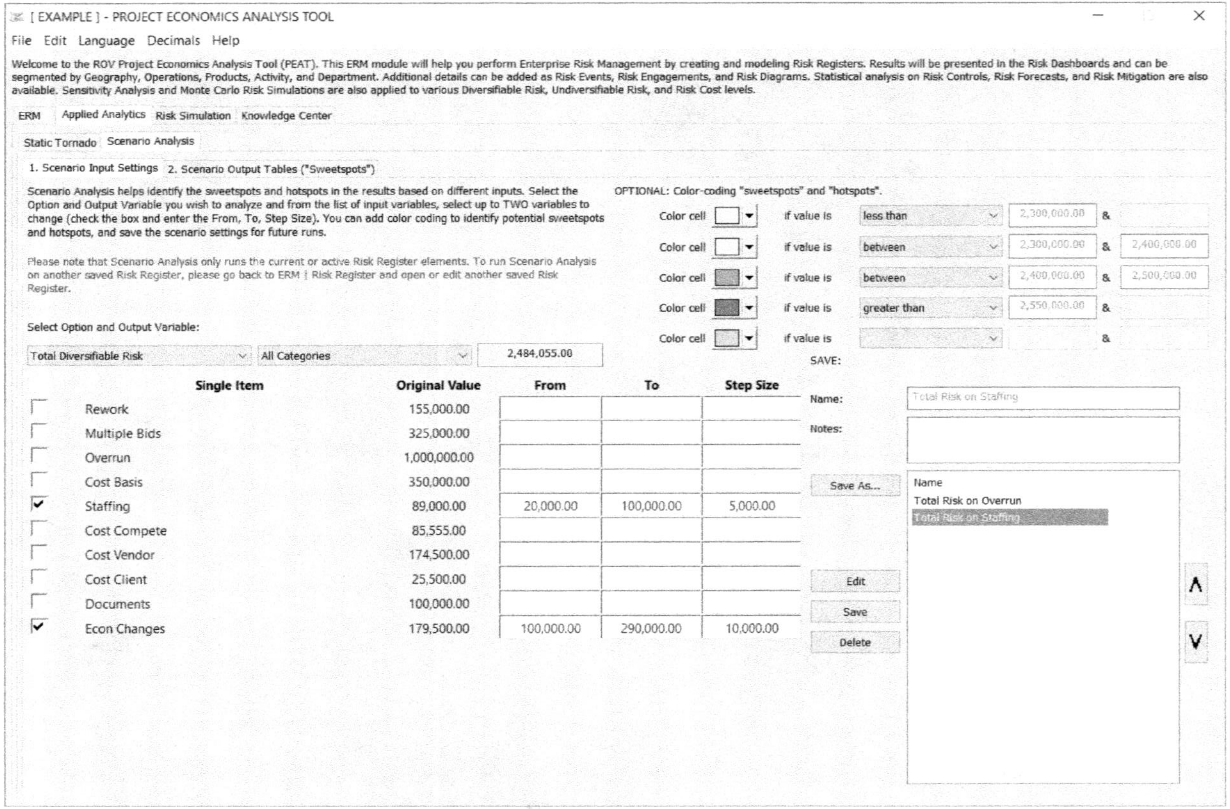

File   Edit   Language   Decimals   Help

Welcome to the ROV Project Economics Analysis Tool (PEAT). This ERM module will help you perform Enterprise Risk Management by creating and modeling Risk Registers. Results will be presented in the Risk Dashboards and can be segmented by Geography, Operations, Products, Activity, and Department. Additional details can be added as Risk Events, Risk Engagements, and Risk Diagrams. Statistical analysis on Risk Controls, Risk Forecasts, and Risk Mitigation are also available. Sensitivity Analysis and Monte Carlo Risk Simulations are also applied to various Diversifiable Risk, Undiversifiable Risk, and Risk Cost levels.

ERM   Applied Analytics   Risk Simulation   Knowledge Center

Static Tornado   Scenario Analysis

1. Scenario Input Settings   2. Scenario Output Tables ("Sweetspots")

Scenario Analysis helps identify the sweetspots and hotspots in the results based on different inputs. Select the Option and Output Variables you wish to analyze and from the list of input variables, select up to TWO variables to change (check the box and enter the From, To, Step Size). You can add color coding to identify potential sweetspots and hotspots, and save the scenario settings for future runs.

Please note that Scenario Analysis only runs the current or active Risk Register elements. To run Scenario Analysis on another saved Risk Register, please go back to ERM | Risk Register and open or edit another saved Risk Register.

OPTIONAL: Color-coding "sweetspots" and "hotspots".

Color cell ▸	If value is	less than ∨	2,390,000.00 &
Color cell ▸	If value is	between ∨	2,300,000.00 &
Color cell ▸	If value is	between ∨	2,400,000.00 &
Color cell ▸	If value is	greater than ∨	2,350,000.00 &
Color cell ▸	If value is	∨	&

Select Option and Output Variable:

Total Diversifiable Risk   ∨   All Categories   ∨

2,484,055.00   ∨

Single Item	Original Value	From	To	Step Size
Rework	155,000.00			
Multiple Bids	325,000.00			
Overrun	1,000,000.00			
Cost Basis	350,000.00			
Staffing	89,000.00	20,000.00	100,000.00	5,000.00
Cost Compete	85,555.00			
Cost Vendor	174,500.00			
Cost Client	25,500.00			
Documents	100,000.00			
Econ Changes	179,500.00	100,000.00	290,000.00	10,000.00

SAVE:

Name: Total Risk on Staffing

Notes:

Save As...

Edit

Save

Delete

Name
Total Risk on Overrun
Total Risk on Staffing

‹   ›

Figure 2.27: Risk Scenario Settings

File   Edit   Language   Decimals   Help

Welcome to the ROV Project Economics Analysis Tool (PEAT). This ERM module will help you perform Enterprise Risk Management by creating and modeling Risk Registers. Results will be presented in the Risk Dashboards and can be segmented by Geography, Operations, Products, Activity, and Department. Additional details can be added as Risk Events, Risk Engagements, and Risk Diagrams. Statistical analysis on Risk Controls, Risk Forecasts, and Risk Mitigation are also available. Sensitivity Analysis and Monte Carlo Risk Simulations are also applied to various Diversifiable Risk, Undiversifiable Risk, and Risk Cost levels.

ERM   Applied Analytics   Risk Simulation   Knowledge Center

Static Tornado   Scenario Analysis

1. Scenario Input Settings   2. Scenario Output Tables ("Sweetspots")

Select one of the saved scenarios to run the scenario table. In the event you make any changes in the inputs or settings, remember to click Update to manually update the scenario table.

Select the Saved Scenario to Compute:

Total Risk on Overrun

Scenario table is for:

Overrun

All Categories

and the Column variable (across) is

Econ Changes

Update   View Full Grid

Show results with   0   decimals

The Row variable (down) is

NOTE:

	100,000	110,000	120,000	130,000	140,000	150,000	160,000	170,000	180,000	190,000	200,000	210,000	220,000	230,000	240,000	250,000	260,000	270,00
800,000	2,204,555	2,214,555	2,224,555	2,234,555	2,244,555	2,254,555	2,264,555	2,274,555	2,284,555	2,294,555	2,304,555	2,314,555	2,324,555	2,334,555	2,344,555	2,354,555	2,364,555	2,374,5
850,000	2,254,555	2,264,555	2,274,555	2,284,555	2,294,555	2,304,555	2,314,555	2,324,555	2,334,555	2,344,555	2,354,555	2,364,555	2,374,555	2,384,555	2,394,555	2,404,555	2,414,555	2,424,5
900,000	2,304,555	2,314,555	2,324,555	2,334,555	2,344,555	2,354,555	2,364,555	2,374,555	2,384,555	2,394,555	2,404,555	2,414,555	2,424,555	2,434,555	2,444,555	2,454,555	2,464,555	2,474,5
950,000	2,354,555	2,364,555	2,374,555	2,384,555	2,394,555	2,404,555	2,414,555	2,424,555	2,434,555	2,444,555	2,454,555	2,464,555	2,474,555	2,484,555	2,494,555	2,504,555	2,514,555	2,524,5
1,000,000	2,404,555	2,414,555	2,424,555	2,434,555	2,444,555	2,454,555	2,464,555	2,474,555	2,484,555	2,494,555	2,504,555	2,514,555	2,524,555	2,534,555	2,544,555	2,554,555	2,564,555	2,574,5
1,050,000	2,454,555	2,464,555	2,474,555	2,484,555	2,494,555	2,504,555	2,514,555	2,524,555	2,534,555	2,544,555	2,554,555	2,564,555	2,574,555	2,584,555	2,594,555	2,604,555	2,614,555	2,624,5
1,100,000	2,504,555	2,514,555	2,524,555	2,534,555	2,544,555	2,554,555	2,564,555	2,574,555	2,584,555	2,594,555	2,604,555	2,614,555	2,624,555	2,634,555	2,644,555	2,654,555	2,664,555	2,674,5
1,150,000	2,554,555	2,564,555	2,574,555	2,584,555	2,594,555	2,604,555	2,614,555	2,624,555	2,634,555	2,644,555	2,654,555	2,664,555	2,674,555	2,684,555	2,694,555	2,704,555	2,714,555	2,724,5
1,200,000	2,604,555	2,614,555	2,624,555	2,634,555	2,644,555	2,654,555	2,664,555	2,674,555	2,684,555	2,694,555	2,704,555	2,714,555	2,724,555	2,734,555	2,744,555	2,754,555	2,764,555	2,774,5
1,250,000	2,654,555	2,664,555	2,674,555	2,684,555	2,694,555	2,704,555	2,714,555	2,724,555	2,734,555	2,744,555	2,754,555	2,764,555	2,774,555	2,784,555	2,794,555			
1,300,000	2,704,555	2,714,555	2,724,555	2,734,555	2,744,555	2,754,555	2,764,555	2,774,555	2,784,555	2,794,555								
1,350,000	2,754,555	2,764,555	2,774,555	2,784,555	2,794,555													
1,400,000																		
1,450,000																		
1,500,000																		
1,550,000																		
1,600,000																		

Figure 2.28: Risk Scenarios

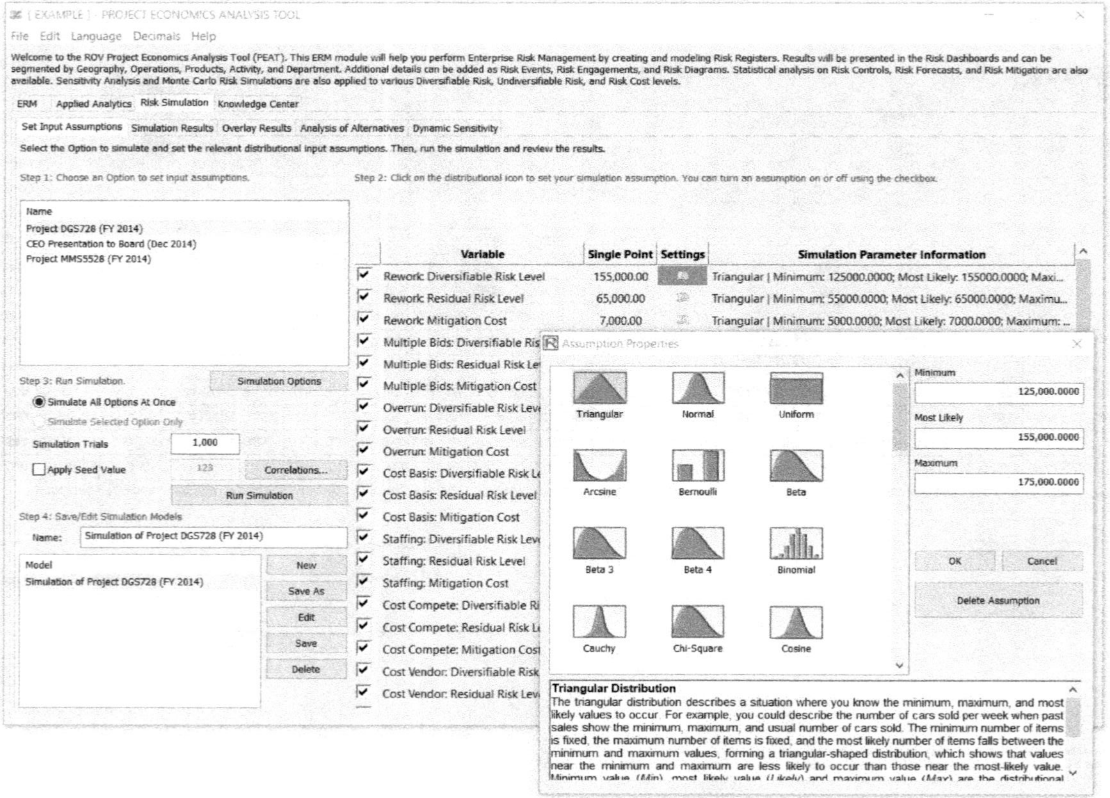

Figure 2.29: Risk Simulation Assumptions

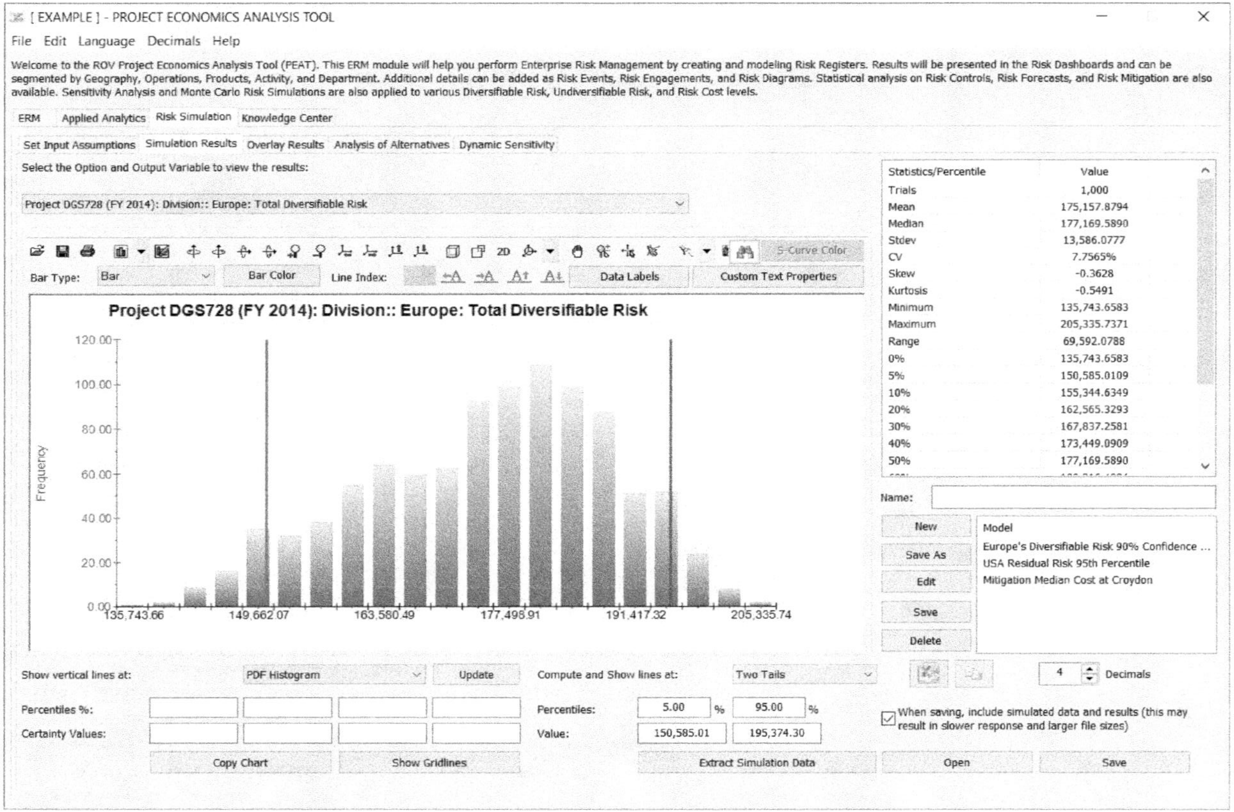

[EXAMPLE] - PROJECT ECONOMICS ANALYSIS TOOL

— □ ×

File Edit Language Decimals Help

Welcome to the ROV Project Economics Analysis Tool (PEAT). This ERM module will help you perform Enterprise Risk Management by creating and modeling Risk Registers. Results will be presented in the Risk Dashboards and can be segmented by Geography, Operations, Products, Activity, and Department. Additional details can be added as Risk Events, Risk Engagements, and Risk Diagrams. Statistical analysis on Risk Controls, Risk Forecasts, and Risk Mitigation are also available. Sensitivity Analysis and Monte Carlo Risk Simulations are also applied to various Diversifiable Risk, Undiversifiable Risk, and Risk Cost levels.

ERM Applied Analytics Risk Simulation Knowledge Center

Set Input Assumptions Simulation Results Overlay Results Analysis of Alternatives Dynamic Sensitivity

Select the Option and Output Variable to view the results:

Project DGS728 (FY 2014): Division:: Europe: Total Diversifiable Risk

Bar Type: | Bar | Bar Color | Line Index: | Data Labels | Custom Text Properties | S-Curve Color

Project DGS728 (FY 2014): Division:: Europe: Total Diversifiable Risk

Statistics/Percentile	Value
Trials	1,000
Mean	175,157.8794
Median	177,169.5890
Stdev	13,586.0777
CV	7.7565%
Skew	-0.3628
Kurtosis	-0.5491
Minimum	135,743.6583
Maximum	205,335.7371
Range	69,592.0788
0%	135,743.6583
5%	150,585.0109
10%	155,344.6349
20%	162,565.3293
30%	167,837.2581
40%	173,449.0909
50%	177,169.5890

Name: [   ]

Model
Europe's Diversifiable Risk 90% Confidence ...
USA Residual Risk 95th Percentile
Mitigation Median Cost at Croydon

New | Save As | Edit | Save | Delete

☑ When saving, include simulated data and results (this may result in slower response and larger file sizes)

[4] Decimals

Open | Save

Show vertical lines at: | [>] | Update | Compute and Show lines at: | Two Tails
Percentiles %: | PDF Histogram | Percentiles: | 5.00 | % | 95.00 | %
Certainty Values: | | Value: | 150,585.01 | | 195,374.30

Copy Chart | Show Gridlines | Extract Simulation Data

Frequency
120.00
100.00
80.00
60.00
40.00
20.00
0.00
135,743.66 149,662.07 163,580.49 177,498.91 191,417.32 205,335.74

Figure 2.30: Risk Simulation Results

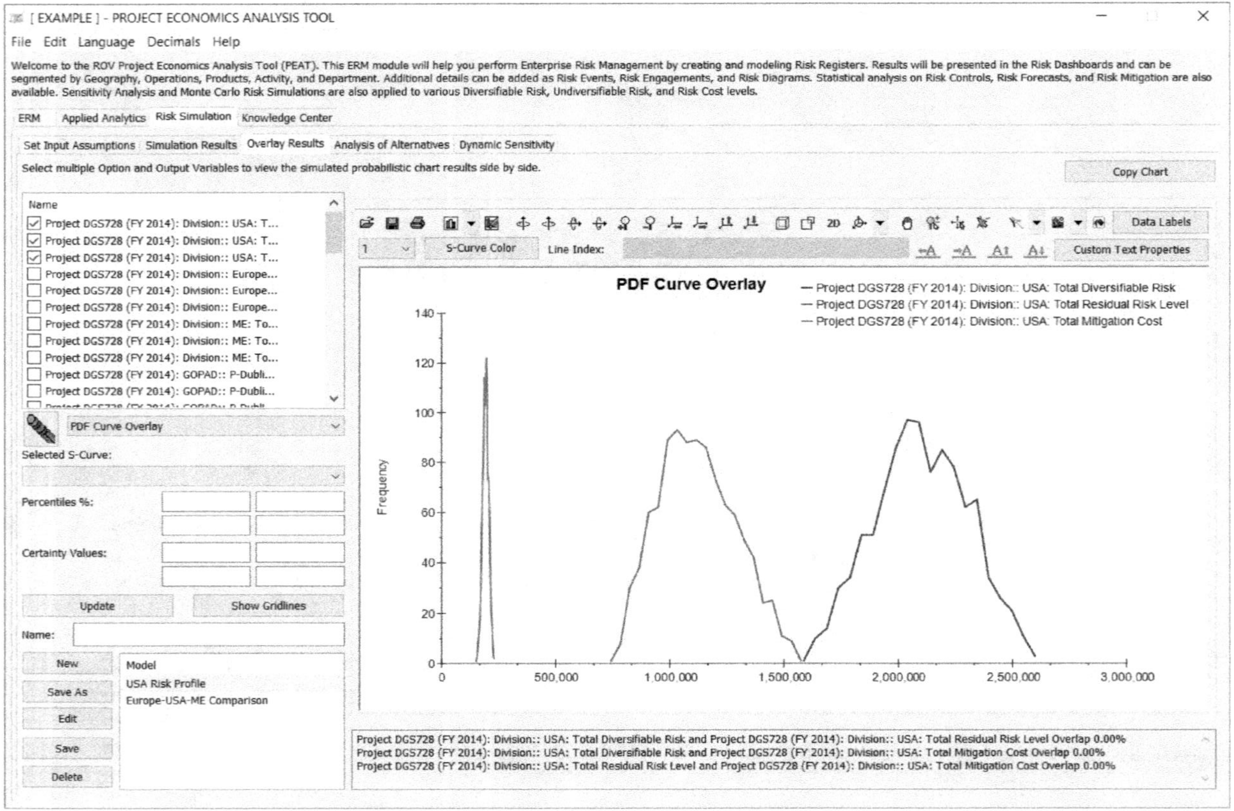

Figure 2.31: Risk Simulation Overlay Comparison

File   Edit   Language   Decimals   Help

Welcome to the ROV Project Economics Analysis Tool (PEAT). This ERM module will help you perform Enterprise Risk Management by creating and modeling Risk Registers. Results will be presented in the Risk Dashboards and can be segmented by Geography, Operations, Products, Activity, and Department. Additional details can be added as Risk Events, Risk Engagements, and Risk Diagrams. Statistical analysis on Risk Controls, Risk Forecasts, and Risk Mitigation are also available. Sensitivity Analysis and Monte Carlo Risk Simulations are also applied to various Diversifiable Risk, Undiversifiable Risk, and Risk Cost levels.

ERM   Applied Analytics   Risk Simulation   Knowledge Center

Set Input Assumptions   Simulation Results   Overlay Results   Analysis of Alternatives   Dynamic Sensitivity

You can compare the dynamic simulated results of all your options. A simulation must first be run before you can obtain any results. Choose if you wish to compare all options as standalone (Analysis of Alternatives) or against a base case (Incremental Analysis).

ANALYSIS OF ALTERNATIVES AND BASE CASE INCREMENTAL ANALYSIS

◉ Analysis of Alternatives (No Base Case)   ○ Incremental Analysis (Choose Base Case):

Economic Results: Division:: USA

OPTIONS	Total Diversifiable Risk	Total Residual Risk Level	Total Mitigation Cost
◉ Mean	2,100,489.72	1,121,820.86	193,205.23
○ Median	2,099,206.68	1,107,387.53	193,463.53
○ Stdev	204,354.76	168,395.55	13,677.43
○ Variance	4.17E+010	2.83E+010	1.87E+008
○ CV	9.73%	15.01%	7.08%
○ Skew	-0.0065	0.2583	-0.0659
○ Kurtosis	-0.5499	-0.5790	-0.1796
○ Minimum	1,586,027.72	741,523.53	151,549.44
○ Maximum	2,597,540.48	1,574,592.01	231,087.72
○ Range	1,011,512.76	833,068.48	79,538.28
○ 0% Percentile	1,586,027.72	741,523.53	151,549.44
○ 5% Percentile	1,755,135.87	860,757.89	171,063.45
○ 10% Percentile	1,830,428.71	907,100.51	175,351.59
○ 20% Percentile	1,919,977.05	972,002.55	181,653.59
○ 30% Percentile	1,993,647.25	1,016,779.47	186,188.08
○ 40% Percentile	2,044,007.97	1,065,807.12	189,758.00
○ 50% Percentile	2,099,206.68	1,107,387.53	193,463.53
○ 60% Percentile	2,154,066.30	1,153,533.60	196,523.26
○ 70% Percentile	2,217,902.89	1,211,773.27	200,335.73
○ 80% Percentile	2,282,038.02	1,277,000.89	205,369.72
○ 90% Percentile	2,366,013.89	1,360,030.40	210,673.29
○ 95% Percentile	2,440,538.12	1,419,980.17	215,233.08
○ 100% Percentile	2,597,540.48	1,574,592.01	231,087.72

Total Diversifiable Risk
2 Decimals

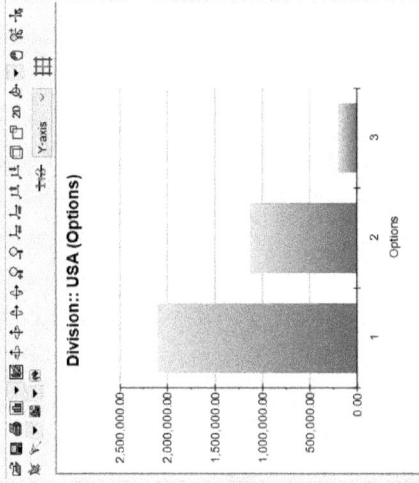

Division:: USA (Options)

2D Bar   Copy Chart

Figure 2.32: Risk Analysis of Alternatives

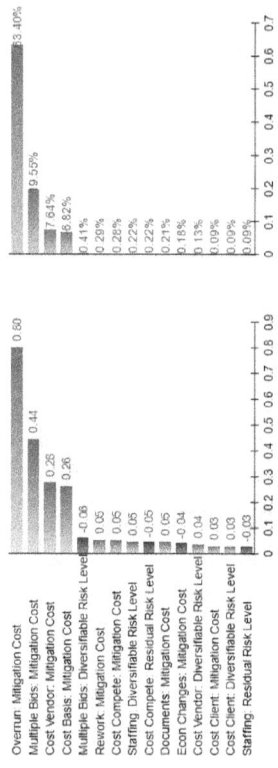

Figure 2.33: Risk Sensitivity

3

COMPLIANCE WITH GLOBAL STANDARDS: BASEL, COSO, ISO, NIST, AND SARBOX

ERM methods deployed by any organization should at least consider compliance with global standards if not exactly mirroring COSO (Committee of Sponsoring Organizations of the Treadway Commission, with respect to their organizing committees at AAA, AICPA, FEI, IMA, and IIA), International Standards ISO 31000:2009, the U.S. Sarbanes–Oxley Act, the Basel III/IV requirements for Operational Risk (from the Basel Committee through the Bank of International Settlements), and NIST 800-37. The parallels and applications of ROV methodologies closely mirror, and at times exceed, these regulatory and international standards.

Figures 3.1–3.10 illustrate some examples of compliance with ISO 31000:2009, Figures 3.11–3.20 show compliance with Basel III and Basel IV requirements, and Figures 3.21–3.29 show compliance with COSO requirements. These figures and the summary lists that follow assume that the reader is already familiar with the IRM methodology employed throughout this book.

- The IRM methodology we employ is in line with ISO 31000:2009 Clauses 2.3 and 2.8 requiring a risk management process (Figure 3.1), as well as Clause 5 (5.4.2 requiring risk identification where we use tornado analysis and scenario analysis; 5.4.3. requiring quantitative risk analysis where we apply Monte Carlo risk simulations; 5.4.4 where existing Excel-based evaluation models are used and overlaid with IRM methodologies such as simulations; etc.).

- ISO 31000:2009 Clause 5.4.4 looks at the risk tolerance levels and comparing various risk levels in a portfolio optimization and efficient frontier analysis employed in our IRM methodology (Figure 3.2).

- Figure 3.3 shows quantified consequences and the likelihoods (probabilities and confidence levels) of potential events that can occur using simulations, as required in ISO 31000:2009 Clauses 2.1 and 5.4.3. (See Chapter 2 for examples of Likelihood and Impact measures.)

- ISO 31000:2009 Clause 5.4.3 requires viewing the analysis from the perspectives of various stakeholders, multiple consequences, and multiple objectives to develop a combined level of risk. These perspectives are achieved through a multicriteria optimization and efficient frontier analysis (Figure 3.4) in the IRM process.

- ISO 31000:2009 Clause 3F requires that historical data and experience as well as stakeholder feedback and observation coupled with expert judgment be used to forecast future risk events. The IRM process employs a family of 16 forecasting methods (Figure 3.5 shows an example of the ARIMA model) coupled with risk simulations with high fidelity to determine the best goodness-of-fit when historical data exist, or using subject matter expert estimates and stakeholder assumptions, we can apply the Delphi method and custom distribution to run risk simulations on the forecasts.

- ISO 31000:2009 Clauses 3C, 5.4.3, 5.5, and 5.5.2 require risk evaluations on risk treatments, options to execute when different types of risks are involved, and selecting and implementing various risk treatment strategic options that are not solely reliant on economics. The IRM's strategic real options methodology allows users to model multiple path-independent and path-dependent implementation strategies or alternate courses of action that are generated to mitigate downside risks and take advantage of upside potentials (Figure 3.6).

- Figure 3.7 illustrates how ISO 31000:2009 Clauses 3D, 3E, and 5.4.3 are satisfied using the IRM process of probability distribution fitting of uncertain variables and how their interdependencies (correlations) are executed.

- Risk controls are required in ISO 31000:2009 Clauses 2.26, 4.43, and 5.4.3 (Figure 3.8). The control charts and Risk Effectiveness calculations in PEAT ERM help decision makers identify if a particular risk mitigation strategy and response that was enacted had sufficiently and statistically significantly affected the outcomes of future risk states.

- Scenarios, cascading, and cumulative effects (consequences) are also the focus of ISO 31000:2009 Clause 5.4.2. The IRM method uses tornado analysis, scenario analysis, dynamic sensitivity analysis, and risk simulations (Figure 3.9) to identify which input(s) have the highest impact on the organization's risks and model their impacts on the total risks of the organization.

- ISO 31000:2009 Clause 5.2 requires proper communication of risk exposures and consequences, and an understanding of the basis and reasons of each risk. The PEAT ERM Risk Dashboards provide details and insights for a better understanding of the issues governing each of the risk issues in an organization (Figure 3.10).

Integrated Risk Management Process

ISO 31000:2009 (Clause 2.3): "Risk Management Framework"

ISO 31000:2009 (Clause 2.8): "Risk Management Process"

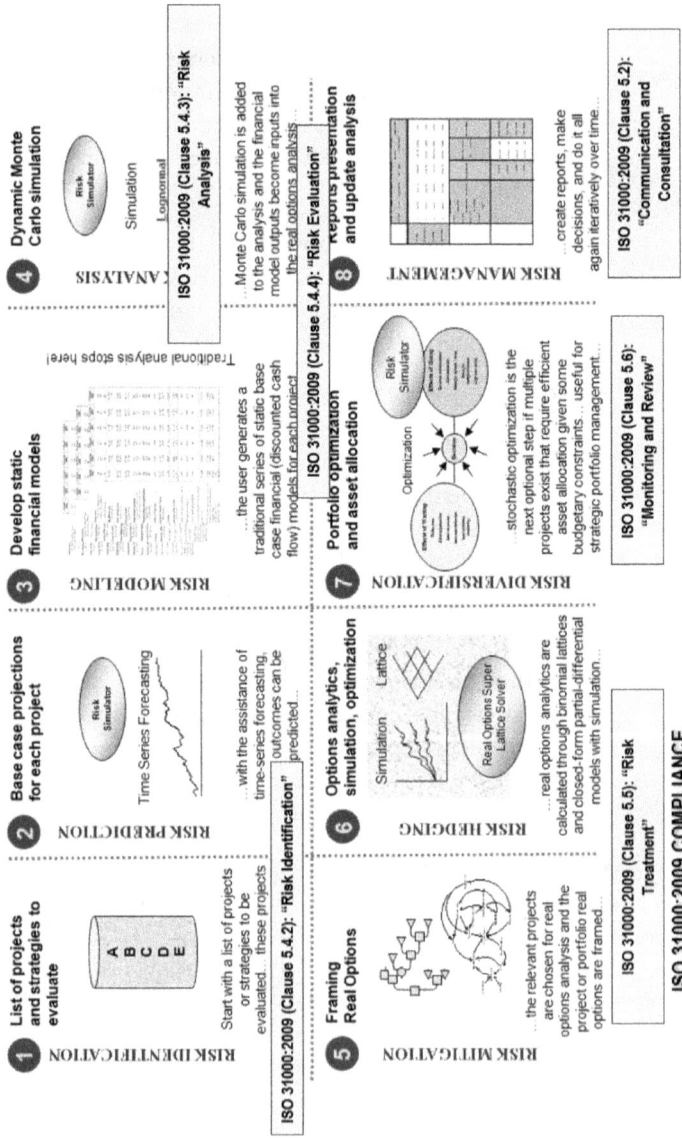

1 **RISK IDENTIFICATION**

List of projects and strategies to evaluate

A
B
C
D
E

Start with a list of projects or strategies to be evaluated... these projects

ISO 31000:2009 (Clause 5.4.2): "Risk Identification"

2 **RISK PREDICTION**

Base case projections for each project

Risk Simulator

Time Series Forecasting

...with the assistance of time-series forecasting, outcomes can be predicted...

3 **RISK MODELING**

Develop static financial models

Traditional analysis stops here!

...the user generates a traditional series of static base case financial (discounted cash flow) models for each project...

4 **RISK ANALYSIS**

Dynamic Monte Carlo simulation

Risk Simulator

Simulation

Lognormal

ISO 31000:2009 (Clause 5.4.3): "Risk Analysis"

...Monte Carlo simulation is added to the analysis and the financial model outputs become inputs into the real options analysis...

5 **RISK MITIGATION**

Framing Real Options

...the relevant projects are chosen for real options analysis and the project or portfolio real options are framed...

6 **RISK HEDGING**

Options analytics, simulation, optimization

Lattice

Simulation

Real Options Super Lattice Solver

...real options analytics are calculated through binomial lattices and closed-form partial-differential models with simulation...

7 **RISK DIVERSIFICATION**

Portfolio optimization and asset allocation

Risk Simulator

Optimization

ISO 31000:2009 (Clause 5.6): "Monitoring and Review"

...stochastic optimization is the next optional step if multiple projects exist that require efficient asset allocation given some budgetary constraints... useful for strategic portfolio management...

8 **RISK MANAGEMENT**

...reports presentation and update analysis

ISO 31000:2009 (Clause 5.4.4): "Risk Evaluation"

ISO 31000:2009 (Clause 5.2): "Communication and Consultation"

...create reports, make decisions, and do it all again iteratively over time...

ISO 31000:2009 (Clause 5.5): "Risk Treatment" COMPLIANCE

ISO 31000:2009 COMPLIANCE

Figure 3.1: ISO 31000:2009—IRM

Investment Efficient Frontiers analysis provides for a variety of budget scenarios when considering portfolios of options

ISO 31000:2009 (Clause 5.4.4): "Risk evaluation involves **comparing the level of risk found** during the analysis process with **risk criteria established** when the context was considered. Based on this comparison, the need for treatment can be considered. Decisions should take account of the wider context of the risk and include consideration of the **tolerance of the risk borne** by parties other then the org that benefits from the risk."

Budget	Comprehensive Score	Tactical Score	Military Score	Allowed Projects	ROI-RANK Objective
$3,800.00	33.15	62.64	58.58	10	$470,235.60
$4,800.00	36.33	68.85	66.86	11	$521,645.92
$5,600.00	38.40	70.46	75.69	12	$623,557.79
$6,800.00	39.94	72.14	82.31	13	$659,947.99
$7,800.00	39.76	70.05	86.54	14	$676,279.81

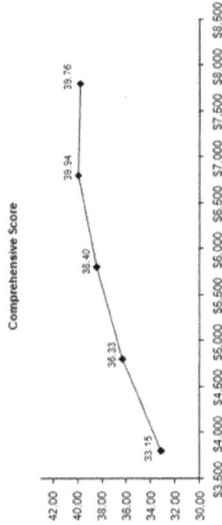

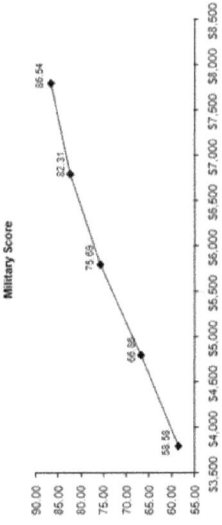

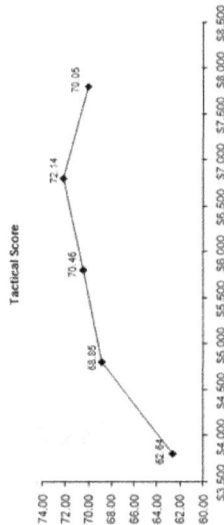

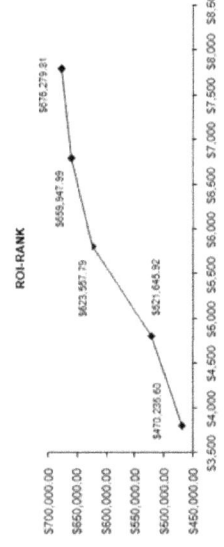

Figure 3.2: ISO 31000:2009—Risk Tolerance

Risk Simulation provides the decision maker with additional data

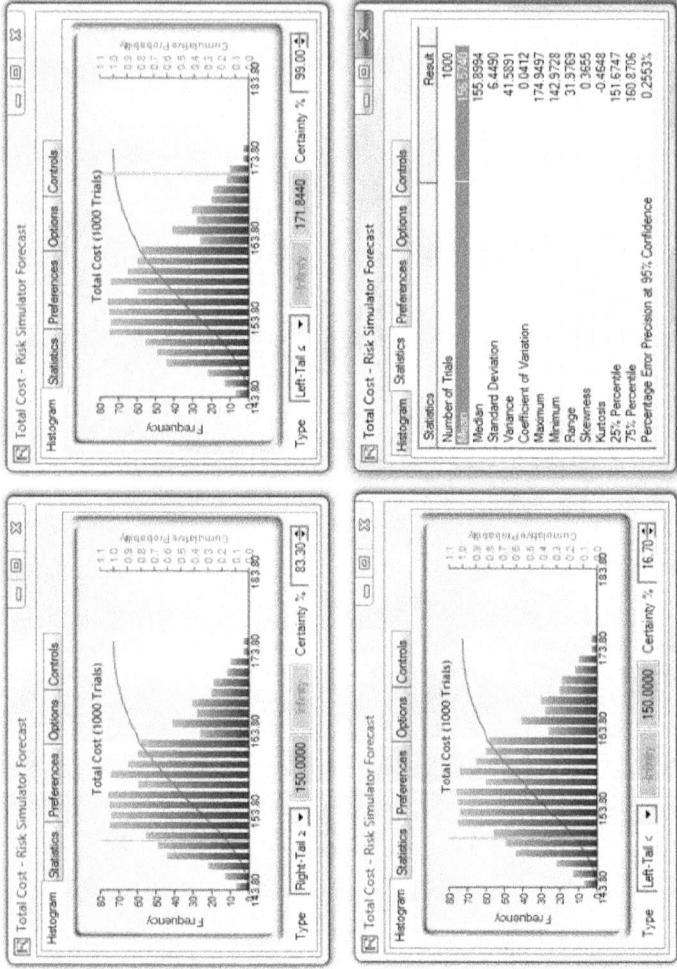

ISO 31000:2009 (Clause 5.4.3): "Factors that affect **consequences and likelihood** should be identified. Risk is analyzed by determining consequences and their likelihood, and other attributes of the risk."

ISO 31000:2009 (Clause 2.1): "Risk is often characterized by reference to **potential events** (2.17) **and consequences** (2.18), or a combination of these."

Figure 3.3: ISO 31000:2009—Consequences and Likelihood

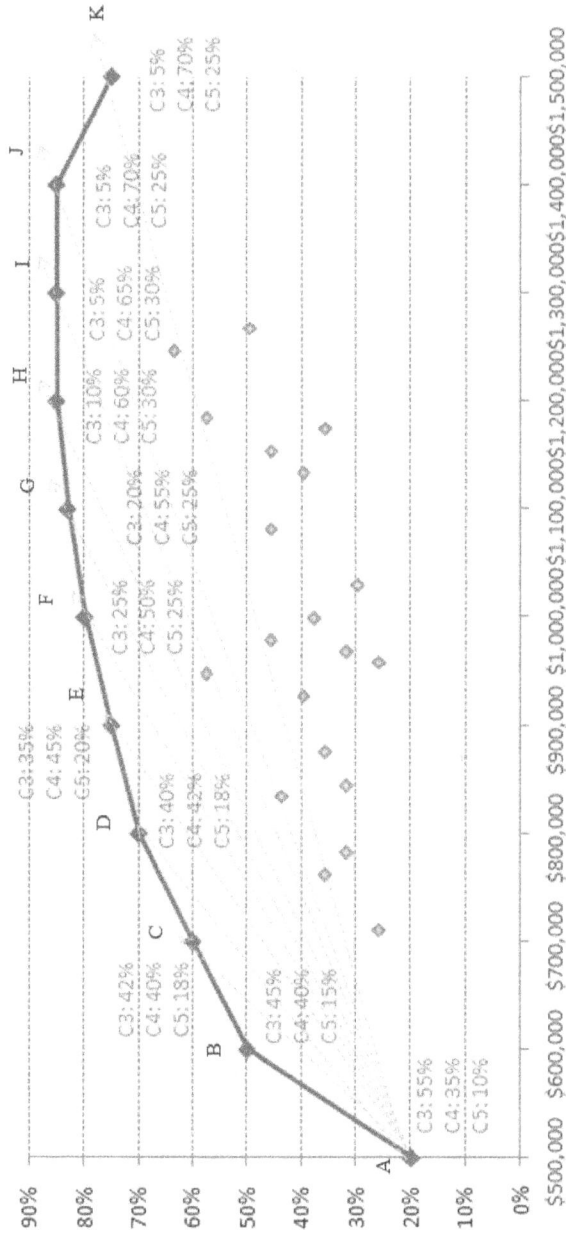

ISO 31000:2009 (Clause 5.4.3): "An event can have **multiple consequences** and can affect **multiple objectives**. The way in which consequences and likelihood are expressed and the way in which they are **combined determine a level of risk...**"

Optimal Portfolio Efficient Frontier

A
C3: 55%
C4: 35%
C5: 10%

B
C3: 42%
C4: 40%
C5: 18%

C
C3: 40%
C4: 42%
C5: 18%

C3: 45%
C4: 40%
C5: 15%

D
C3: 35%
C4: 45%
C5: 20%

E
C3: 25%
C4: 50%
C5: 25%

F
C2: 20%
C4: 55%
C5: 25%

G
C5: 10%
C4: 60%
C5: 30%

H
C3: 5%
C4: 65%
C5: 30%

I

J
C3: 5%
C4: 70%
C5: 25%

K
C3: 5%
C4: 70%
C5: 25%

$500,000 $600,000 $700,000 $800,000 $900,000 $1,000,000 $1,100,000 $1,200,000 $1,300,000 $1,400,000 $1,500,000

Figure 3.4: ISO 31000:2009—Multiple Stakeholder Objectives and Consequences

ACTUAL SALES VS. ECONOMETRIC FORECAST
With linkage to the overall economy indicators

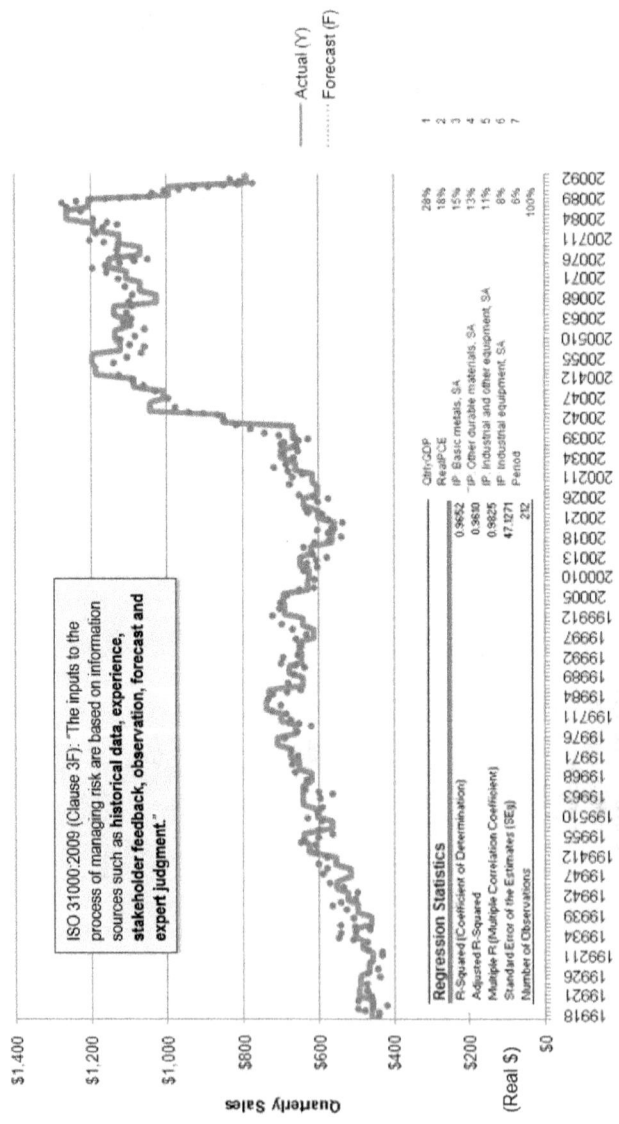

ISO 31000:2009 (Clause 3F): "The inputs to the process of managing risk are based on information sources such as **historical data, experience, stakeholder feedback, observation, forecast and expert judgment**."

Regression Statistics	
R-Squared (Coefficient of Determination)	0.9652
Adjusted R-Squared	0.9630
Multiple R (Multiple Correlation Coefficient)	0.9825
Standard Error of the Estimates (SEε)	47.1271
Number of Observations	212

Qtr-GDP	28%	1
RealPCE	18%	2
IP Basic metals, SA	15%	3
IP Other durable materials, SA	13%	4
IP Industrial and other equipment, SA	11%	5
IP Industrial equipment, SA	8%	6
Period	6%	7
	100%	

Figure 3.5: ISO 31000:2009—Historical Data and Future Forward Forecast

ISO 31000:2009 (Clause 5.4.3): "Risk analysis provides and input to risk evaluation and to decisions on whether risks need to be treated, and on the most appropriate risk treatment strategies and methods. Risk analysis can also provide an input into making decisions where choices must be made and the options involve different types and levels of risk."

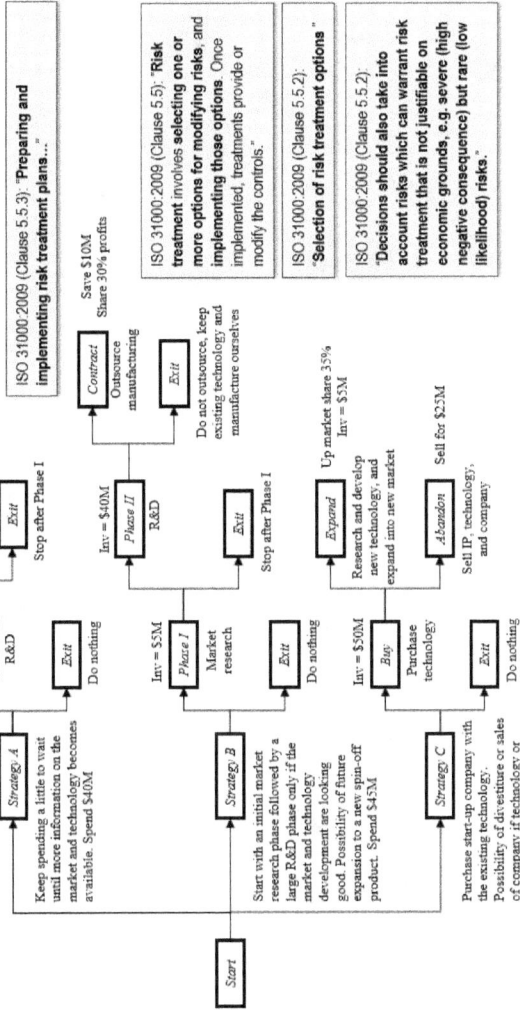

ISO 31000 2009 (Clause 5.5.3): "Preparing and implementing risk treatment plans..."

ISO 31000:2009 (Clause 5.5): "Risk treatment involves selecting one or more options for modifying risks, and implementing those options. Once implemented, treatments provide or modify the controls."

ISO 31000:2009 (Clause 5.5.2): "Selection of risk treatment options"

ISO 31000:2009 (Clause 5.5.2): "Decisions should also take into account risks which can warrant risk treatment that is not justifiable on economic grounds, e.g. severe (high negative consequence) but rare (low likelihood) risks."

ISO 31000:2009 (Clause 3C): "RM is part of decision making. RM helps decision makers make informed choices, prioritize actions and distinguish among alternative courses of action."

Start

Strategy A
Keep spending a little to wait until more information on the market and technology becomes available. Spend $40M

Strategy B
Start with an initial market research phase followed by a large R&D phase only if the market and technology development are looking good. Possibility of future expansion to a new spin-off product. Spend $45M

Strategy C
Purchase start-up company with the existing technology. Possibility of divestiture or sales of company if technology or market fails, or ability to focus on another new technology if market is there. Spend $50M

Inv = $10M
Phase I
Small-scale R&D

Exit
Do nothing

Inv = $10M
Phase II
Small-scale R&D

Exit
Stop after Phase I

Inv = $10M
Phase III
Small-scale R&D

Exit
Stop after Phase II

Inv = $10M
Phase IV
Small-scale R&D

Exit
Stop after Phase III

Inv = $5M
Phase I
Market research

Exit
Do nothing

Inv = $40M
Phase II
R&D

Exit
Stop after Phase I

Contract
Outsource manufacturing
Save $10M
Share 30% profits

Exit
Do not outsource, keep existing technology and manufacture ourselves

Inv = $50M
Buy
Purchase technology

Exit
Do nothing

Expand
Research and develop new technology, and expand into new market
Up market share 35%
Inv = $5M

Abandon
Sell IP, technology, and company
Sell for $25M

Figure 3.6: ISO 31000:2009—Multiple Options, Strategies, and Alternatives

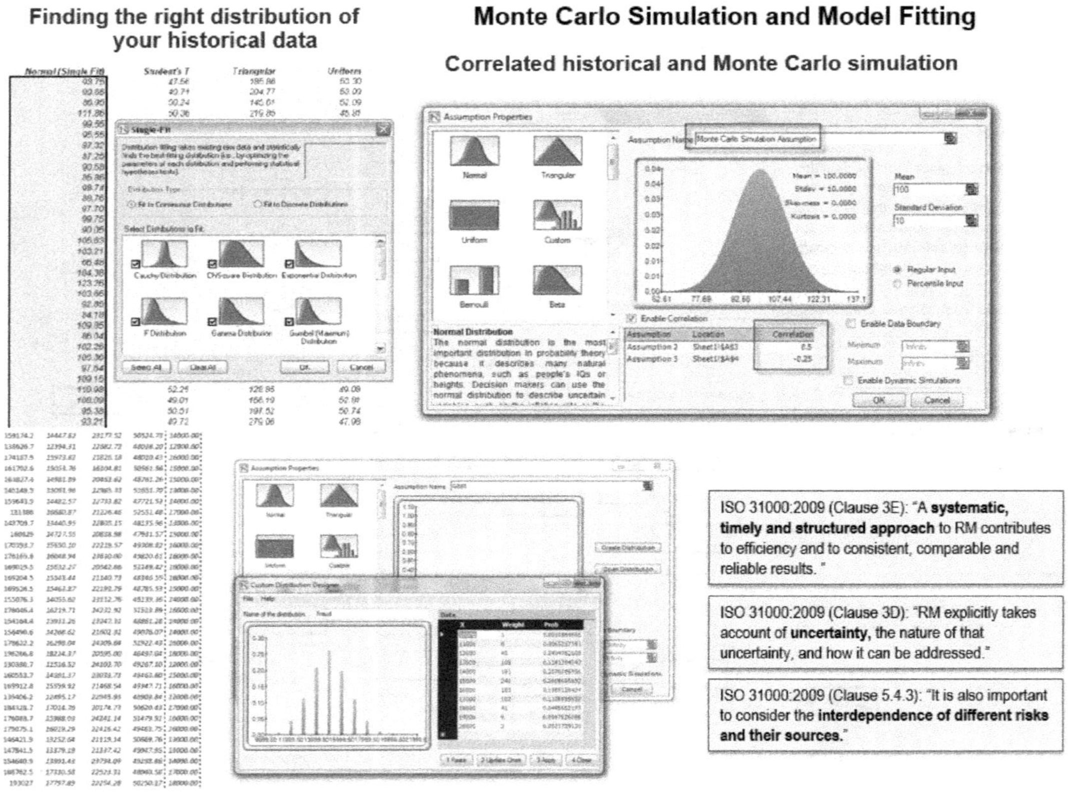

Figure 3.7: ISO 31000:2009 Structured Approach, Probability Fitting, and Correlations

Operational Risk Controls

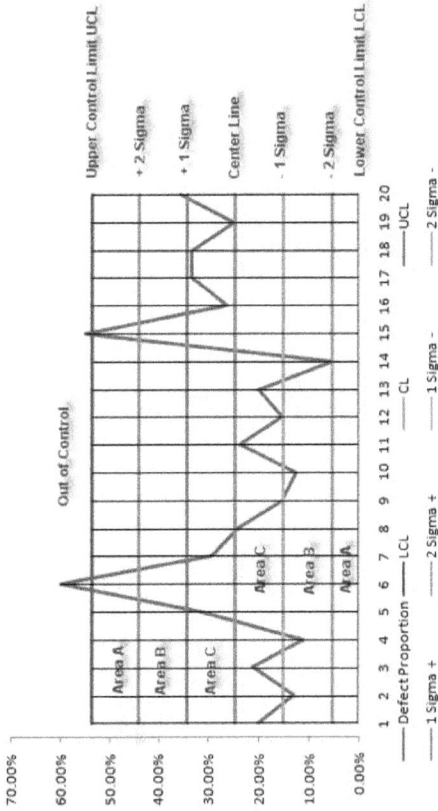

Out of Control

Area A

Area B

Area C

Area C

Area B

Area A

70.00%
60.00%
50.00%
40.00%
30.00%
20.00%
10.00%
0.00%

1 2 3 4 5 6 7 8 9 10 11 12 13 14 15 16 17 18 19 20

Upper Control Limit UCL

+ 2 Sigma

+ 1 Sigma

Center Line

- 1 Sigma

- 2 Sigma

Lower Control Limit LCL

— Defect Proportion —— LCL —— UCL

—— -1 Sigma + —— 2 Sigma + —— CL —— 1 Sigma - —— 2 Sigma -

ISO 31000:2009 (Clause 2.26): **"Controls...measures that modify risk..."**

ISO 31000:2009 (Clause 4.4.3): "Implementing and maintaining the RM process and ensuring the **adequacy, effectiveness and efficiency of any controls.**"

ISO 31000:2009 (Clause 5.4.3): "**Existing controls and their effectiveness and efficiency** should also be taken into account. The way in which consequences and likelihood are expressed and the way in which they are combined determine a **level of risk** should reflect the type of risk, the information available and the purpose for which the risk assessment output is to be used. These should all be consistent with the risk criteria.

Figure 3.8: ISO 31000:2009—Risk Control Efficiency and Effectiveness

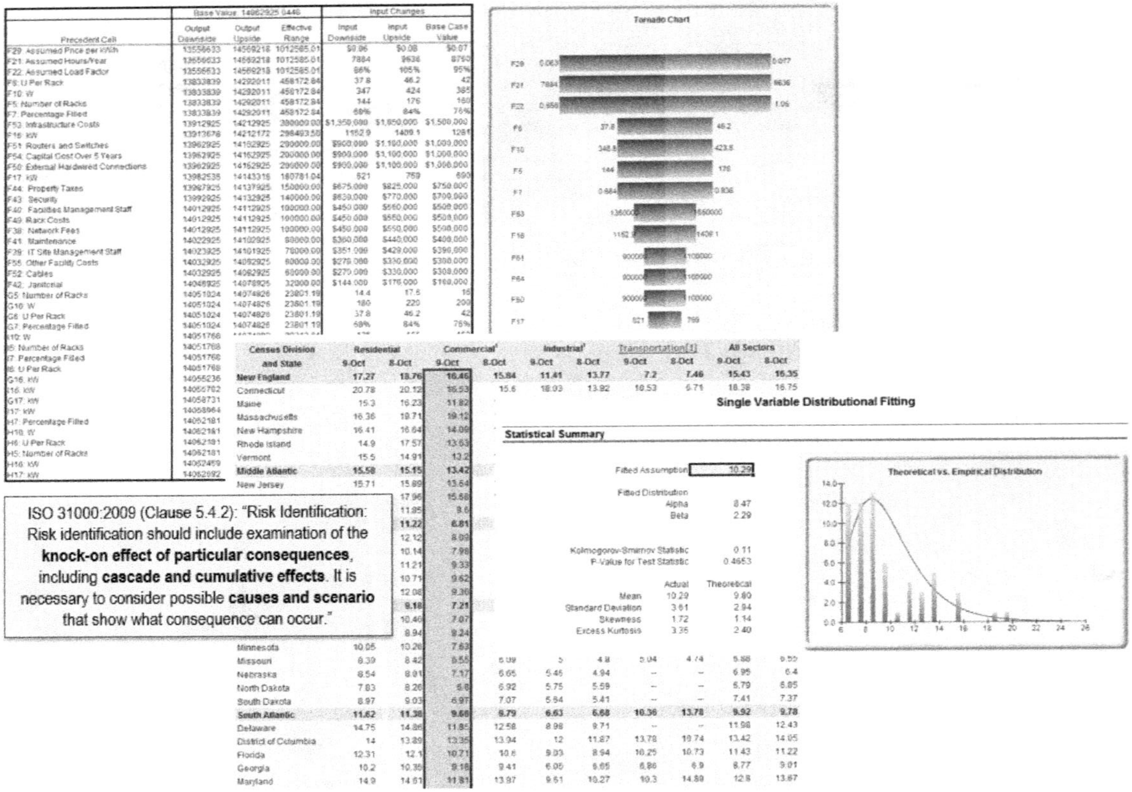

ISO 31000:2009 (Clause 5.4.2): "Risk Identification:
Risk identification should include examination of the
knock-on effect of particular consequences,
including **cascade** and **cumulative effects.** It is
necessary to consider possible **causes** and **scenario**
that show what consequence can occur."

Tornado Chart

Single Variable Distributional Fitting

Statistical Summary

Theoretical vs. Empirical Distribution

Figure 3.9: ISO 31000:2009—Consequences, Cascades, and Scenarios

Management Dashboards

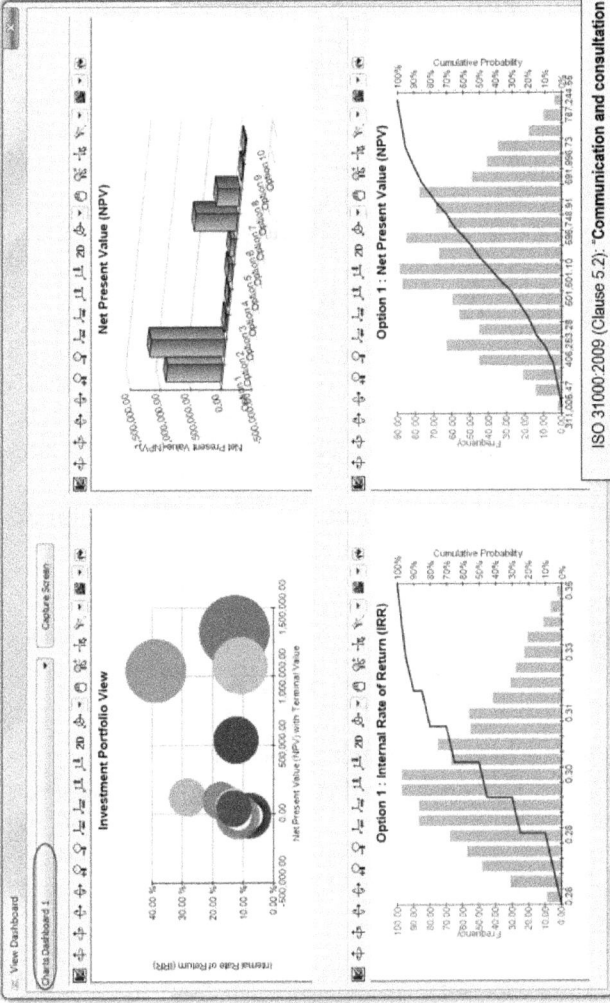

You can retrieve any of the saved dashboards and these dashboards will be populated only if the appropriate models have been run...

ISO 31000:2009 (Clause 5.2): "**Communication and consultation** with external and internal stakeholders should take place during all stages of the RM process. These should **address issues relating to the risk itself, its causes, its consequences (if known), and the measures being taken to treat it.** Stakeholders need to **understand the basis on which decisions are made, and the reasons why particular actions are required.**"

Figure 3.10: ISO 31000:2009—Communication and Consultation

COMPLIANCE WITH BASEL III
AND BASEL IV FRAMEWORK

The following provides a quick summary of Basel III and Basel IV compliance when using the IRM methodology:

- Figure 3.11 shows Monte Carlo risk simulations applied to determine confidence levels, percentiles, and probabilities of occurrence using historically fitted data or forecast expectations. These methods are in line with Basel III and Basel IV requirements Sections 16 and 161 concerning the use of historical simulations, Monte Carlo simulations, and 99th percentile confidence intervals.

- Figure 3.12 shows a correlated simulation of a portfolio of assets and liabilities, where asset returns are correlated against one another in a portfolio and optimization routines were run on the simulated results. These processes provide compliance with Basel III and Basel IV requirements Sections 178, 232, and 527(f) involving correlations, Value at Risk (VaR) models, portfolios of segments, and pooled exposures (assets and liabilities).

- Figure 3.13 shows Value at Risk percentile and confidence calculations using structural models and simulation results that are in line with Basel III and Basel IV requirements Sections 179, 527(c), and 527(f).

- Figure 3.14 shows the computations of probability of default (PD) as required in the Basel Accords, specifically Basel III and Basel IV Section 733 and Annex 2's Section 16. PD can be computed using structural models or based on historical data through running basic ratios to more advanced binary logistic models.

- Figure 3.15 shows the simulation and generation of interest rate yield curves using Risk Simulator and Modeling Toolkit models. These methods are in line with Basel III and Basel IV requirements Section 763 requiring the analysis of interest rate fluctuations and interest rate shocks.

- Figure 3.16 shows additional models for volatile interest rates, financial markets, and other liquid instruments' instantaneous shocks using Risk Simulator's stochastic process models. These analyses conform to Basel III and Basel IV requirements Sections 155, 527(a), and 527(b).

- Figure 3.17 shows several forecast models with high predictive and analytical power, which is a part of the Risk Simulator family of forecast methods. Such modeling provides compliance with Basel III and Basel IV requirements Section 417 requiring models of good predictive power.

- Figure 3.18 shows the list of financial and credit models available in the ROV Modeling Toolkit and ROV Real Options SLS software applications. These models conform to Basel III and Basel IV requirements Sections 112, 203, and 527(e) requiring the ability to value and model over-the-counter (OTC) derivatives, nonlinear equity derivatives and convertibles, hedges, and embedded options.

- Figure 3.19 shows the modeling of foreign exchange instruments and hedges to determine the effectiveness of foreign exchange hedging vehicles and their impact on valuation, portfolio profitability, and VaR, in line with Basel III and Basel IV Sections 131 and 155 requiring the analysis of different currencies, correlations, volatility, and hedges.

- Figure 3.20 shows the option-adjusted spread (OAS), credit default swaps (CDS), and credit spread options (CSO) models in ROV Modeling Toolkit. These models provide compliance with Basel III and Basel IV requirements Sections 140 and 713 pertaining to modeling and valuing credit derivatives and credit hedges.

Basel III Compliance

Monte Carlo Simulation and Model Fitting

Finding the right distribution of your historical data

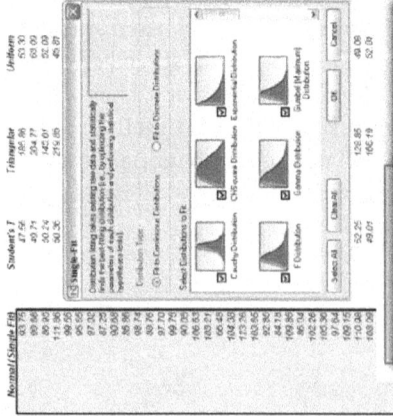

Correlated historical and Monte Carlo simulation

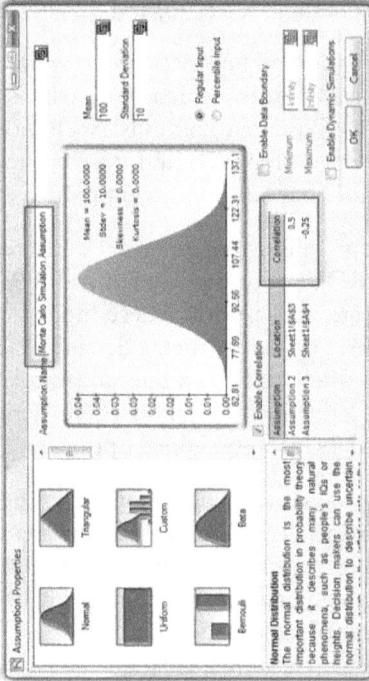

Basel II & III Section 161:

No particular type of model is prescribed. So long as each model used captures all the material risks run by the bank, banks will be free to use models based on, for example, **historical simulations and Monte Carlo simulations**

Basel II & III Section 16:

After reviewing a variety of methodologies, the Committee decided to use **Monte Carlo simulations** to calibrate both the monitoring and trigger levels for each credit **risk assessment category**. In particular, the proposed monitoring levels were derived from the **99th percentile confidence interval** and the trigger level benchmark from the 99.9th percentile confidence interval

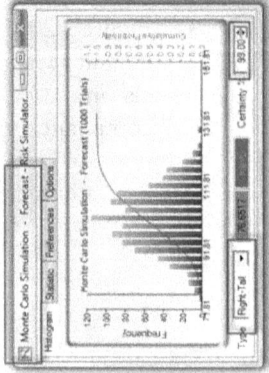

Figure 3.11: Basel III and Basel IV Confidence Levels, Monte Carlo Simulations, and Credit Risk

Basel III Compliance

Correlated Portfolio Optimization

TAIL VALUE AT RISK MODEL (BASEL II REQUIREMENT)

Line of Business	Mean Required Capital	99.95th Percentile	Capital Required	Allocation Weights	Minimum Allowed	Maximum Allowed	
Business 1	$10.50	$36.52	$26.01	10.00%	5.00%	15.00%	3.48
Business 2	$11.12	$47.52	$36.39	10.00%	5.00%	15.00%	4.27
Business 3	$11.77	$48.99	$37.22	10.00%	5.00%	15.00%	4.16
Business 4	$10.77	$37.34	$26.56	10.00%	5.00%	15.00%	3.47
Business 5	$13.49	$49.52	$36.03	10.00%	5.00%	15.00%	3.67
Business 6	$14.24	$55.59	$41.35	10.00%	5.00%	15.00%	3.91
Business 7	$15.60	$60.24	$44.64	10.00%	5.00%	15.00%	3.86
Business 8	$14.95	$64.69	$49.74	10.00%	5.00%	15.00%	4.33
Business 9	$14.15	$61.02	$46.87	10.00%	5.00%	15.00%	4.31
Business 10	$10.09	$35.37	$25.29	10.00%	5.00%	15.00%	3.51
Portfolio Total	$12.67	$49.68	$37.01	100.00%			
Total Capital Required			$14.00				

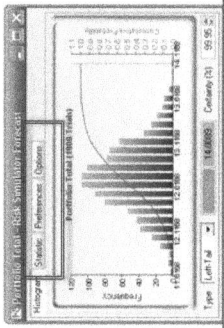

Correlation Matrix

	1	2	3	4	5	6	7	8	9	10
1										
2	-2.20									
3	-0.13	0.35								
4	-0.05	0.01	0.00							
5	0.21	0.50	0.15	0.00						
6	0.00	0.00	-0.15	0.00	0.03					
7	0.25	0.00	-0.28	0.01	0.19	-0.10				
8	0.36	-0.25	-0.60	-0.30	0.00	0.00	-0.15			
9	-2.01	-2.20	0.16	0.04	-0.01	0.01	0.00	0.00		

This model shows the capital requirements per Basel II (99.95 percentile capital adequacy based on a specific holding period). Without running risk-based historical and Monte Carlo simulation using Risk Simulator, the required capital is $37.01M as compared to only $14.00M is required. This is due to the cross-correlations between assets and business lines, and can only be modeled using Risk Simulator. To run the model click on Simulation and select Run Simulation (if you had other models open, make sure you first click on Simulation, Change Simulation Profile, and select the Tail VaR profile before starting). This model will not run unless Risk Simulator is initiated.

Basel II & III Section 178:

As an alternative to the use of standard or own-estimate haircuts, banks may be permitted to use a VaR models approach to reflect the price volatility of the exposure and collateral for repo-style transactions, taking into account correlation effects between security positions. This approach would apply to repo-style transactions covered by bilateral netting agreements on a counterparty-by-counterparty basis.

Basel II & III Section 232

The exposure must be one of a large pool of exposures, which are managed by the bank on a pooled basis... Furthermore, it must not be managed individually in a way comparable to corporate exposures, but rather as part of a portfolio segment or pool of exposures with similar risk characteristics for purposes of risk assessment and quantification.

Basel II & III Section 527 (f):

Subject to supervisory review, equity portfolio correlations can be integrated into a bank's internal risk measures. The use of explicit correlations (e.g., utilization of a variance/covariance VaR model) must be fully documented and supported using empirical analysis. The appropriateness of implicit correlation assumptions will be evaluated by supervisors in their review of model documentation and estimation techniques.

Figure 3.12: Basel III and Basel IV Correlated Portfolios and Correlated Simulations

Basel III Compliance

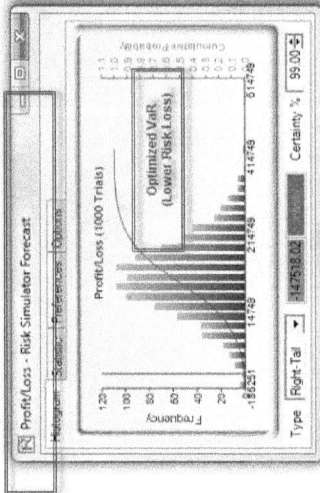

Value at Risk

Basel II & III Section 179:
The quantitative and qualitative criteria for recognition of internal market risk models for repo-style transactions and other similar transactions are in principle the same as under the Market Risk Amendment. With regard to the holding period, the minimum will be 5-business days for repo-style transactions, rather than the 10-business days under the Market Risk Amendment. For other transactions eligible for the VaR models approach, the 10-business day holding period will be retained.

Basel II & III Section 527 (c):
No particular type of **VaR model** (e.g. **variance-covariance, historical simulation, or Monte Carlo**) is prescribed. However, the model used must be able to capture adequately all of the material risks embodied in equity returns including both the general market risk and specific risk exposure of the institution's **equity portfolio**. Internal models must adequately explain historical price variation, capture both the magnitude and changes in the composition of potential concentrations, and be robust to adverse market environments. The population of risk exposures represented in the data used for estimation must be closely matched to or at least comparable with those of the bank's equity exposures

Basel II & III Section 527 (f):
Subject to supervisory review, equity portfolio correlations can be integrated into a bank's internal risk measures. The use of explicit correlations (e.g., utilization of a **variance/covariance VaR model**) must be fully documented and supported using empirical analysis. The appropriateness of implicit **correlation** assumptions will be evaluated by supervisors in their review of model documentation and estimation techniques.

VALUE AT RISK WITH ASSET ALLOCATION OPTIMIZATION MODEL

VALUE AT RISK (VARIANCE-COVARIANCE METHOD)

This model is used to compute the portfolio's Value at Risk at a given percentile for a specific holding period, after accounting for the cross-correlation effects between the assets. The daily volatility is the annualized volatility divided by the square root of trading days per year.

Figure 3.13: Basel III and Basel IV Value at Risk and Percentiles

Financial Engineering: Credit Risk

Probability of Default

STEP ONE:

Default Probability and Credit Risk Model for Basel II

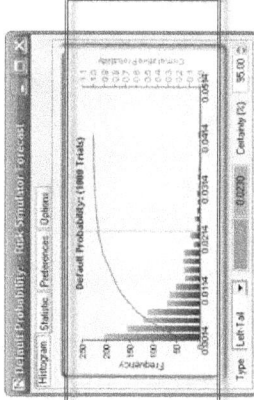

Available market and corporate data stating that we have:

Market Capitalization	$3,000	(in millions)
Equity Volatility (computed)	45.64%	(annualized)
Total Liabilities	$10,000	(in millions)

This value is obtained from market data on the firm's capitalization
This value is computed in the Volatility or LPVA worksheets
This is the firm's book value of debt

Inputs in the real options model:

	Solved	Starting	Optimized
Call Value	$2,451		
Asset Value*	$12,000	$12,000	$12,509
Strike Value	$10,000		
Maturity	1		
Volatility of Asset*	10.00%	10.00%	11.53%
Risk-free Rate	5.0%		
Dividend Rate	0%		

This is the value of the option and should be set to the equity value using optimization
This is the value to be solved* and is hence set as a decision variable in Risk Simulator
This is set as the book value of debt
For simplicity, we set this as 1 year, to obtain the 1-year default probability
This is the value to be solved* and is hence set as a decision variable in Risk Simulator
This is the corresponding risk-free rate for the maturity of the option being analyzed
For simplicity, we assume a zero dividend rate

Optimization parameters:

Call value	$3,000	This is the target result
Computed value	$2,451	This is the computed result
Minimize Absolute Difference	$609	Objective to Minimize (we minimize this error function to solve the simultaneous equations)

Decision Variable Constraints:

	Min	Max	
Asset Value	$10,000	$15,000	These are decision variable constraints, set at appropriate levels based on the input parameters
Volatility	5%	35%	These are decision variable constraints, set at appropriate levels based on the input parameters

Optimization Constraints:

Set value	39.29% to be exactly 45.64% which is the equity volatility

STEP TWO:

Default Probability is computed using the Risk Simulator Distribution Analysis tool on:

Anticipated Growth	7%	Enter in the expected annualized cumulative growth rate of the firm's assets
Standardized Value	-2.4732	This an intermediate computed value
Default Probability	0.6695%	This is the computed probability of default

Distance to Default:	**2.47**	This is the computed distance to default in standard deviations

Basel II & III Annex 2 – Section 16:

After reviewing a variety of methodologies, the Committee decided to use **Monte Carlo simulations** to calibrate both the monitoring and trigger levels for each **credit risk assessment** category. In particular, the proposed monitoring levels were derived from the **99th percentile confidence interval** and the trigger level benchmark from the 99.5th percentile confidence interval.

Basel II & III Section 733:
Credit risk: Banks should have methodologies that enable them to assess the **credit risk** involved in exposures to **individual borrowers or counterparties** as well as at the **portfolio** level. For more sophisticated banks, the credit review assessment of capital adequacy, at a minimum, should cover four areas: risk rating systems, portfolio analysis/aggregation, securitization/complex credit derivatives, and large exposures and risk concentrations.

Figure 3.14: Basel III and Basel IV Credit Risk Analysis

Financial Engineering: Market Risk

Interest Rate and Yield Curve Analytics

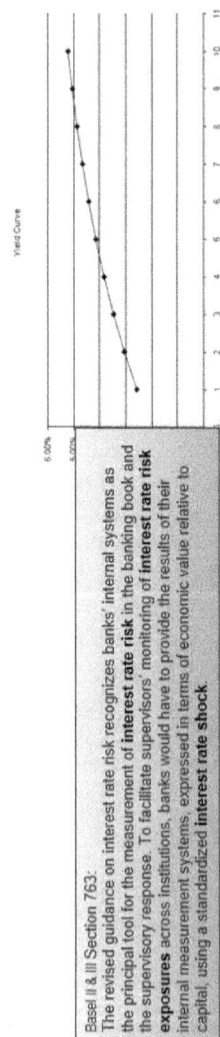

Splined Curve

YIELD CURVE - INTERPOLATION MODEL

This is the Bliss Interpolation model for generating the term structure of interest rates and yield curve estimation. This model requires several input parameters, whereby their estimations require some econometric modeling techniques to calibrate their values.

Function used: B2YieldCurveBliss(Beta 0, Beta 1, Beta 2, Lambda 1, Lambda 2)

Time	Rate
1	3.91%
2	7.96%

Yield Curve

VASICEK MODEL
YIELD CURVE CONSTRUCTION

Input Assumptions

Time to Maturity of the Bond or Debt (Years)	1.00
Riskfree Rate (Short Rate)	2.00%
Long-run Mean Rate	8.00%
Annualized Volatility of Interest Rate	2.00%
Market Price of Interest Rate Risk	0.00%
Rate of Mean Reversion	20.00%

Yield of Zero Coupon Bond 2.5563%

This is the Vasicek model used to compute the term structure of interest rates and yield curve. The Vasicek model assumes a mean-reverting stochastic interest rate. The rate of reversion and long-run mean rates can be determined using Risk Simulator's statistical analysis tool. If the long-run rate is higher than the current short rate, the yield curve is upward sloping, and vice versa.

Function call: B2BondVasicekBondYields (Maturity, Riskfree, Longterm Rate, Volatility, Market Price of Risk, Rate of Mean Reversion)

Years	Rate
1	2.56%
2	3.03%
3	3.45%
4	3.81%
5	4.12%
6	4.40%
7	4.64%
8	4.86%
9	5.05%
10	5.22%
15	5.83%
20	6.21%
25	6.46%
30	6.63%

Basel II & III Section 763:
The revised guidance on interest rate risk recognizes banks' internal systems as the principal tool for the measurement of **interest rate risk** in the banking book and the supervisory response. To facilitate supervisors' monitoring of **interest rate risk exposures** across institutions, banks would have to provide the results of their internal measurement systems, expressed in terms of economic value relative to capital, using a standardized **interest rate shock**.

Figure 3.15: Basel III and Basel IV Interest Rate Risk and Market Shocks

Financial Engineering: Market Risk

Stochastic Forecasting

- ARIMA
- GARCH Volatility
- Brownian Motion Random Walk
- Cubic Spline Yield Curves
- Implied Yield Curves from Debt
- Mean-Reverting Interest Rates
- Jump-Diffusion Prices
- Mixed Stochastic Processes
- Time-Series Decomposition

Stochastic Process Forecasting

Statistical Summary

A stochastic process is a sequence of events or paths generated by probabilistic laws. That is, random events can occur over time but are governed by specific statistical and probabilistic rules. The main stochastic processes include Random Walk or Brownian Motion, Mean-Reversion, and Jump-Diffusion. These processes can be used to forecast a multitude of variables that seemingly follow random trends but are restricted by probabilistic laws.

The Random Walk Brownian Motion process can be used to forecast stock prices, prices of commodities, and other stochastic time-series data given a drift or growth rate and a volatility around the drift path. The Mean-Reversion process can be used to reduce the fluctuations of the Random Walk process by allowing the path to target a long-term value. The Jump-Diffusion process is useful for forecasting time-series variables that have a long-term rate such as interest rates and inflation rates and inflation rates where there are sporadic target rates. In systems automatically (or the market). The Jump-Diffusion process is useful for forecasting time-series data where the variable can occasionally exhibit random jumps, such as oil prices or price of electricity (prices spike up and down when supply and demand are mixed and matched or not spike). Finally, these three stochastic processes can be mixed and matched as required.

The results on the right indicate the mean and standard deviation of all the forecasts generated at each time step of the Brownian motion / geometric random walk stochastic time-series of the forecast journey, with 20 shown in a separate worksheet. This graph generated below shows a sample set of forecast pathways.

Stochastic Process, Brownian Motion (Random Walk with Drift)

Start Value	100	Steps	50.00	Jump Rate	N/A
Drift Rate	5.00%	Iterations	10.00	Jump Size	N/A
Volatility	25.00%	Reversion Rate	N/A	Random Seed	1720682443
Horizon	5	Long-Term Value	N/A		

Time	Mean	Stdev
0.0000	100.00	0.00

Figure 3.16: Basel III and Basel IV Volatility and Adverse Instantaneous Shocks

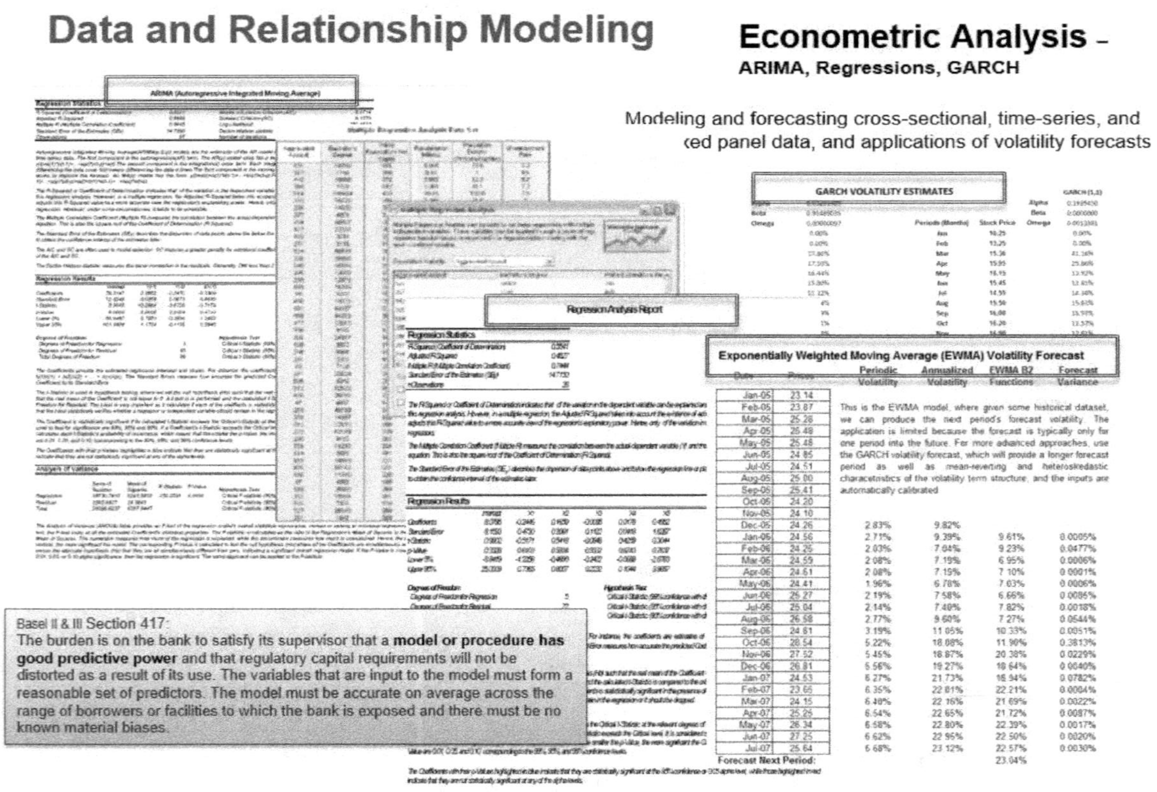
Data and Relationship Modeling
Econometric Analysis -
ARIMA, Regressions, GARCH
Modeling and forecasting cross-sectional, time-series, and
ced panel data, and applications of volatility forecasts
ARIMA (Autoregressive Integrated Moving Average)
Regression Analysis Report
GARCH VOLATILITY ESTIMATES
Exponentially Weighted Moving Average (EWMA) Volatility Forecast
This is the EWMA model, where given some historical dataset, we can produce the next period's forecast volatility. The application is limited because the forecast is typically only for one period into the future. For more advanced approaches, use the GARCH volatility forecast, which will provide a longer forecast period as well as mean-reverting and heteroskedastic characteristics of the volatility term structure, and the inputs are automatically calibrated.
Forecast Next Period:
Basel II & III Section 417:
The burden is on the bank to satisfy its supervisor that a model or procedure has good predictive power and that regulatory capital requirements will not be distorted as a result of its use. The variables that are input to the model must form a reasonable set of predictors. The model must be accurate on average across the range of borrowers or facilities to which the bank is exposed and there must be no known material biases.

Figure 3.17: Basel III and Basel IV Forecast Models with Strong Predictive Power

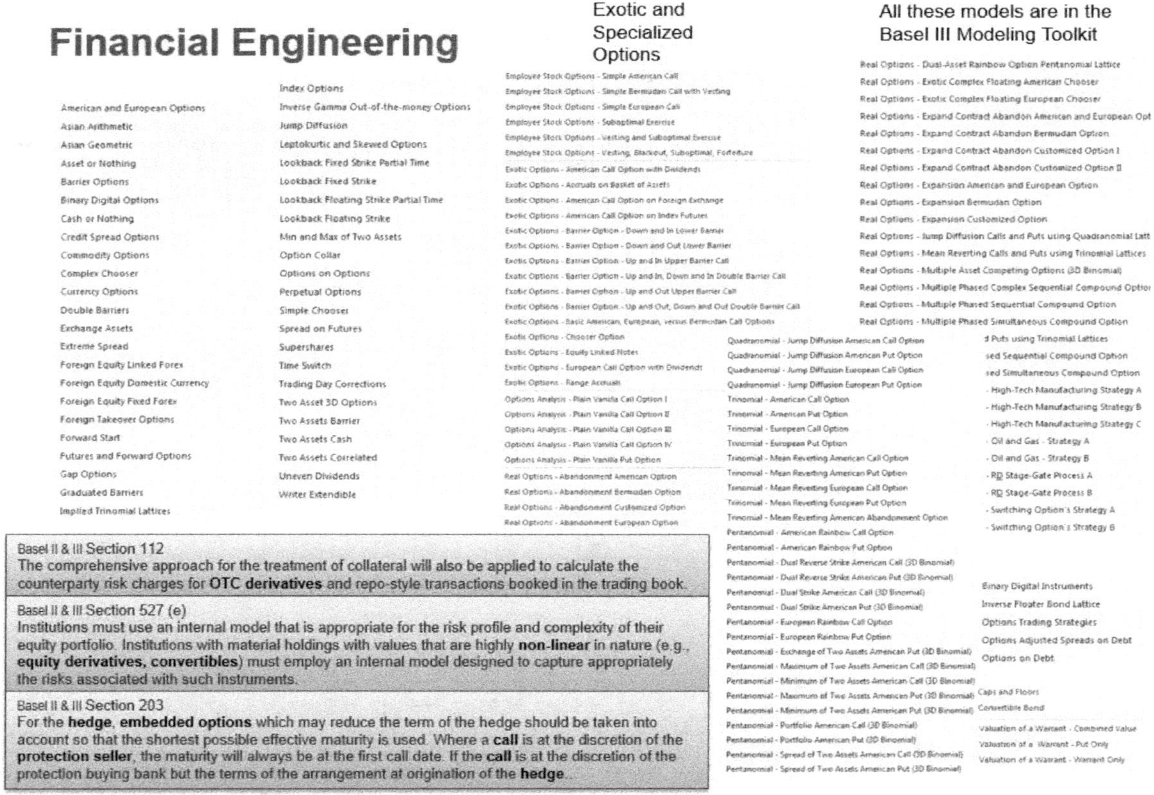

Financial Engineering

- American and European Options
- Asian Arithmetic
- Asset or Nothing
- Barrier Options
- Binary Digital Options
- Cash or Nothing
- Credit Spread Options
- Commodity Options
- Complex Chooser
- Currency Options
- Double Barriers
- Exchange Assets
- Extreme Spread
- Foreign Equity Limited Forex
- Foreign Equity Domestic Currency
- Foreign Equity Fixed Forex
- Foreign Takeover Options
- Forward Start
- Futures and Forward Options
- Gap Options
- Graduated Barriers
- Implied Trinomial Lattices
- Index Options
- Inverse Gamma Out-of-the-money Options
- Jump Diffusion
- Leptokurtic and Skewed Options
- Lookback Fixed Strike Partial Time
- Lookback Fixed Strike
- Lookback Floating Strike Partial Time
- Lookback Floating Strike
- Min and Max of Two Assets
- Option Collar
- Options on Options
- Perpetual Options
- Simple Chooser
- Spread on Futures
- Supershares
- Time Switch
- Trading Day Corrections
- Two Asset 3D Options
- Two Assets Barrier
- Two Assets Cash
- Two Assets Correlated
- Uneven Dividends
- Writer Extendable

Exotic and Specialized Options

- Employee Stock Options - Simple American Call
- Employee Stock Options - Simple Bermudan Call with Vesting
- Employee Stock Options - Simple European Call
- Employee Stock Options - Subsidtised Exercise
- Employee Stock Options - Vesting, Blackout, Suboptimal, Forfeiture
- Exotic Options - American Call Option with Dividends
- Exotic Options - Accruals on Basket of Assets
- Exotic Options - American Call Option on Foreign Exchange
- Exotic Options - American Call Option on Index Futures
- Exotic Options - Barrier Option- Down and In Lower Barrier
- Exotic Options - Barrier Option- Down and Out Lower Barrier
- Exotic Options - Barrier Option- Up and In Upper Barrier Call
- Exotic Options - Barrier Option- Up and In, Down and In Double Barrier Call
- Exotic Options - Barrier Option- Up and Out Upper Barrier Call
- Exotic Options - Barrier Option- Up and Out, Down and Out Double Barrier Calls
- Exotic Options - Basic American, European, versus Bermudan Call Options
- Exotic Options - Chooser Option
- Exotic Options - Equity Linked Notes
- Exotic Options - European Call Option with Dividends
- Exotic Options - Range Accruals
- Options Analysis - Plain Vanilla Call Option I
- Options Analysis - Plain Vanilla Call Option II
- Options Analysis - Plain Vanilla Call Option III
- Options Analysis - Plain Vanilla Call Option IV
- Options Analysis - Plain Vanilla Put Option
- Real Options - Abandonment American Option
- Real Options - Abandonment Bermudan Option
- Real Options - Abandonment Customized Option
- Real Options - Abandonment European Option

All these models are in the Basel III Modeling Toolkit

- Real Options: - Dual-Asset Rainbow Option Pentanomial Lattice
- Real Options: - Exotic Complex Floating American Chooser
- Real Options: - Exotic Complex Floating European Chooser
- Real Options: - Expand Contract Abandon American and European Out
- Real Options: - Expand Contract Abandon Bermudan Option
- Real Options: - Expand Contract Abandon Customized Option I
- Real Options: - Expand Contract Abandon Customized Option II
- Real Options: - Expansion American and European Option
- Real Options: - Expansion Bermudan Option
- Real Options: - Expansion Customized Option
- Real Options: - Jump Diffusion Calls and Puts using Quadranomial Latt
- Real Options: - Mean Reverting Calls and Puts using Trinomial Lattices
- Real Options: - Multiple Asset Competing Options (3D Binomial)
- Real Options: - Multiple Phased Complex Sequential Compound Optio
- Real Options: - Multiple Phased Sequential Compound Option
- Real Options: - Multiple Phased Simultaneous Compound Option
- 3 Paths using Trinomial Lattices
- ...ied Sequential Compound Option
- ...ied Simultaneous Compound Option
- High-Tech Manufacturing Strategy A
- High-Tech Manufacturing Strategy B
- High-Tech Manufacturing Strategy C
- Oil and Gas - Strategy A
- Oil and Gas - Strategy B
- RG Stage-Gate Process A
- RG Stage-Gate Process B
- Switching Options 5 Strategy A
- Switching Options 5 Strategy B
- Quadranomial - Jump Diffusion American Call Option
- Quadranomial - Jump Diffusion American Put Option
- Quadranomial - Jump Diffusion European Call Option
- Quadranomial - Jump Diffusion European Put Option
- Trinomial - American Call Option
- Trinomial - American Put Option
- Trinomial - European Call Option
- Trinomial - European Put Option
- Trinomial - Mean Reverting American Call Option
- Trinomial - Mean Reverting American Put Option
- Trinomial - Mean Reverting European Call Option
- Trinomial - Mean Reverting European Put Option
- Pentanomial - American Rainbow Call Option
- Pentanomial - American Rainbow Put Option
- Pentanomial - Dual Reverse Strike American Call (3D Binomial)
- Pentanomial - Dual Reverse Strike American Put (3D Binomial)
- Pentanomial - Dual Strike American Call (3D Binomial)
- Pentanomial - Dual Strike American Put (3D Binomial)
- Pentanomial - European Rainbow Call Option
- Pentanomial - European Rainbow Put Option
- Pentanomial - Exchange of Two Assets American Call (3D Binomial)
- Pentanomial - Maximum of Two Assets American Call (3D Binomial)
- Pentanomial - Minimum of Two Assets American Call (3D Binomial)
- Pentanomial - Maximum of Two Assets American Put (3D Binomial)
- Pentanomial - Minimum of Two Assets American Put (3D Binomial)
- Pentanomial - Portfolio American Call (3D Binomial)
- Pentanomial - Portfolio American Put (3D Binomial)
- Pentanomial - Spread of Two Assets American Call (3D Binomial)
- Pentanomial - Spread of Two Assets American Put (3D Binomial)

- Binary Digital Instruments
- Inverse Floater Bond Lattice
- Options Trading Strategies
- Options Adjusted Spreads on Debt
- Options on Debt
- Call and Floors
- Convertible Bond
- Valuation of a Warrant - Combined value
- Valuation of a Warrant - Put Only
- Valuation of a Warrant - Warrant Only

Basel II & III Section 112
The comprehensive approach for the treatment of collateral will also be applied to calculate the counterparty risk charges for OTC **derivatives** and repo-style transactions booked in the trading book.

Basel II & III Section 527 (e)
Institutions must use an internal model that is appropriate for the risk profile and complexity of their equity portfolio. Institutions with material holdings with values that are highly **non-linear** in nature (e.g. **equity derivatives, convertibles**) must employ an internal model designed to capture appropriately the risks associated with such instruments.

Basel II & III Section 203
For the **hedge, embedded options** which may reduce the term of the hedge should be taken into account so that the shortest possible effective maturity is used 'Where a **call** is at the discretion of the **protection seller**, the maturity will always be at the first call date. If the **call** is at the discretion of the protection buying bank but the terms of the arrangement at origination of the **hedge**.

Figure 3.18: Basel III and Basel IV Modeling OTC Derivatives and Exotic Convertibles

Foreign Exchange Risk

Hedging Foreign Exchange Exposure with Currency Options

Months	Jan	Feb	Mar	April	May
FX Spot Rate (HKD/USD)	7.80	7.40	7.60	7.30	7.10
FX Strike Rate (HKD/USD)	7.80	7.80	7.80	7.80	7.80
Maturity (Y ears)	0.5833	0.5000	0.4167	0.3333	0.2500
Risk Free Rate US	6.08%	6.08%	6.08%	6.08%	6.08%
Risk Free Rate HK	5.58%	5.58%	5.58%	5.58%	5.58%
Volatility	15.00%	15.00%	15.00%	15.00%	15.00%
Quantity of Options Hedge Position	10,000,000	10,000,000	10,000,000	10,000,000	10,000,000

	Jan	Feb	Mar	April	May
Currency Put Option Value (HKD/USD)	0.3229	0.5191	0.3795	0.5533	0.7912
Market Value of Hedge	3,229,135	5,191,089	3,794,813	5,532,845	7,012,229
Intrinsic Value	0	4,000,000	2,000,000	5,000,000	7,000,000
Time Value	3,229,135	1,191,089	1,794,813	532,845	12,229

FINANCIAL STATEMENTS IMPACTS - MARK TO MARKET

Balance Sheet (in 000's)

	Jan	Feb	Mar	April	May
Option Contract	3,229,135	5,191,089	3,794,813	5,532,845	7,012,229
Other Comp Income (SE)		4,000,000	2,000,000	5,000,000	7,000,000

Income Statement (in 000's)

Hedge Effectiveness gain or loss per period		(2,038,128)		
Hedge Effectiveness sum of all periods		603,865	(1,261,969)	(626,615)
Market Cost of Hedge (Current Period)				
Income from Option Exercise				
Net Valuation of Hedging				
Income from Hedging				
Income from No Hedging				
Loss Distribution from Hedging				
Loss Distribution from No Hedge				

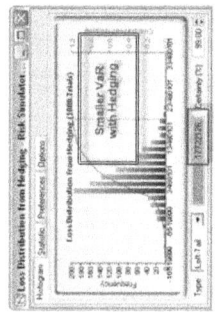

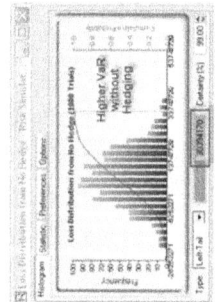

EQUITY LINKED FOREIGN EXCHANGE OPTIONS IN DOMESTIC CURRENCY

Input Assumptions	
Fixed Exchange Rate	1.50
Asset Price	$70.00
Strike Price	1.25
Maturity	6.50
Domestic Risk Free Rate	5.50%
Foreign Risk Free	6.00%
Desired Rate	1.50%
Volatility of Asset	25.00%
Volatility of Currency	10.00%
Correlation	0.25

Foreign Equity Linked Call Option	$17.5633
Foreign Equity Linked Put Option	$0.1777

Functions

B2EquityLinkedFXCallOptionDomesticValue
B2EquityLinkedFXPutOptionDomesticValue

3.225.1: Foreign Exchange Rate Hedged at 0.85 (Simulation Results)

	Name	Net Present Value
770.0X	Enabled	Yes
74,770.0X	Cell	8066
3,229.1X	Kurtosis Precision	
4,000.0X	Precision Level	
	Error Level	

Number of Datapoints	1000
Mean	2496.6775
Median	2495.3256
Standard Deviation	132.8299
Variance	17651.7424
Average Deviation	106.1536
Maximum	2847.7774
Minimum	1979.9491
Range	867.8243
Skewness	0.0053
Kurtosis	-0.0340
25% Percentile	2316.1631
75% Percentile	2486.2391
Error Precision at 95%	0.6624

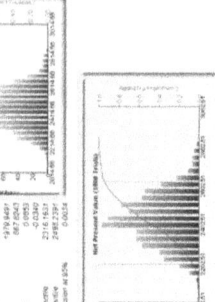

Basel II & III Section 131: Additionally where the exposure and collateral are held in **different currencies** an additional downwards adjustment must be made to the volatility adjusted collateral amount to take account of **possible future fluctuations in exchange rates.**

Basel II & III Section 155: Banks must estimate the **volatility** of the collateral instrument or **foreign exchange** mismatch individually. estimated **volatilities** for each transaction must not take into account the **correlations** between unsecured exposure, collateral and **exchange rates.**

Figure 3.19: Basel III and Basel IV Modeling Foreign Exchange Fluctuations

Credit Derivatives

OPTIONS ADJUSTED SPREAD WITH YIELD CURVE AND VOLATILITY TERM STRUCTURE

Face Value:	$100.00	Coupon Per Period	$2.50	Delta T	0.50/6	Modeling Toolkit Functions:		
Maturity	4	Market Price of Debt	$100.00	Straight Spread	0.6900%	2.3387%		
Total Steps	8	Callable Price	$101.00	Callable Spread	0.6900%	2.3896%		
		Callable Step	6		Compute Spreads			

Certain types of debt come with an option-embedded provision, for instance, a bond might be callable if the market price rises or if it is more profitable for the issuing company to call the debt and reissue new debt at the lower rate or prepayment allowance. You can compute the option adjusted spread (i.e. the additional premium that should be charged on the option provision).

Interest Rates (Yields)	2.60%	2.60%	2.60%	2.60%	2.60%	2.60%	2.60%	2.60%
Interest Volatilities	N/A	20.00%	20.00%	20.00%	20.00%	20.00%	20.00%	20.00%

Steps 0 1 2 3 4 5 6 7

Short Rate Lattice

2.60%	2.95%	3.14%	3.48%	3.80%	4.17%	4.51%	5.07%
	2.34%	2.57%	2.83%	3.11%	3.43%	3.79%	4.15%
		2.11%	2.32%	2.55%	2.81%	3.09%	3.49%
			1.90%	2.09%	2.30%	2.53%	2.79%
				1.71%	1.88%	2.07%	2.28%
					1.54%	1.69%	1.87%
						1.39%	1.53%
							1.25%

Straight Using Function: 110.06

Price Lattice 110.06

110.06	107.95	105.91	104.26	102.73	101.45	100.49	99.87
	110.64	108.00	106.13	104.43	102.95	101.72	100.78
		108.66	107.68	105.85	104.19	102.74	101.53
			108.97	107.82	106.22	103.59	102.15
				107.99	106.97	104.29	102.56
					106.77	104.86	103.08
						105.34	103.43
							103.71

Callable Debt Using Function: 110.03

Price Lattice 110.03

110.03	107.93	105.63	105.15	103.77	102.32	100.48	99.87
	109.68	107.99	106.48	105.21	104.20	103.10	100.78

CREDIT DEFAULT SWAP (CDS) SPREADS

Input Assumptions

Bond Yield	7.00%
Annual Coupon Rate	10.00%
Coupon Payments Per Year	2
Risk-free Yield	5.00%
Recovery Rate at Default	80.00%

Credit Default Swap Spread	1.7690%

A credit default swap or CDS which allows the holder of the instrument to sell a bond or debt at par value when a credit event or default occurs. This model computes the valuation of the CDS spread. A CDS does not protect against movements of the credit spread (only a credit spread option can do that) but

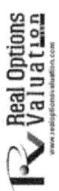

CREDIT SPREAD OPTIONS (CSO)

Input Assumptions

Credit Spread	3.00%
Strike Spread	2.90%
Duration (Spread to Currency Conversion Rate)	1000.00
Probability of Default	2.50%
Maturity	1.00
Risk-free Rate	5.00%
Volatility	25.00%

Credit Spread Call Option	$3.2102
Credit Spread Put Option	$2.7828

B2CreditSpreadCallOption
B2CreditSpreadPutOption

Credit spread options or CSO are exotic options where the payoff depends on a credit spread or the price of the underlying asset that is sensitive to interest rate movements such as floating or inverse floating rate notes and debt. A CSO call provides a return to the holder if the prevailing reference credit spread exceeds the predetermined strike rate, and the duration input variable is used to translate the percentage spread into a notional currency amount. The CSO expires when there is a credit default event

---

Forward Asset Price at Maturity	$1,000.00
Strike Price	$900.00
Probability of Default	2.50%
Maturity	1.00
Risk-free Rate	5.00%
Volatility	25.00%

Credit Asset Spread Call Option	$141.6406
Credit Asset Spread Put Option	$48.8957

CSO can only protect against any movements in the reference spread and not a default event. Only a credit default swap (CDS) can do that. Typically, to hedge against defaults and spread movements, both CDS and CDO are used. In some cases, when the CSO covers a reference entity's underlying asset value and not the spread itself, the credit asset spread options are used instead

---

Basel II & III Section 140: Where guarantees or credit derivatives are direct, explicit, irrevocable and unconditional, and supervisors are satisfied that banks fulfill certain minimum operational conditions relating to risk management processes they may allow banks to take account of such **credit protection in calculating capital requirements.**

Basel II & III Section 713: Specific **risk capital charges for positions hedged by credit derivatives.** Full allowance will be recognized when the values of two legs (i.e. long and short) always move in the opposite direction and broadly to the same extent.

Figure 3.20: Basel III and Basel IV Credit Derivatives and Hedging

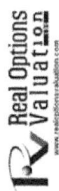

The following provides a quick summary of COSO Integrated ERM Framework compliance when using the IRM methodology:

- Figure 3.21 shows the PEAT ERM module's Risk Register tab where mitigation costs and benefits (gross risks reduced to residual risk levels), likelihood and impact measures, and spreads with varying precision levels ready for Monte Carlo risk simulation are situated, in compliance with COSO ERM Framework Sections 5 & 6.

- Figure 3.22 shows the PEAT ERM module where the likelihood and impact within a risk map is generated, in compliance with COSO AT/Exhibit 5.13.

- Figure 3.23 shows compliance with COSO AT/Exhibit 6.5 and COSO ERM Integrated Framework Section 6, where entity-wide portfolio and business unit, department, and functional areas' gross and residual risks are computed.

- Figure 3.24, a sample of the Risk Dashboard reports, also shows compliance with COSO AT/Exhibit 6.5 and COSO ERM Integrated Framework Section 6, where entity-wide portfolio and business unit, department, and functional areas' gross and residual risks are computed and compared against each other.

- Figure 3.25 shows the PEAT DCF module's efficient frontier model, consistent with COSO AT/Exhibit 3.7 requiring an analysis of the capital investment in relation to the returns within a diversified (optimized) portfolio.

- Figure 3.26 shows the PEAT ERM and DCF module's simulated results, where Value at Risk, percentiles, and statistical probabilities can be obtained, in compliance with COSO AT/Exhibit 5.5 requiring a range of outcomes based on distributional assumptions, and COSO ERM Integrated Framework Exhibit 5.2 requiring historical or simulated outcomes of future behaviors under probabilistic models.

- Figure 3.27 shows compliance with COSO AT/Exhibit 3.1 requiring the use of scenario modeling and stress testing.

- Figure 3.28 shows the CMOL module in PEAT where scenario analysis, stress testing, and gap analysis are performed, in compliance with COSO AT/Exhibit 5.10, to complement probabilistic models.

- Figure 3.29 shows compliance with COSO AT/Exhibits 5.8 and 5.9 requiring the modeling of operational and credit loss distributions with back-testing or historical simulation, sensitivity analysis, and Value at Risk calculations.

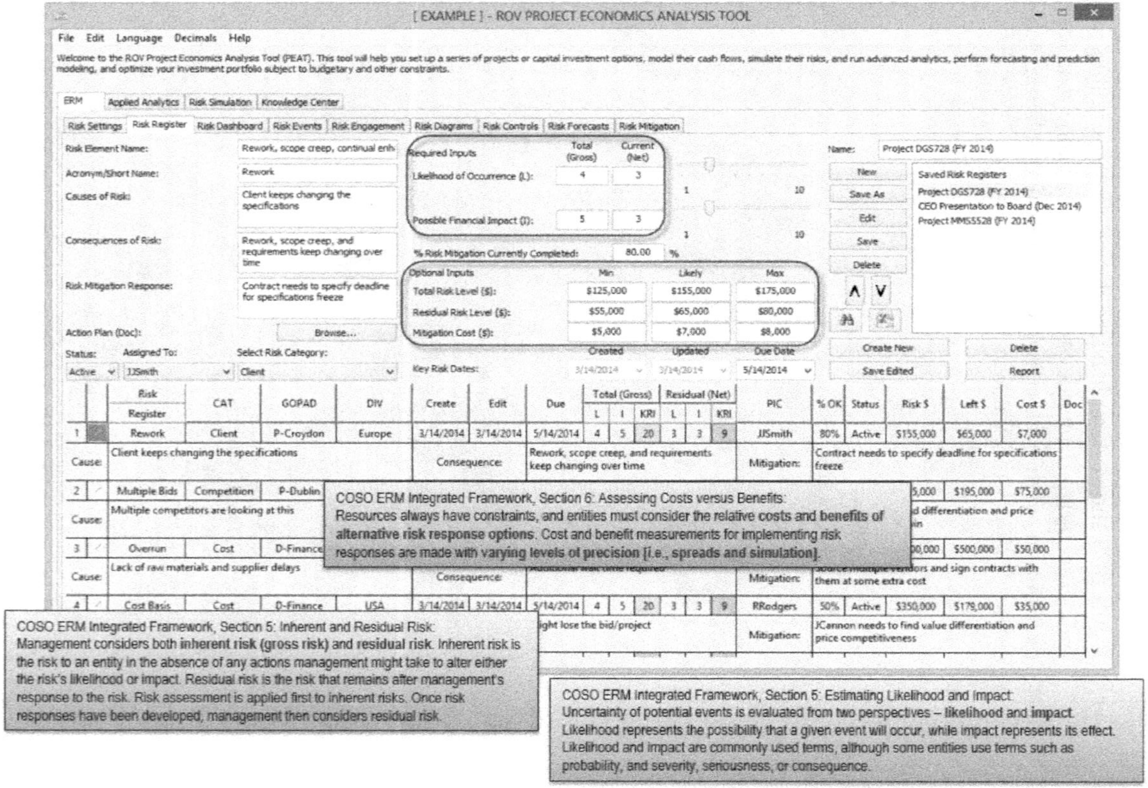

Figure 3.21: PEAT ERM and COSO Integrated Framework

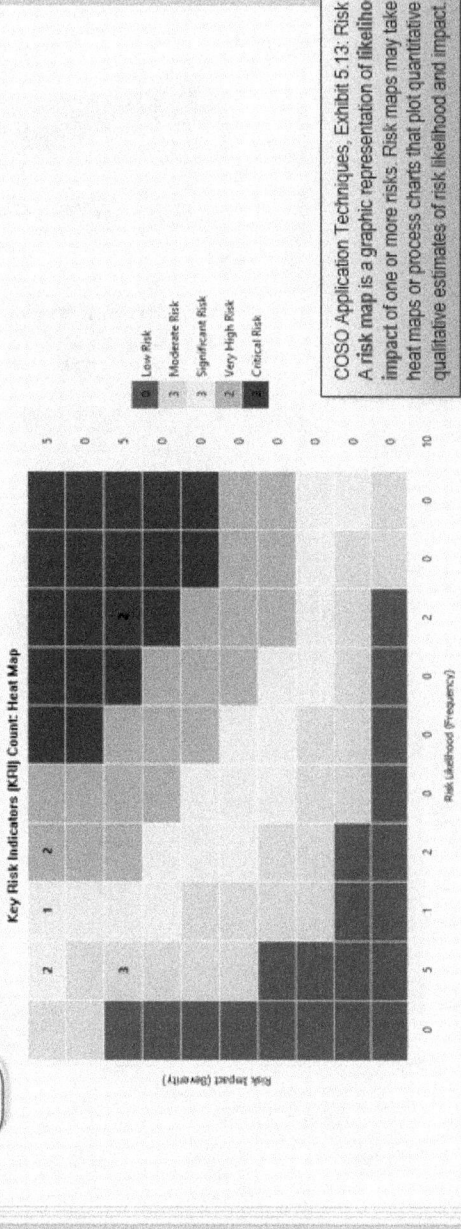

Figure 3.22: PEAT ERM Heat Map and Risk Matrix

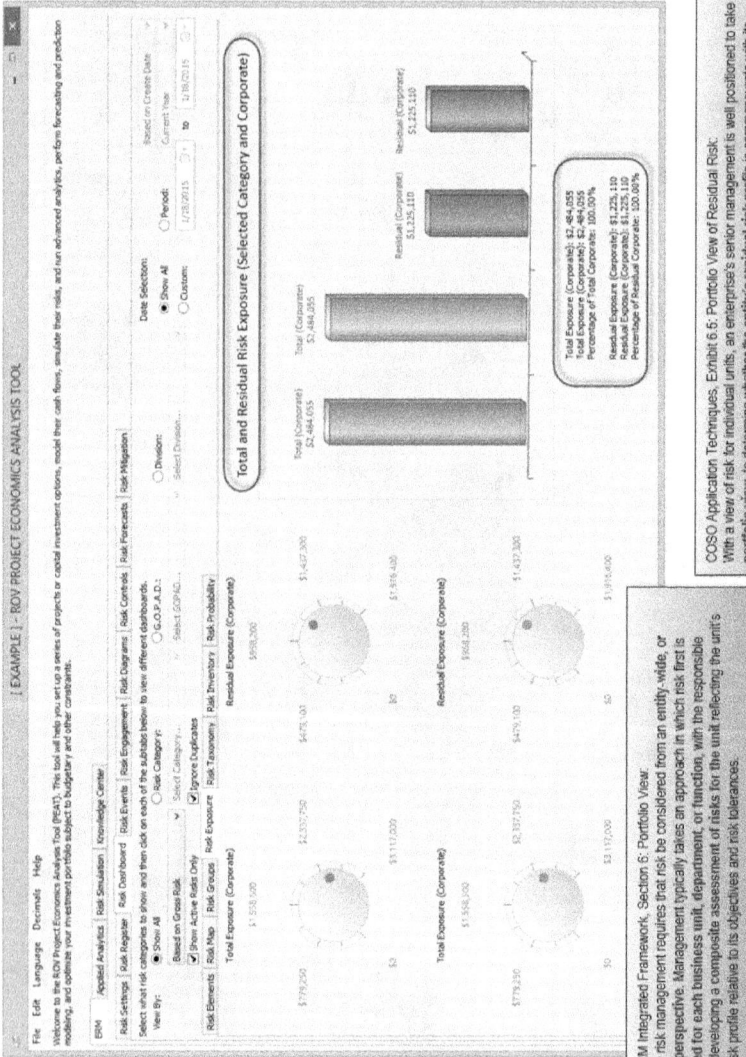

Figure 3.23: PEAT ERM Corporate Portfolio View of Gross and Residual Risk

[EXAMPLE] - ROV PROJECT ECONOMICS ANALYSIS TOOL

File   Edit   Language   Decimals   Help

Welcome to the ROV Project Economics Analysis Tool (PEAT). This tool will help you set up a series of projects or capital investment options, model the cash flows, simulate their risks, and run advanced analytics, perform forecasting and prediction modeling, and estimate your investment portfolio subject to budgetary and other constraints.

ERM
Applied Analytics | Risk Simulation | Knowledge Center

Risk Settings | Risk Dashboard | Risk Register | Risk Events | Risk Engagement | Risk Diagrams | Risk Controls | Risk Forecasts | Risk Mitigation

Select what risk categories to show and then click on each of the subfolders below to view different dashboards.

View By:
○ Show All   ○ Risk Category:
● Based on Gross Risk

☑ Show Active Risks Only
☑ Ignore Duplicates

Risk Elements | Risk Map | Risk Groups | Risk Exposure | Risk Taxonomy | Risk Inventory | Risk Probability
● Risk Elements View   ○ Pareto Chart View

Date Selection:
○ G.O.P.A.D.:
○ P-O'clock

Divisions:

● Show All
○ Custom:

Period: 1/28/2015   to   1/18/2015
Current Year

Based on Create Date

Key Risk Indicators

Cost Client   64
Multiple Bids   64
Econ Changes   40
Cost Vendor   40
Documents   30
Cost Basis   20
Reage   20
Overrun   16
Cost Compute   16
Staffing   16

Total Corporate Risk

38.9%
14.72%
21.47%
24.64%

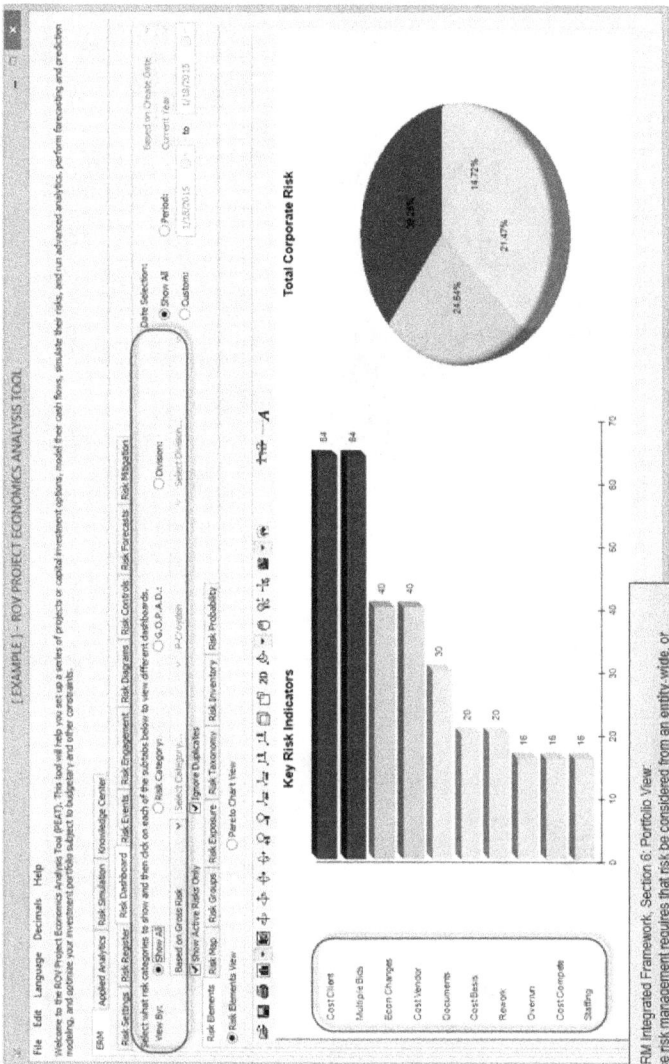

COSO ERM Integrated Framework, Section 6: Portfolio View:
Enterprise risk management requires that risk be considered from an entity-wide, or portfolio perspective. Management typically takes an approach in which risk first is considered for each business unit, department, or function, with the responsible manager developing a composite assessment of risks for the unit reflecting the units residual risk profile relative to its objectives and risk tolerances.

COSO Application Techniques, Exhibit 6.5: Portfolio View of Residual Risk:
With a View of risk for individual units, an enterprise's senior management is well positioned to take a portfolio view, to determine whether the entity's residual risk profile is commensurate with its overall risk appetite relative to its objectives.

Figure 3.24: PEAT ERM View by Department, Business Unit, Function, and Portfolio

COSO Application Techniques, Exhibit 3.7: Efficient Frontier.
The analysis illustrates how a company views capital at risk versus return in relation to risk appetite. The company strives to diversify its portfolio to earn a return that lines up along the target profile.

[EXAMPLE 1 - ROV PROJECT ECONOMICS ANALYSIS TOOL]

File   Edit   Projects   Report   Tools   Language   Decimals   Help

Welcome to the ROV Project Economics Analysis Tool (PEAT). This tool will help you set up a series of projects or capital investment options, model their cash flows, simulate their risks, and run advanced analytics, perform forecasting and prediction modeling, and optimize your investment portfolio subject to budgetary and other constraints.

Discounted Cash Flow | Applied Analytics | Risk Simulation | Options Valuation | Forecast Prediction | Portfolio Optimization | Dashboard | Knowledge Center

Optimization Settings | Optimization Results | Advanced Custom Optimization

Risk Optimizer Report: Date Sun Jan 18 23:27:24 2015 Runtime: 0.56 seconds

Problem Title: PEAT Portfolio Optimization

Problem Parameters:
Number of variables   10
Number of functions   2
Objective function will be maximized

Starting values

Functions:

No.	Function Name	Status	Type	Initial Value	Lower Bound	Upper Bound
1	G		RNGE	1.97662e+006	-1.79769e+308	2e+006
2	G		OBJ	6.12864		

Chart Type: Standard 2D Line

☐ Show Values on Chart

The optimization run has been completed. Optimize Time: 1s.

	6.1286	6.7465	6.9478	6.9478	6.9478	6.9478
Objective Function						
Frontier Variable	2,000,000	2,500,000	3,000,000	3,000,000	3,500,000	4,000,000
Optimized Constraint	1,976,618	2,487,042	2,718,646	2,718,646	2,718,646	2,718,646
Option1	1	1	1	1	1	1
Option2	0	1	1	1	1	1
Option3	1	1	1	1	1	1
Option4	1	1	1	1	1	1
Option5	1	1	1	1	1	1
Option6	0	0	1	1	1	1
Option7	0	0	0	0	0	0
Option8	1	1	1	1	1	1
Option9	0	0	1	1	1	1
Option10	0	1	1	1	1	1

Figure 3.25: PEAT DCF Module's Portfolio Optimization and Efficient Frontier

COSO Application Techniques, Exhibit 5.5: Value at Risk. Value-at-risk (VaR) models are based on distributional assumptions about change in the value of an item or group of items, which is not expected to be exceeded with a given confidence level over a defined time period. These models are used to estimate extreme ranges of value change expected to occur infrequently, such as the estimated level of loss that would not be expected to be exceeded with 95% or 99% confidence.

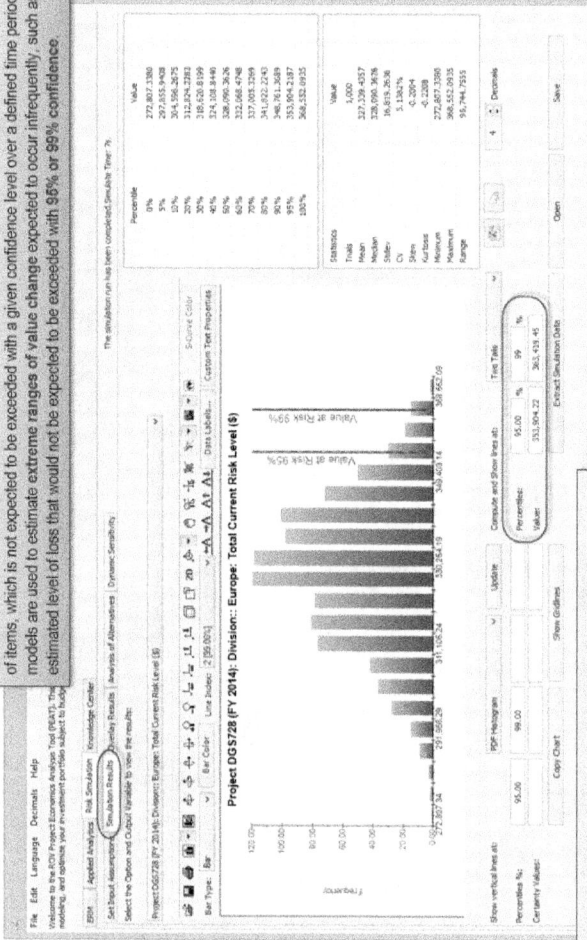

File   Edit   Language   Decimals   Help

Welcome to the ROV Project Economics Analysis Tool (PEAT). This modeling, and optimize your investment portfolio subject to budge

ERM   Applied Analytics   Risk Simulation   Knowledge Center

Set Input Assumptions   Simulation Results   Overlay Results   Analysis of Alternatives   Dynamic Sensitivity

Select the Option and Output Variable to view the results:

Project DGS728 (FY 2014): Division:: Europe: Total Current Risk Level ($)

Bar Type: Bar   Bar Color   Line Index: 2 [99.00%]   Custom Text Properties

PDF Histogram
Show vertical lines at: 95.00
Percentiles %:   99.00
Certainty Value:

Copy Chart   Show Gridlines

Update

Compute and Show from at:
Percentiles: 95.00 %   99 %   Tree Table
Values: 353,904.22   361,439.45

Extract Simulation Data

Project DGS728 (FY 2014): Division:: Europe: Total Current Risk Level ($)

Value at Risk 99%
Value at Risk 95%

-$27,857.34   29,986.29   311,105.24   330,254.19   340,403.14   349,662.09

Frequency

The simulation run has been completed. Simulate Time: 7s

Percentile	Value
0%	272,807.3380
5%	297,955.9408
10%	304,596.2675
20%	312,674.2383
30%	318,620.8199
40%	324,108.8440
50%	328,090.3626
60%	332,668.4748
70%	337,003.3269
80%	341,622.2243
90%	348,761.3689
95%	353,904.2187
100%	368,552.0935

Statistics	Value
Trials	1,000
Mean	327,328.4357
Median	328,090.3626
Stdev	16,619.2536
CV	3.1362%
Skew	-0.2004
Kurtosis	-0.2208
Minimum	272,807.3380
Maximum	368,552.0935
Range	95,744.7555

Decimals   Save

Open   Save

COSO ERM Integrated Framework, Exhibit 5.2: Probabilistic Models: Probabilistic models associate a range of events based on certain assumptions. Likelihood with the likelihood of those events based on certain assumptions. Likelihood and impact are assessed based on historical data or simulated outcomes reflecting assumptions of future behavior. Examples of probabilistic models include value at risk, cash flow at risk, earnings at risk, and development of credit and operational loss distributions.

COSO Application Techniques, Exhibit 5.5: Quantitative Probability Models: Probability-based techniques measure the likelihood and impact of a range of outcomes based on distributional assumptions of the behavior of events.

Figure 3.26: PEAT ERM and DCF Module's Risk Simulation and Value at Risk

[EXAMPLE] - ROV PROJECT ECONOMICS ANALYSIS TOOL

File   Edit   Language   Decimals   Help

Welcome to the ROV Project Economics Analysis Tool (PEAT). This tool will help you set up a series of projects or capital investment options, model their cash flows, simulate their risks, and run advanced analytics, perform forecasting and prediction modeling, and optimize your investment portfolio subject to budgetary and other constraints.

ERM   Applied Analytics   Scenario Analysis   Risk Simulation   Knowledge Center

Static Tornado   Scenario Analysis

1. Scenario Input Settings   2. Scenario Output Tables ("Sweetspots")

Select one of the saved scenarios to run the scenario table. In the event you make any changes in the inputs or settings, remember to click Update to manually update the scenario table.

Select the Saved Scenario to Compute:

Show results with   0   decimals

NOTE: The Row variable (down) is

Scenario table is for: Total Risk on Overrun
Overrun

and the Column variable (across) is

All Categories   Update   Econ Changes

	100,000	110,000	120,000	130,000	140,000	150,000	160,000	170,000	180,000	190,000	200,000	210,000	220,000	230,000	240,000	250,000	260,000	270,000	280,000	290,000
800,000	2,204,555	2,214,555	2,224,555	2,234,555	2,244,555	2,254,555	2,264,555	2,274,555	2,284,555	2,294,555	2,304,555	2,314,555	2,324,555	2,334,555	2,344,555	2,354,555	2,364,555	2,374,555	2,384,555	2,394,555
850,000	2,254,555	2,264,555	2,274,555	2,284,555	2,294,555	2,304,555	2,314,555	2,324,555	2,334,555	2,344,555	2,354,555	2,364,555	2,374,555	2,384,555	2,394,555	2,404,555	2,414,555	2,424,555	2,434,555	2,444,555
900,000	2,304,555	2,314,555	2,324,555	2,334,555	2,344,555	2,354,555	2,364,555	2,374,555	2,384,555	2,394,555	2,404,555	2,414,555	2,424,555	2,434,555	2,444,555	2,454,555	2,464,555	2,474,555	2,484,555	2,494,555
950,000	2,354,555	2,364,555	2,374,555	2,384,555	2,394,555	2,404,555	2,414,555	2,424,555	2,434,555	2,444,555	2,454,555	2,464,555	2,474,555	2,484,555	2,494,555	2,504,555	2,514,555	2,524,555	2,534,555	2,544,555
1,000,000	2,404,555	2,414,555	2,424,555	2,434,555	2,444,555	2,454,555	2,464,555	2,474,555	2,484,555	2,494,555	2,504,555	2,514,555	2,524,555	2,534,555	2,544,555	2,554,555	2,564,555	2,574,555	2,584,555	2,594,555
1,050,000	2,454,555	2,464,555	2,474,555	2,484,555	2,494,555	2,504,555	2,514,555	2,524,555	2,534,555	2,544,555	2,554,555	2,564,555	2,574,555	2,584,555	2,594,555	2,604,555	2,614,555	2,624,555	2,634,555	2,644,555
1,100,000	2,504,555	2,514,555	2,524,555	2,534,555	2,544,555	2,554,555	2,564,555	2,574,555	2,584,555	2,594,555	2,604,555	2,614,555	2,624,555	2,634,555	2,644,555	2,654,555	2,664,555	2,674,555	2,684,555	2,694,555
1,150,000	2,554,555	2,564,555	2,574,555	2,584,555	2,594,555	2,604,555	2,614,555	2,624,555	2,634,555	2,644,555	2,654,555	2,664,555	2,674,555	2,684,555	2,694,555	2,704,555	2,714,555	2,724,555	2,734,555	2,744,555
1,200,000	2,604,555	2,614,555	2,624,555	2,634,555	2,644,555	2,654,555	2,664,555	2,674,555	2,684,555	2,694,555	2,704,555	2,714,555	2,724,555	2,734,555	2,744,555	2,754,555	2,764,555	2,774,555	2,784,555	2,794,555
1,250,000	2,654,555	2,664,555	2,674,555	2,684,555	2,694,555	2,704,555	2,714,555	2,724,555	2,734,555	2,744,555	2,754,555	2,764,555	2,774,555	2,784,555	2,794,555					
1,300,000	2,704,555	2,714,555	2,724,555	2,734,555	2,744,555	2,754,555	2,764,555	2,774,555	2,784,555	2,794,555										
1,350,000	2,754,555	2,764,555	2,774,555	2,784,555	2,794,555															
1,400,000																				
1,450,000																	3,004,555	3,014,555	3,024,555	3,044,555
1,500,000											3,004,555	3,014,555	3,024,555	3,034,555	3,044,555	3,054,555	3,064,555	3,074,555	3,084,555	3,094,555
1,550,000	3,004,555	3,014,555	3,024,555	3,034,555	3,044,555	3,054,555	3,064,555	3,074,555	3,084,555	3,094,555	3,104,555	3,114,555	3,124,555	3,134,555	3,144,555	3,154,555	3,164,555	3,174,555	3,184,555	3,194,555
1,600,000	3,004,555	3,014,555	3,024,555	3,034,555	3,044,555	3,054,555	3,064,555	3,074,555	3,084,555	3,094,555	3,104,555	3,114,555	3,124,555	3,134,555	3,144,555	3,154,555	3,164,555	3,174,555	3,184,555	3,194,555

Figure 3.27: PEAT ERM and DCF Module's Scenario Analysis and Heat Map Regions

COSO Application Techniques, Exhibit 3.1: Scenarios, Stress Testing, Modeling

Using scenario analysis, modeling, and stress testing, management compared the results of each option in relation to the impact on return on capital employed. Management identified the distribution of potential return outcomes.

EXAMPLE I - ROV CREDIT, MARKET, LIQUIDITY RISK

Credit Risk (ERC)　Market Risk　Asset Liability Management　Analytical Models　Operational Risk　KRI Dashboard

Interest Rate Risk　Liquidity Risk

Input Assumptions　Scenario Analysis　Stress Testing　Gap Analysis　Charts

ASSETS	Month 1	Month 2	Month 3	Month 4	Month 5	Month 6	Month 7	Month 8	Month 9	Month 10	Month 11	Month 12
Month												
LOANS												
Available	21.95%	2.13%	13.32%	23.54%	-2.51%	-22.69%	13.12%	-10.69%	0.72%	2.00%	-6.20%	6.96%
Individual Firm Notes	-8.26%	-2.88%	-0.95%	0.38%	4.32%	2.87%	1.44%	1.99%	-0.95%	4.75%	-1.76%	-1.72%
Discounted Notes	-8.26%	-2.88%	-0.95%	0.38%	4.32%	2.87%	1.44%	1.99%	-0.95%	4.75%	-1.76%	-1.72%
Mortgages	0.39%	0.47%	0.05%	-0.23%	-0.22%	-0.41%	-0.52%	-0.82%	-1.01%	-0.97%	-0.80%	-0.83%
Pledges	-0.05%	2.52%	-1.79%	-1.82%	-3.76%	-3.17%	-4.79%	-3.62%	-3.47%	-3.51%	-4.03%	-3.43%
Cards	7.92%	0.27%	7.46%	-4.09%	10.82%	3.95%	9.76%	-2.48%	-0.16%	1.20%	17.39%	0.69%
Personal	4.19%	2.91%	-1.19%	-0.56%	-0.45%	-1.09%	-1.26%	-0.89%	-0.31%	1.54%	2.26%	1.15%

LIABILITIES	Month 1	Month 2	Month 3	Month 4	Month 5	Month 6	Month 7	Month 8	Month 9	Month 10	Month 11	Month 12
Month												
REGULAR DEPOSITS												
Public Sector	41.75%	-19.84%	-1.39%	10.22%	-7.67%	8.14%	-12.88%	7.85%	-2.84%	-10.50%	0.49%	15.82%
Private Sector	17.24%	-8.16%	-0.32%	3.79%	-4.86%	3.87%	-1.05%	3.97%	-2.45%	-6.84%	1.63%	7.83%
TIME DEPOSITS												
Public Sector	-21.17%	19.94%	-0.78%	-22.00%	2.69%	-6.38%	27.78%	16.77%	5.27%	-0.56%	1.08%	3.30%
Private Sector	-2.21%	13.10%	2.77%	-3.29%	-1.98%	4.76%	-2.33%	8.35%	4.63%	-1.24%	0.45%	-0.22%

Select the analysis Dataset

Sample Dataset

◉ Enter scenarios using % change
○ Enter scenarios using actual values

Add Scenario:

Scenario 1

List of Saved Scenarios

Scenario
Scenario 1
Scenario 2

Save As

New　Delete
Edit　Save

COSO Application Techniques, Exhibit 5.10: Scenario Testing and Stress Testing
Scenario analysis assesses the effect on an objective of one or more events. **Stress testing** assesses the impact of events having extreme impact. Stress testing differs from scenario analysis in that it focuses on the direct impact of a change in only one event or activity under extreme circumstances, as opposed to focusing on changes on a more normal scale as in scenario analysis. Stress testing generally is used as a complement to probabilistic measures to examine the results of low likelihood, high impact events that might not be captured adequately by distributional assumptions used with probabilistic techniques.

Figure 3.28: CMOL Module's Scenario Analysis and Stress Testing

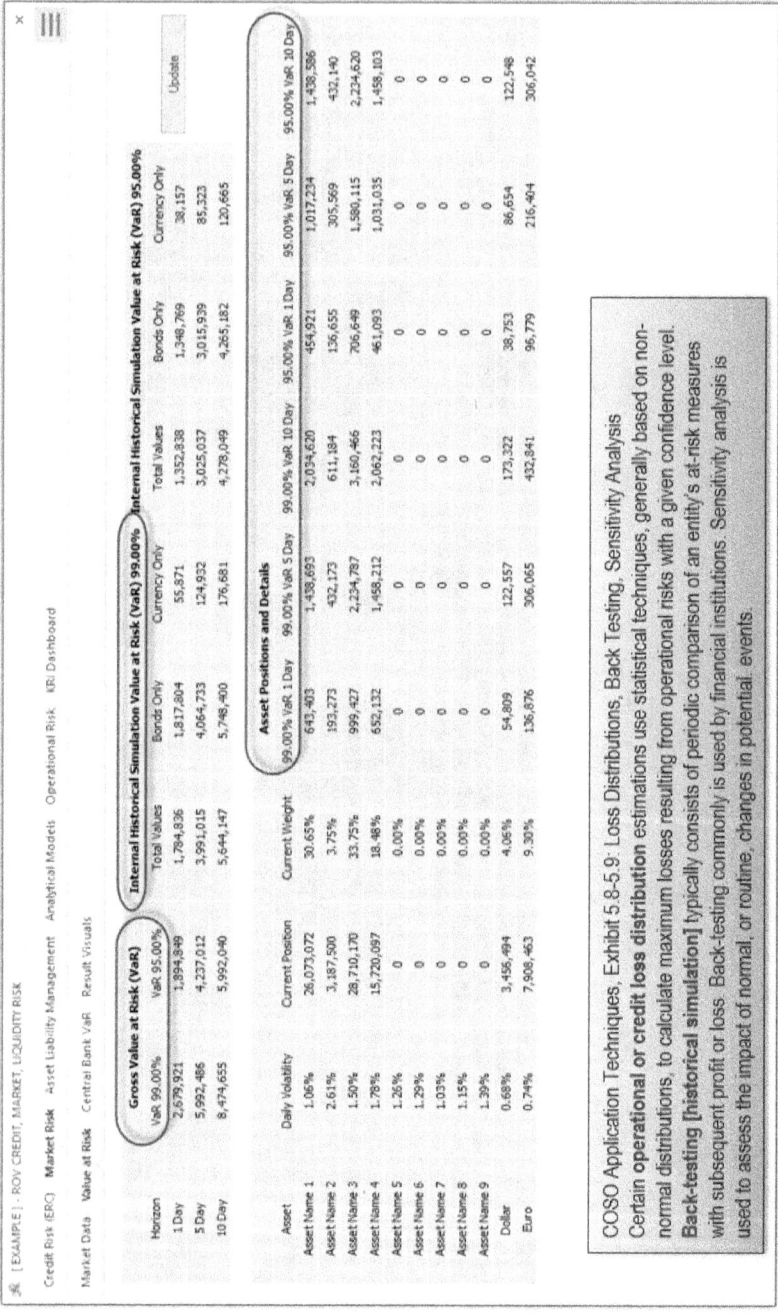

Figure 3.29: CMOL Module's Value at Risk and Back-Testing Historical Simulations

[EXAMPLE] - ROV CREDIT, MARKET, LIQUIDITY RISK

Credit Risk (ERC)　Market Risk　Asset Liability Management　Analytical Models　Operational Risk　KRI Dashboard

Market Data　Value at Risk　Central Bank VaR　Result Visuals

Gross Value at Risk (VaR)

Horizon	VaR 99.00%	VaR 95.00%
1 Day	2,679,921	1,894,849
5 Day	5,992,486	4,237,012
10 Day	8,474,655	5,992,040

Internal Historical Simulation Value at Risk (VaR) 99.00%

Horizon	Total Values	Bonds Only	Currency Only
1 Day	1,784,836	1,817,804	55,871
5 Day	3,991,015	4,064,733	124,932
10 Day	5,644,147	5,748,400	176,681

Internal Historical Simulation Value at Risk (VaR) 95.00%

Total Values	Bonds Only	Currency Only
1,352,838	1,348,769	38,157
3,025,037	3,015,939	85,323
4,278,049	4,265,182	120,665

Update

Asset Positions and Details

Asset	Daily Volatility	Current Position	Current Weight	99.00% VaR 1 Day	99.00% VaR 5 Day	99.00% VaR 10 Day	95.00% VaR 1 Day	95.00% VaR 5 Day	95.00% VaR 10 Day
Asset Name 1	1.06%	26,073,072	30.65%	643,403	1,438,693	2,034,620	454,921	1,017,234	1,438,586
Asset Name 2	2.61%	3,187,500	3.75%	193,273	432,173	611,184	136,655	305,569	432,140
Asset Name 3	1.50%	28,710,170	33.75%	999,427	2,234,787	3,160,466	706,649	1,580,115	2,234,620
Asset Name 4	1.78%	15,720,097	18.48%	652,132	1,458,212	2,062,223	461,093	1,031,035	1,458,103
Asset Name 5	1.26%	0	0.00%	0	0	0	0	0	0
Asset Name 6	1.29%	0	0.00%	0	0	0	0	0	0
Asset Name 7	1.03%	0	0.00%	0	0	0	0	0	0
Asset Name 8	1.15%	0	0.00%	0	0	0	0	0	0
Asset Name 9	1.39%	0	0.00%	0	0	0	0	0	0
Dollar	0.68%	3,456,494	4.06%	54,809	122,557	173,322	38,753	86,654	122,548
Euro	0.74%	7,908,463	9.30%	136,876	306,065	432,841	96,779	216,404	306,042

COSO Application Techniques, Exhibit 5.8-5.9: Loss Distributions, Back Testing, Sensitivity Analysis
Certain operational or credit loss distribution estimations use statistical techniques, generally based on non-normal distributions, to calculate maximum losses resulting from operational risks with a given confidence level. **Back-testing [historical simulation]** typically consists of periodic comparison of an entity's at-risk measures with subsequent profit or loss. Back-testing commonly is used by financial institutions. Sensitivity analysis is used to assess the impact of normal, or routine, changes in potential events.

DYNAMIC EVALUATION OF ENTERPRISE RISK MANAGEMENT AT ELETROBRAS FURNAS IN BRAZIL

This case study was written by Dr. Nelson Albuquerque and Dr. Johnathan Mun, with the cooperation of Eletrobrás Furnas SA, which allowed us access to this enterprise risk management project and its officers, Welington Cristiano Lima and José Roberto Teixeira Nunes. We would like to also acknowledge the thorough review conducted by Professor Pedro Bello, also of Eletrobrás. It is intended to describe the methodology applied in automating Enterprise Risk Management (ERM) for Eletrobrás Furnas, the largest utility company in Brazil. The ERM approach uses Real Options Valuation, Inc. (ROV) PEAT software's ERM module, and adapts the Risk Matrix model currently used by the Eletrobrás group to the concept of expected value of risk, pushing the envelope from qualitative risk assessment to more quantitative risk management.

The PEAT ERM module was built according to the concept of Expected Risk—which uses the concept of quantification of risks— enabling plans for risk mitigation, statistical evaluation, strategic real options, and analysis of alternatives, as well as optimizing the portfolios of multiple projects.

To get started, ERM requires a two-dimensional input of the Likelihood (L) or Frequency of a risk event occurring and the Impact (I) or the Severity in terms of financial, economic, and non-economic effects of the risk. These L and I concepts are industry standard and used even in regulatory environments such as the Basel III and Basel IV Accords (initiated by the Bank of International Settlements in Switzerland and accepted by most Central Banks around the world as regulatory reporting standards for operational risks).

However, Eletrobrás is a utility company and is not subject to stringent banking and financial regulations; therefore, in place of the probability scale of Likelihood or Frequency, Eletrobrás uses the concept of *Vulnerability* (V). Consequently, the typical ERM risk matrix is modified slightly as shown in Figure 4.1.

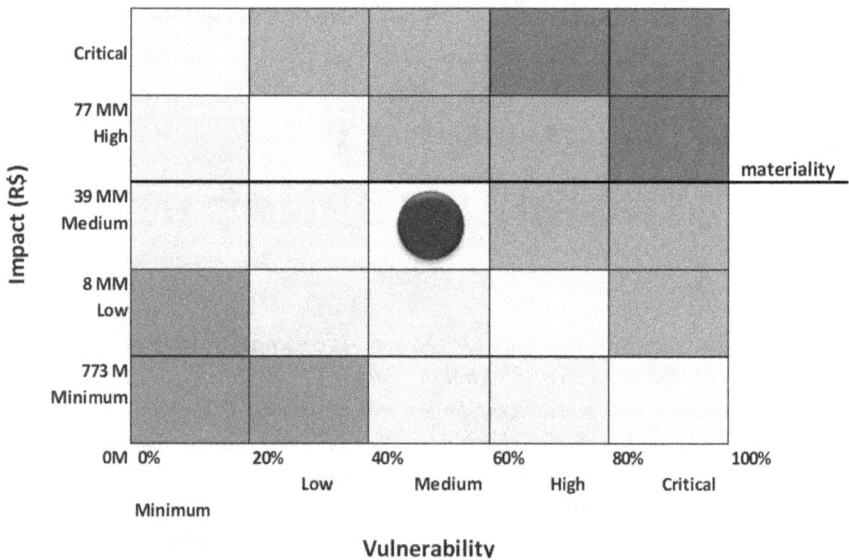

Figure 4.1: Modified Eletrobrás Risk Matrix

Using Likelihood or Vulnerability produces similar results and the choice of which to use is entirely up to the organization. However, we do observe several advantages to using the concept of Vulnerability, especially as it facilitates the existing audit activity in Eletrobrás because the degree of vulnerability metric within the company has already been associated with the evaluation of easily auditable controls and has been in use for several years.

This case study explores how the PEAT ERM module was customized and applied at Eletrobrás, allowing its managers to not only document the major risk factors but to also push the envelope of risk analytics and perform sensitivity analysis, Monte Carlo risk simulation, and quantitative analytics, as well as to assess the dynamics of its business risks, risk controls, and overall enterprise risk management.

For the sole purpose of this case study, we will adapt and use the concept of Vulnerability associated with items related to internal control standards and guidelines already established in Brazil and internationally (e.g., ISO-31000, COSO, COBIT, and SOX or the Sarbanes–Oxley Act). The purpose of this customization is to make it possible to qualify and quantify the degree of implementation in each of the Risk Elements (RE) attached to specific company-wide programs at Eletrobrás.

Uncertainty, Risk, and Vulnerability

In enterprise risk assessment of the quantitative risk environment, the concept of *uncertainty* is associated with the Likelihood (L) of an event happening in the future. The uncertainties of repetitive events observed in nature over a long period of time can sometimes become predictable but usually not with absolute certainty. Such observances can be associated with mathematical functions that reflect the statistical properties of something likely to occur at a future time.

The risk of an event occurring is connected to two parameters: the Impact (I) caused by an uncertain event and the probability of an event occurring or its Likelihood (L). Given some known probability of a risk event occurring, the higher the impact, the greater the risk. If the impact is zero, the risk will be zero even though the event has a high probability of occurring. The reverse argument is also true. If the probability of a risk event occurring is equal to zero, the risk is zero (this is an environment of pure certainty), regardless of the magnitude of the impact.

In other words, uncertainty is measured in terms of Likelihood of occurrence, and unless there is some financial or non-economic but observable Impact, there is no risk, just uncertainty.

Within the realm of Eletrobrás, the concept of Vulnerability (V) is associated with the risk of an event. Put another way, Vulnerability is associated with an organization's susceptibility to the consequences of a risk event. Risk is reduced through the mitigation of risk, either by decreasing the Likelihood of an event occurring (e.g., rather than leaving the car parked on a deserted street at night, put it in a garage under camera surveillance) or by reducing its Impact (e.g., purchasing auto theft insurance) to protect your capital.

The mitigation of the risk consequences can be scaled according to the predictable value of risk. For example, say we have a specific risk event where its maximum financial impact is valued at $100, with a 10% probability of occurring. Further suppose that there is a minimum or residual value of $5 with 90% probability, which implies that there is an expected value of $14.5. Thus, mitigation measures can be designed to try to neutralize this exposure. Clearly, there are two ways to reduce the risk: reduce the Impact or reduce the Likelihood.

Impact reduction means taking preventive measures (e.g., entering into contractual agreements to reduce legal liability), and Likelihood reduction may mean changing organizational processes and behaviors (e.g., changing processes that have a high probability of disaster). Nevertheless, regardless of the steps used to reduce the Likelihood or Impact, if the possibility still exists of the risk event occurring, the risk should be assessed on two levels: the mitigated risk and the residual risk. Mitigation measures are meant to reduce the first level of risk to its residual risk whenever possible.

Proposed Mechanism for Dynamic Risk Indicators

Institutional rules or guidelines that address business risk with only a qualitative view do not indicate a method to evaluate this exposure quantitatively. In the traditional qualitative analysis, the measure of the riskiness of a company is a snapshot at a point in time. Mitigation measures are evaluated later, often from audits to verify the degree of compliance on previous snapshots. The effort to implement these mitigation measures is typically not dynamically evaluated, nor are its results compared to what was expected within the range of risks vis-à-vis the cost of mitigation.

The PEAT ERM module intends not only to document the state of vulnerability of a company to the events that may lead to risk losses, whether economic or non-economic, but also to quantify and measure the uncertainties of the risks and their mitigation costs. All of this is done dynamically, whereby the company may periodically make adjustments to achieve its targeted goals for reducing exposure and pushes the envelope from qualitative assessment to quantitative risk analysis.

PEAT ERM allows dynamic assessments and measures the degree of vulnerability of the company over time using the "% Risk Mitigation Currently Completed" parameter for each risk control and their respective weights in the Risk Register window (see Figure 4.5), which assumes the function of the measurement parameter of Vulnerability as applied within Eletrobrás. This percentage parameter is interpreted as "% Mitigation Completed = 100% − % Vulnerability" indicating a reduction in risk exposure due to the company having implemented measures to reduce its exposure to the risks identified.

This parameter ranges from 0% Complete (i.e., 100% Vulnerable), indicating that the company is exposed to the Total Risk Value, up to 100%, to 100% Complete, indicating a 0% Vulnerability measure, where the risk is reduced to an exposure at its minimum level, also known as the Residual Value Risk.

Accounting for Corporate Risk

The set of Key Risk Indicators (KRI) provides an overview of financial risk to which the company is subject. Figure 4.2 shows an example of the residual risk exposure in PEAT ERM. In the following example, we present the risk exposure of the Finance Department due to the Risk Element of Cost Overrun. In the example, the Gross Value of Risk is $1,000,000 and its Residual Value is $500,000. The Corporate Risk, composed of all the risk factors of the company, is $1,480,000.

In this example, KRI Overrun is measured as $(L = 4) \times (I$ or $V = 4) = (KRI = 16)$ and can be shown in the Risk Matrix. In this case, it is classified as a Moderate Risk, and a reduction factor of 50% will reduce the risk exposure to $750,000 or a KRI of 12.

The model of dynamic measurement of exposure to corporate risk has the graphical representation as shown in Figure 4.3.

In this case, the company can assess its risk exposure dynamically by implementing the mitigation of Risk Factors, which may be marked by international standards and controls (e.g., SOX, COBIT). Thus, the Vulnerability used by Eletrobrás is associated with compliance with the controls. Dynamically this can be represented by Figure 4.4.

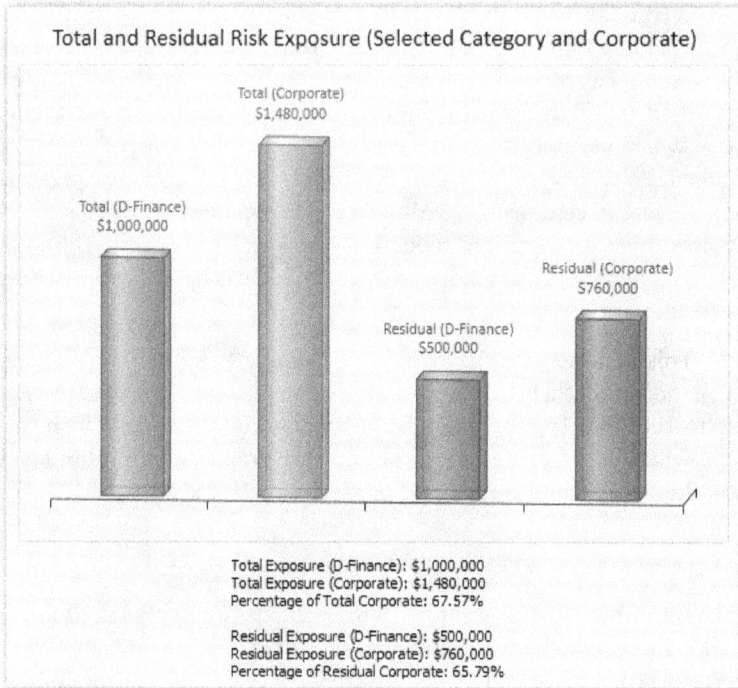

Figure 4.2: Financial Impact KRI

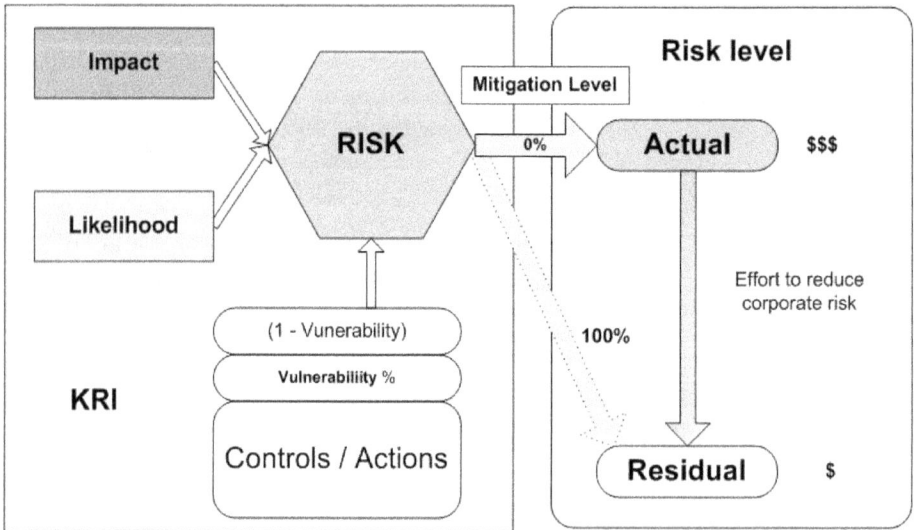

Figure 4.3: Model of Dynamic Measurement of Risk Exposure

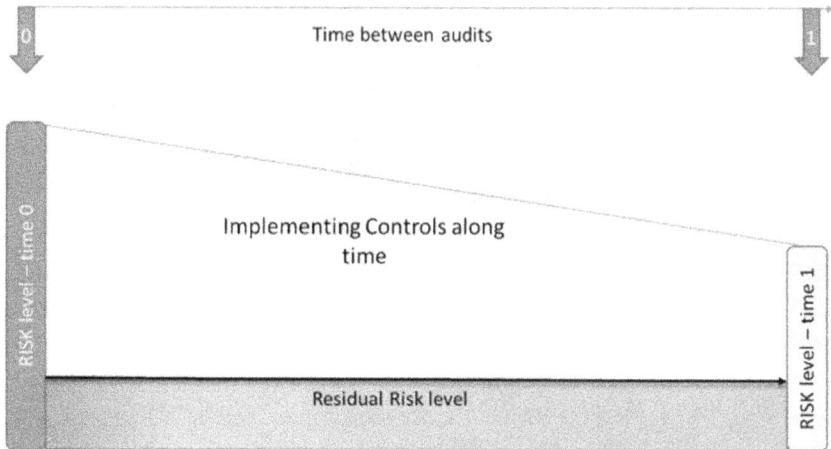

Figure 4.4: Dynamic Mitigation of Risk Factors

By means of an audit, be it external or internal, the company can show the evolution of the measures taken to mitigate the risk and reduce its financial exposure.

Dynamic Assessment of Vulnerability: An Illustration

The Vulnerability Factor (VF) is associated with a set of controls ($Cr_{i,j}$), based on international standards or internal rules that must be fulfilled to reduce the Risk Element (RE_j) to a level of residual risk. Each control ($Cr_{i,j}$) by RE_j selected should be associated with a weight ($w_{i,j}$) equal to one, two, or four, depending on the degree of importance attached to it. The use of weights allows us to distinguish between controls that are more difficult to be implemented or which would have a much greater impact on risk mitigation. Our suggestion is to rank the controls by the degree of impact: minor impact should be classified as having a weight identical to unity; the average impact, a weight equal to 2 (two); and, finally, if any, high impact with a weight of 4 (four), providing a sense of geometric growth. After an audit, controls may have different degrees of conformity ($GC_{i,j}$), namely, implemented (0%), partially implemented (50%), and non-deployed (100%). The RE_j audited Vulnerability Factor ($VF_{i,j}$) is calculated using the following formula:

$$VF_j = \frac{\sum_{i=1}^{n} Cr_{i,j} * w_{i,j} * GC_{i,j}}{\sum w_j}$$

Figure 4.5 illustrates a manual computation of several sample Risk Elements, their respective Risk Controls, Weights, Vulnerability %, and the computed Vulnerability Factor (%VF) and Degree of Mitigation (%DM). It also shows a screenshot of the PEAT ERM Risk Register tab showing how these assumptions can be entered and the subsequent simple steps required to set up the ERM Risk Register.

Explanation Details

- A Risk Register comprises multiple Risk Elements. Figure 4.6's PEAT ERM shows three sample saved Risk Registers, with the highlighted Risk Register being actively edited (e.g., Risk Register *Project DGS728* is currently selected).

- A Risk Element means an actual or anticipated risk. In the table, we see there are *n* Risk Elements in a single Risk Register. The first Risk Element example is a catastrophic fire risk event at one of the plants or utility facilities, another risk is employee accidents at the plants (Risk Element 2), and so forth, ending with legal risks (Risk Element *N*).

- In the first Risk Element, the catastrophic fire, let's say, for illustration purposes, there are three problems relating to this fire: destruction and loss of assets (Assets), loss of production and output (Production), and loss of human productivity (Productivity).

	Control 1	Control 2	Control 3	Vulnerability Factor (%VF)	Degree of Mitigation (%DM)
Risk Element 1 (Catastrophic Fire)					
Weight	6	3	1		
Vulnerability %	0%	100%	100%	40%	60%
Risk Element 2 (Plant Accidents)	Control 1	Control 2	Control 3	Vulnerability Factor (%VF)	Degree of Mitigation (%DM)
Weight	6	1	3		
Vulnerability %	55%	65%	85%	65%	35%
...					
Risk Element N (Legal Problems)	Control 1	Control 2	Control 3	Vulnerability Factor (%VF)	Degree of Mitigation (%DM)
Weight %	60%	10%	30%		
Vulnerability %	55%	65%	85%	65%	35%

Figure 4.5: PEAT ERM Risk Register

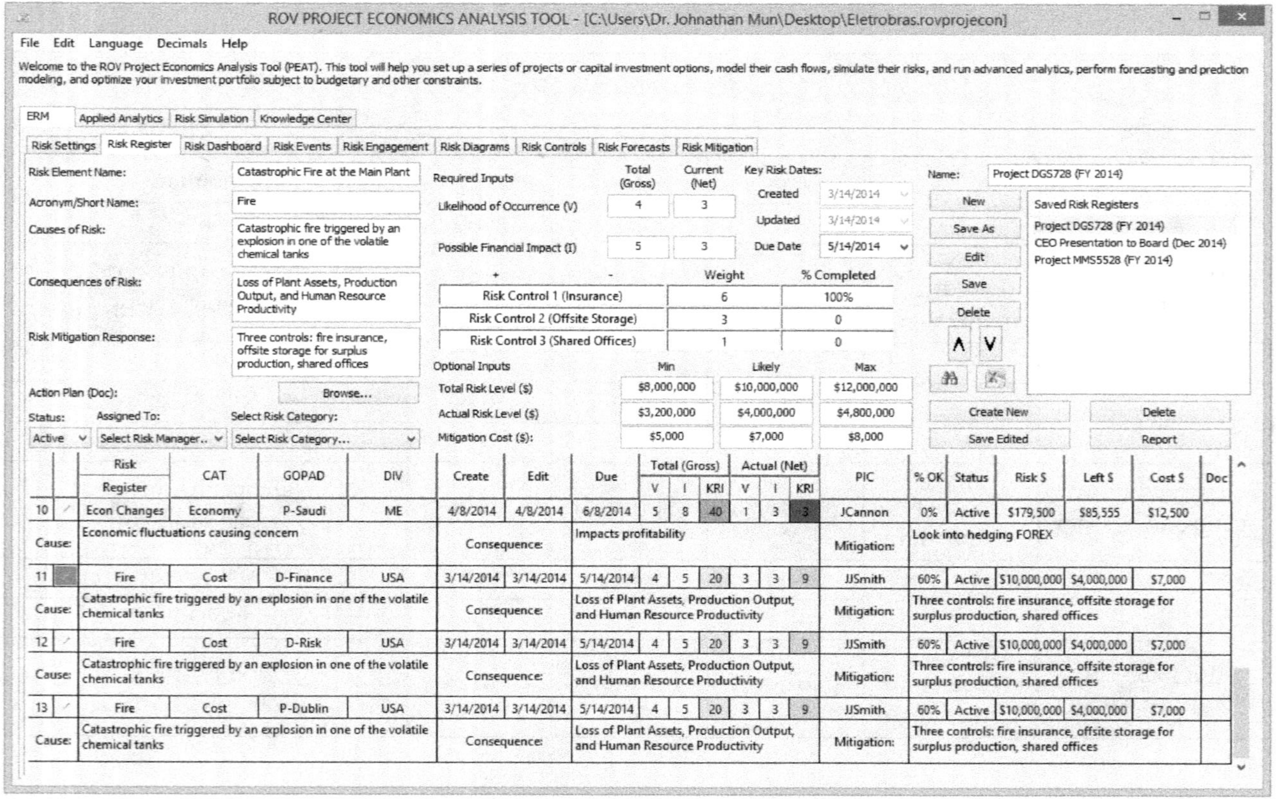

Figure 4.6: PEAT ERM Risk Register

- Each problem is mitigated by a control. Control 1 mitigates losses in Assets by purchasing fire insurance; Control 2 mitigates losses in Production by installing capacitors and storage areas in a different off-site location that can store excess production and handle demand for the next 90 days after a catastrophic fire; and Control 3 mitigates Productivity losses by initiating a joint venture with a partner company to house all the employees at a temporary workplace while at the same time migrating all IT systems to a cloud-based environment for instant restoration of proprietary data such that employees can get back to work almost immediately.

- Let's further assume a simple scenario involving Risk Element 1 where the estimated total and complete catastrophic fire event will mean a loss of $6M in Assets, $3M in Production, and $1M in Productivity. These amounts were obtained through an audit by the risk personnel by performing inventory of the assets, financial analysis of production rates and loss revenues, and human resource estimations. Using these estimates, we can enter the relevant weights, either as numerical values or percentages. For instance, Control 1 has a weight of 6, Control 2 has a weight of 3, and Control 3 has a weight of 1, commensurate with the total gross risk covered and impact mitigated by each control for this single Risk Element. Of course, each company may have its own paradigm in setting the weights, as long as it is consistent throughout its ERM implementation. In this simple example we look at weighting the risk-reduction impact, whereas different organizations who do not have such impact numbers may similarly use degree of difficulty to execute the control, complication, or cost to implement (in which case the weights will be different than in the example above).

- Furthering our example, let's say that Control 1 (fire insurance) is very simple to execute and coverage was already purchased for the full amount of the Assets, which means that the % Mitigation Completed (%M) is 100% or, alternatively, % Vulnerability (%V) is 0%. Controls 2 and 3 are more difficult to complete and take time and money, and, as of right now, they are 0% completed (0% mitigated or 100% vulnerable if a fire occurs).

- As a side note, %M and %V are complementary to each other (i.e., 1 − %V = %D), and expressing either vulnerability or degree of mitigation is a matter of preference (%M takes a more optimistic point of view whereas %V takes a more pessimistic point of view, but converting from one measure to another is very simple as described).

- See Figure 4.5 for Risk Element 2 (employee accidents at the plant) for another sample set of inputs. Finally, Risk Element N intentionally showcases the same weighting levels but here a percentage weight is used instead. Therefore, instead of a numerical weight of 6, 1, 3 (which sums to 10), we can alternatively input these as 60%, 10%, and 30% (this is equivalent to 6/10, 1/10, and 3/10). This is a user preference and can be set in PEAT ERM's *Global Settings* tab.

- Then, the PEAT ERM module automatically computes the Vulnerability Factor (%VF) and the Degree of Mitigation (%DM) for each of the Risk Elements. The following shows their respective calculations:

Risk Element 1: Catastrophic Fire.

- $\%VF = (6 \times 0\% + 3 \times 100\% + 1 \times 100\%) \div (6 + 3 + 1) = 40\%$

- $\%DM = 1 - \%VF = 100\% - 40\% = 60\%$, or, similarly, we have:

- $\%DM = 1 - (6 \times 0\% + 3 \times 100\% + 1 \times 100\%) \div (6 + 3 + 1) = 60\%$

Risk Element 2: Plant Accidents.

- $\%VF = (6 \times 55\% + 1 \times 65\% + 3 \times 85\%) \div (6 + 1 + 3) = 65\%$

- $\%DM = 1 - \%VF = 100\% - 65\% = 35\%$, or, similarly, we have:

- $\%DM = 1 - (6 \times 55\% + 1 \times 65\% + 3 \times 85\%) \div (6 + 1 + 3) = 35\%$

Risk Element N: Legal Issues. In this example, we use % weights instead of numerical.

- $\%VF = (60\% \times 55\% + 10\% \times 65\% + 30\% \times 85\%) = 65\%$

- $\%DM = 1 - \%VF = 100\% - 65\% = 35\%$, or, similarly, we have:

o $\%DM = 1 - (60\% \times 55\% + 10\% \times 65\% + 30\% \times 85\%) = 35\%$

As a side note, the numerical weight can take on any positive integer and does not have any further restrictions, whereas the % weight each needs to be between 0% and 100%, and the total weights for each Risk Element must sum to 100%.

- The monetary Gross Risk for Risk Element 1 (catastrophic fire) is, of course, $6M + $3M + $1M = $10M. And in the example above, we see that only Control 1 (fire insurance) was 100% mitigated (0% vulnerable). This means the entire $6M has been mitigated and the risk no longer exists, at least financially speaking. Thus, the Remaining or Residual Risk is $3M + $1M = $4M. Alternatively, we can compute the *Residual Risk = Gross Risk × % Vulnerability Factor*.

  Of course, this is the same as saying *Residual Risk = Gross Risk × (1 − % Degree of Mitigation)*. That is, we can compute *Residual Risk* = $10M × 40% = $10M × (1 − 60%) = $4M. This $4M is the Remaining or Residual Risk or the risk that remains after the Risk Controls are in place. As a side note, COSO requirements specifically state to use Impact and Likelihood measures and define Gross Risk as Inherent Risk, and Residual Risk as the remaining risks after management executes whatever controls they have executed. (See Chapter 3 for specifications of how PEAT complies with Basel III/IV, ISO 31000:2009, and COSO global standards.) Regardless of the definitions used in the example here, clearly, different companies have different paradigms; the important thing is to be consistent in defining them. If we compute the Remaining Risk in the example above, the user has the option to change the name "Residual Risk" to something like "Actual or Remaining Risk" in the PEAT ERM's *Global Settings* tab to avoid any confusion.

Procedures

The following shows how to use PEAT ERM to input Risk Elements and Risk Controls into a Risk Register (Figure 4.6):

- Step 1: In the relevant Risk Register, users can input new Risk Elements in the data grid or edit an existing Risk Element (click on the pencil icon in the data grid for the relevant row to edit). Each Risk Element is shown as a new row in the Risk Register's data grid.

- Step 2: Enter the *Risk Controls, Weight,* and *% Mitigation Completed* for each control item (weights can be entered as integers or percentages depending on user settings in the *Global Settings* tab). The *% Degree of Mitigation* is automatically computed and shown in the data grid under the *%OK* column.

- Step 3: Users can optionally enter the monetary Gross Risk amounts if required and known, as well as a spread that will be used later in running Monte Carlo risk simulations. For instance, enter $8M, $10M, and $12M, where the most likely Gross Risk is $10M as illustrated in this example (the sum of the Assets, Production, and Productivity).

- Step 4: Users can then optionally enter the monetary Residual Risk amounts if required. This is very simple to enter: simply take the Gross Risk amounts and multiply by $(1 - \%DM)$. In this example, the Residual Risk spreads will be:

  - *Minimum Residual Risk = $8M × (1 − 60%) = $3.2M.*

  - *Most Likely Residual Risk = $10M × (1 − 60%) = $4.0M.*

  - *Maximum Residual Risk = $12M × (1 − 60%) = $4.8M.*

- Step 5: Depending on whether the user has previously selected the *Impact and Vulnerability* or the *Impact and Likelihood* settings for the Risk Matrix in the *Global Settings* tab of PEAT ERM, users can either use the $4M computed Actual Risk or Residual Risk amount or the %OK (i.e., % Vulnerability Factor for the Risk Element after performing the weighted average computation of the various Risk Controls), or they can use their own specified categories and enter either the V or I value. For example, the following is a simple example of company-specific V and I values, which can be tied to net income, revenues, or other financial metrics and are obviously unique to each company and may change over time. These categorizations will be decided by the company's risk committee (the example below is for a 5 × 5 risk matrix):

Risk Categories	When Net Income = $6.24M	
Critical Risk (I = 5)	> 1.0%	≥ 62M
High Risk (I = 4)	≥ 0.1%	6.2M – 62M
Medium Risk (I = 3)	≥ 0.01%	0.6M – 6.2M
Low Risk (I = 2)	≥ 0.001%	62K – 0.6M
Minimal Risk (I = 1)	< 0.001%	≤ 62K

Vulnerability Factor	V Index
≪ 20%	1
20% – 40%	2
40% – 60%	3
60% – 80%	4
≫80%	5

- Step 6: Continue adding more Risk Elements in the Risk Register, perform the tornado and scenario analyses and the simulation analysis, and run the various Risk Dashboard reports.

Dynamic Evaluation of the Impact

The impact is always associated with the wealth of the decision maker. For example, a company that moves billions of dollars every month in its business of mining or oil extraction has a very different risk appetite than does a bakery or pharmacy. The levels of impact designed in the Risk Matrix should be associated with the appropriate financial impact scale. These financial ranges can be indexed, for example, to the turnover of the company, so that the monetary values of risk are related to or are always updated with the size of the company, since the KRIs are absolute and their evolution will depend only on the implementation of the risk mitigation measures and the nonvolatile wealth of the company.

Dynamic Evaluation of Probability

The probability of an event is associated with a measure of whether it will occur regardless of the actions of the company's managers. It may be the result of a Monte Carlo risk simulation (in the case of measuring the VaR [Value at Risk] or other associated probability and confidence intervals) or it may be a subjective evaluation by those responsible for its management. Usually, experts have some sensitivity, based on their experience, about the chances of a risk event occurring. This value can then be the result of an analytical assessment or research and expert consensus.

An example of setting the levels of event probability can be established by the following table:

Range of Probability		Qualitative Classifica- tion		Equivalent Scale
> 80%	→	critical	↔	5
60% - 80%	→	high	↔	4
40% - 60%	→	medium	↔	3
20% - 40%	→	low	↔	2
< 20%	→	minimum	↔	1

Dynamic Evaluation of the Measurement of KRI (Risk)

A quantitative assessment of the risk or the KRI is associated with mitigation or reduction of risk exposure. These measures can be understood or organized in a listed group, whereby risks are assessed as "OK" or "Low" for those events, if they occur, that are not relevant to the financial health or the image of the company, or "Critical" to "Acceptable" for those that are very severe and may compromise the survival of the company. The group's risk managers should define measures of exclusion or mitigation of risks so that they are always on the "Critical" to "Acceptable" level, and the level of investment to be made by the company in mitigating actions should be less than the decrease of the expected risk.

5

BANKING OPERATIONAL AND ENTERPRISE RISK

OPERATIONAL RISK AT BANKS

The case of operational risk is undoubtedly the most difficult to measure and model. The opposite of market risk, by its definition, operational risk data is not only scarce, but biased, unstable, and unchecked in the sense that the most relevant operational risk events do not come identified in the balance sheet of any financial institution. Since the modeling approach is still based on VaR logic, whereby the model utilizes past empirical data to project expected results, modeling operational risk is a very challenging task. As stated, market risk offers daily, publicly audited information to be used and modeled. Conversely, operational risk events are, in most cases, not public, not identified in the general ledger, and, in many instances, not identified at all. But the utmost difficulty comes from the proper definition of operational risk. Even if we managed to go about the impossible task of identifying each and every operational risk event, we would still have very incomplete information. The definition of operational risk entails events generated by failures in people, processes, systems, and external events. With market risk, asset prices can either go up or down, or stay unchanged. With operational risk, an unknown event that has never occurred before can take place in the analysis period and materially affect operations even without its being an extreme tail event.

So, the logic of utilizing similar approaches for such different information availability and behavior requires very careful definitions and assumptions. With this logic in mind, the Basel Committee has defined that in order to model operational risk properly, banks need to have four sources of operational risk data: internal losses, external losses, business environment and internal control factors, and stressed scenarios. Known as the four elements of operational risk, the Basel Committee recommends that they are taken into account when modeling. For smaller banks, and smaller countries, this recommendation poses a definitive challenge, because many times these elements are not developed enough, or not present at all. In this light, most banks have resorted to just using internal data to model operational risk. This approach comes with some shortcomings and more assumptions and should be taken as an initial step that considers the later development of the other elements as they become available. The example shown in Figure 5.1 looks at the modeling of internal losses as a simplified approach usually undertaken by smaller institutions. Since operational risk information is scarce and biased, it is necessary to "complete" the loss distributions with randomly generated data. The most common approach for the task is the use of Monte Carlo risk simulations (Figures 5.2, 5.3, and 5.4) that allow for the inclusion of more stable data and for the fitting of the distributions into predefined density functions.

Basel III and Basel IV regulations allow for the use of multiple approaches when it comes to computing capital charge on operational risk, defined by the Basel Committee as losses resulting from inadequate or failed internal processes, people, and systems or from external events, which includes legal risk, but excludes any strategic and reputational risks.

- Basic Indicator Approach (BIA) uses the positive Gross Income of the last 3 years applied to an Alpha multiplier.

- The Standardized Approach (TSA) uses the positive Gross Income of 8 distinct business lines with its own Beta risk-weighted coefficients.

- Alternate Standardized Approach (ASA) is based on the TSA method and uses Gross Income but applies Total Loans and Advances for the Retail and Commercial business lines, adjusted by a multiplier, prior to using the same TSA beta risk-weighted coefficients.

- Revised Standardized Approach (RSA) uses Income and Expenses as proxy variables to obtain the Business Indicator required in computing the risk capital charge.

- Advanced Measurement Approach (AMA) is open-ended in that individual banks can utilize their own approaches subject to regulatory approval. The typical approach, and the same method used in the ALM-CMOL software application, is to use historical loss data to perform probability distribution-fitting on the frequency and severity of losses, which is then convoluted through Monte Carlo Risk simulation to obtain probability distributions of future expected losses. The tail event VaR results can be obtained directly from the simulated distributions.

Figure 5.1 illustrates the BIA, TSA, ASA, and RSA methods as prescribed in Basel III/IV. The BIA uses total annual gross income for the last 3 years of the bank and multiplies it with an Alpha coefficient (15%) to obtain the capital charge. Only positive gross income amounts are used. This is the simplest method and does not require prior regulatory approval. In the TSA method, the bank is divided into 8 business lines (*corporate finance, trading and sales, retail banking, commercial banking, payment and settlement, agency services, asset management,* and *retail brokerage*); each business line's positive total annual gross income values for the last 3 years are used, and each business line has its own Beta coefficient multiplier. These beta values are proxies based on industry-wide relationships between operational risk loss experience for each business line and aggregate gross income levels. The total capital charge based on the TSA is simply the sum of the weighted average of these business lines for the last 3 years. The ASA is similar to the TSA except that the retail banking and commercial banking business lines use *total loans and advances* instead of using annual total gross income. These total loans and advances are first multiplied by a 3.50% factor prior to being beta-weighted, averaged, and summed. The ASA is also useful in situations where the bank has extremely high or low net interest margins (NIM), whereby the gross income for the retail and commercial business lines are replaced with an asset-based proxy (total loans and advances multiplied by the 3.50% factor). In addition, within the ASA approach, the 6 business lines can be aggregated into a single business line as long as it is multiplied by the highest beta coefficient (18%), and the 2 remaining loans and advances (retail and commercial business lines) can be aggregated and multiplied by the 15% Beta coefficient. In other words, when using the ALM-CMOL software, you can aggregate the 6 business lines and enter it as a single row entry in Corporate Finance, which has an 18% multiplier, and the 2 loans and advances business lines can be aggregated as the Commercial business line, which has a 15% multiplier.

The main issue with BIA, TSA, and ASA methods is that, on average, these methods are undercalibrated, especially for large and complex banks. For instance, these three methods assume that operational risk exposure increases linearly and proportionally with gross income or revenue. This assumption is invalid because certain banks may experience a decline in gross income due to systemic or bank-specific events that may include losses from operational risk events. In such situations, a falling gross income should be commensurate with a higher operational capital requirement, not a lower capital charge. Therefore, the Basel Committee has allowed the inclusion of a revised method, the RSA. Instead of using gross income, the RSA uses both income and expenditures from multiple sources, as shown in Figure 5.1. The RSA uses inputs from an *interest* component (interest income less interest expense), a *services* component (sum of fee income, fee expense, other operating income, and other operating expense), and a *financial* component (sum of the absolute value of net profit and losses on the trading book, and the absolute value of net profit and losses on the banking book). The calculation of capital charge is based on the calculation of a *Business Indicator* (BI), where the BI is the sum of the absolute values of these three components (thereby avoiding any counterintuitive results based on negative contributions from any component). The purpose of a BI calculation is to promote simplicity and comparability using a single indicator for operational risk exposure that is sensitive to the bank's business size and business volume, rather than static business line coefficients regardless of the bank's size and volume. Using the computed BI, the risk capital charge is determined from 5 predefined buckets from Basel III/IV, increasing in value from 10% to 30%, depending on the size of the BI (ranging from €0 to €30 billion). These Basel predefined buckets are denoted in thousands of euros, with each bucket having its own weighted Beta coefficients. Finally, the risk capital charge is computed based on a marginal incremental or layered approach (rather than a full cliff-effect when banks migrate from one bucket to another) using these buckets.

Figures 5.2, 5.3, and 5.4 illustrate the Operational Risk Loss Distribution analysis when applying the AMA method. Users start at the Loss Data tab where historical loss data can be entered or pasted into the data grid. Variables include losses in the past pertaining to operational risks, segmentation by divisions and departments, business lines, dates of losses, risk categories, and so on. Users then activate the controls to select how the loss data variables are to be segmented (e.g., by risk categories and risk types and business lines), the number of simulation trials to run, and seed values to apply in the simulation if required, all by selecting the relevant variable columns. The distributional fitting routines can also be selected as required. Then the analysis can be run and distributions fitted to the data. As usual, the model settings and data can be saved.

Figure 5.3 illustrates the Operational Risk—Fitted Loss Distribution subtab. Users start by selecting the fitting segments for setting the various risk category and business line segments, and, based on the selected segment, the fitted distributions and their p-values are listed and ranked according to the highest p-value to the lowest p-value, indicating the best to the worst statistical fit to the various probability distributions. The empirical data and fitted theoretical distributions are shown graphically, and the statistical moments are shown for the actual data versus the theoretically fitted distribution's moments. After deciding on which distributions to use, users can then run the simulations.

Figure 5.4 shows the Operational Risk—Risk Simulated Losses subtab using convolution of frequency and severity of historical losses, where, depending on which risk segment and business line was selected, the relevant probability distribution results from the Monte Carlo risk simulations are displayed, including the simulated results on Frequency, Severity, and the multiplication between frequency and severity, termed Expected Loss Distribution, as well as the Extreme Value Distribution of Losses (this is where the extreme losses in the dataset are fitted to the extreme value distributions—see Chapter 4 for details on extreme value distributions and their mathematical models). Each of the distributional charts has its own confidence and percentile inputs where users can select one-tail (right-tail or left-tail) or two-tail confidence intervals and enter the percentiles to obtain the confidence values (e.g., user can enter right-tail 99.90% percentile to receive the VaR confidence value of the worst-case losses on the left tail's 0.10%).

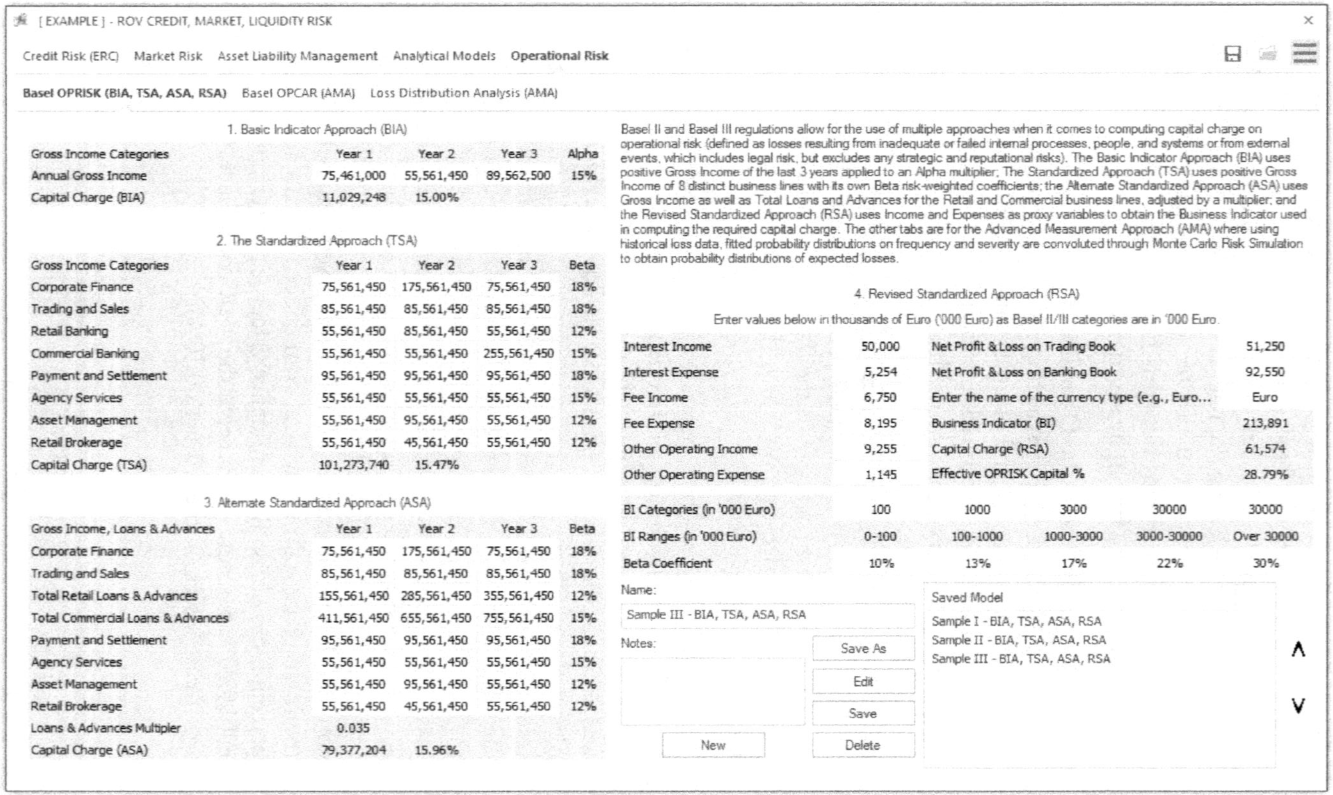

Credit Risk (ERC)   Market Risk   Asset Liability Management   Analytical Models   Operational Risk

Basel OPRISK (BIA, TSA, ASA, RSA)   Basel OPCAR (AMA)   Loss Distribution Analysis (AMA)

Basel II and Basel III regulations allow for the use of multiple approaches when it comes to computing capital charge on operational risk (defined as losses resulting from inadequate or failed internal processes, people, and systems or from external events, which includes legal risk, but excludes any strategic and reputational risks). The Basic Indicator Approach (BIA) uses positive Gross Income of the last 3 years applied to an Alpha coefficient. The Standardized Approach (TSA) uses positive Gross Income of 8 distinct business lines with its own Beta risk-weighted coefficients; the Alternate Standardized Approach (ASA) uses Gross Income as well as Total Loans and Advances for the Retail and Commercial business lines, adjusted by a multiplier and the Revised Standardized Approach (RSA) uses Income and Expenses as proxy variables to obtain the Business Indicator used in computing the required capital charge. The other tabs are for the Advanced Measurement Approach (AMA) where using historical loss data, fitted probability distributions on frequency and severity are convoluted through Monte Carlo Risk Simulation to obtain probability distributions of expected losses.

1. Basic Indicator Approach (BIA)

Gross Income Categories	Year 1	Year 2	Year 3	Alpha
Annual Gross Income	75,461,000	55,561,450	89,562,500	15%
Capital Charge (BIA)	11,029,248	15.00%		

2. The Standardized Approach (TSA)

Gross Income Categories	Year 1	Year 2	Year 3	Beta
Corporate Finance	75,561,450	175,561,450	75,561,450	18%
Trading and Sales	85,561,450	85,561,450	85,561,450	18%
Retail Banking	55,561,450	85,561,450	55,561,450	12%
Commercial Banking	55,561,450	55,561,450	255,561,450	15%
Payment and Settlement	95,561,450	95,561,450	95,561,450	18%
Agency Services	55,561,450	55,561,450	55,561,450	15%
Asset Management	55,561,450	95,561,450	55,561,450	12%
Retail Brokerage	55,561,450	45,561,450	55,561,450	12%
Capital Charge (TSA)	101,273,740	15.47%		

3. Alternate Standardized Approach (ASA)

Gross Income, Loans & Advances	Year 1	Year 2	Year 3	Beta
Corporate Finance	75,561,450	175,561,450	75,561,450	18%
Trading and Sales	85,561,450	85,561,450	85,561,450	18%
Total Retail Loans & Advances	155,561,450	285,561,450	355,561,450	12%
Total Commercial Loans & Advances	411,561,450	655,561,450	755,561,450	15%
Payment and Settlement	95,561,450	95,561,450	95,561,450	18%
Agency Services	55,561,450	55,561,450	55,561,450	15%
Asset Management	55,561,450	55,561,450	55,561,450	12%
Retail Brokerage	55,561,450	45,561,450	55,561,450	12%
Loans & Advances Multiplier	0.035			
Capital Charge (ASA)	79,377,204	15.96%		

4. Revised Standardized Approach (RSA)

Enter values below in thousands of Euro ('000 Euro) as Basel II/III categories are in '000 Euro

Interest Income	50,000	Net Profit & Loss on Trading Book	51,250
Interest Expense	5,254	Net Profit & Loss on Banking Book	92,550
Fee Income	6,750	Enter the name of the currency type (e.g., Euro...	Euro
Fee Expense	8,195	Business Indicator (BI)	213,891
Other Operating Income	9,255	Capital Charge (RSA)	61,574
Other Operating Expense	1,145	Effective OPRISK Capital %	28.79%

BI Categories (in '000 Euro)	100	1000	3000	30000	
BI Ranges (in '000 Euro)	0-100	100-1000	1000-3000	3000-30000	Over 30000
Beta Coefficient	10%	13%	17%	22%	30%

Name:

Sample III - BIA, TSA, ASA, RSA

Notes:

Save As   Edit   Save   Delete   New

Saved Model
Sample I - BIA, TSA, ASA, RSA
Sample II - BIA, TSA, ASA, RSA
Sample III - BIA, TSA, ASA, RSA

Figure 5.1: Basel III/IV BIA, TSA, ASA, RSA Methods

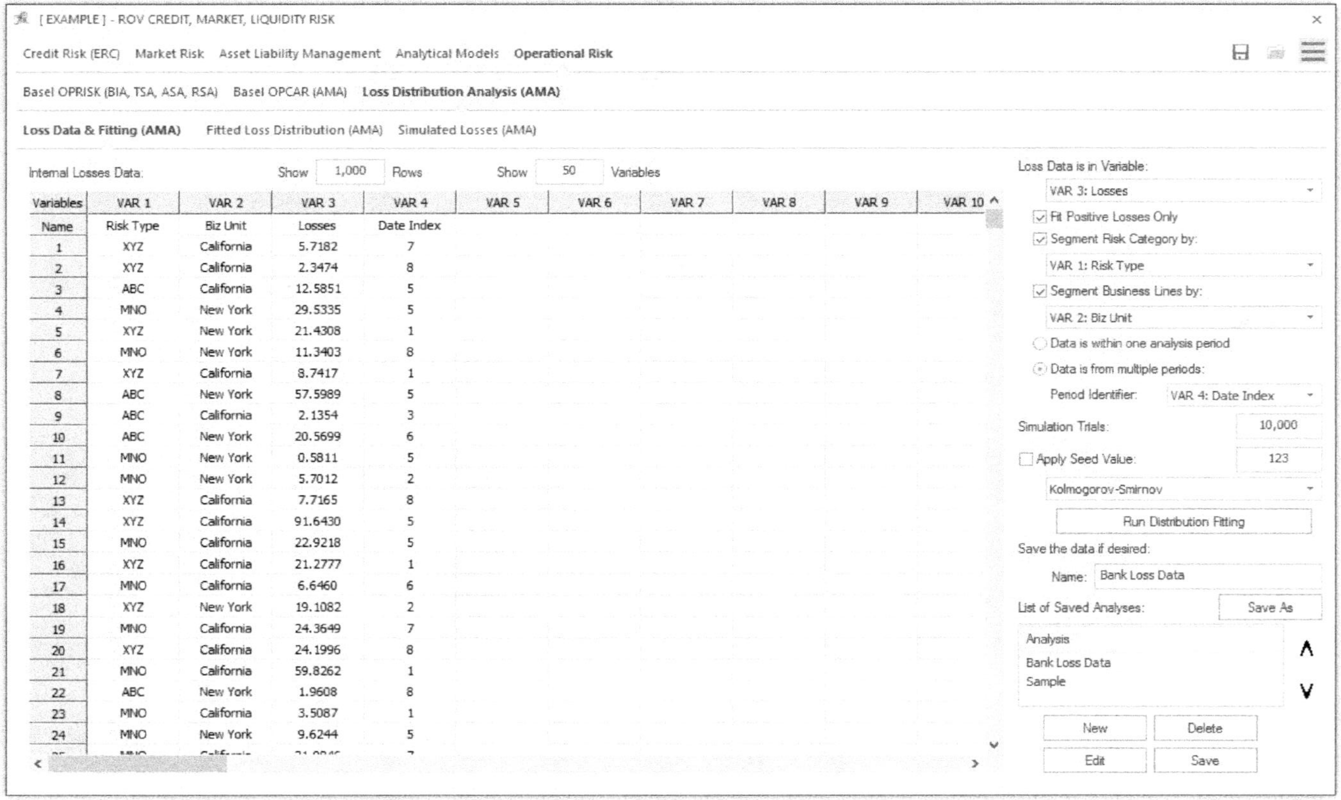

Credit Risk (ERC)   Market Risk   Asset Liability Management   Analytical Models   **Operational Risk**

Basel OPRISK (BIA, TSA, ASA, RSA)   Basel OPCAR (AMA)   **Loss Distribution Analysis (AMA)**

Loss Data & Fitting (AMA)   Fitted Loss Distribution (AMA)   Simulated Losses (AMA)

Internal Losses Data.   Show 1,000 Rows   Show 50 Variables

Variables	VAR 1	VAR 2	VAR 3	VAR 4	VAR 5	VAR 6	VAR 7	VAR 8	VAR 9	VAR 10
Name	Risk Type	Biz Unit	Losses	Date Index						
1	XYZ	California	5.7182	7						
2	XYZ	California	2.3474	8						
3	ABC	California	12.5851	5						
4	MNO	New York	29.5335	5						
5	XYZ	New York	21.4308	1						
6	MNO	New York	11.3403	8						
7	XYZ	California	8.7417	1						
8	ABC	New York	57.5989	5						
9	ABC	California	2.1354	3						
10	ABC	New York	20.5699	6						
11	MNO	New York	0.5811	5						
12	MNO	New York	5.7012	2						
13	XYZ	California	7.7165	8						
14	XYZ	California	91.6430	5						
15	MNO	California	22.9218	5						
16	XYZ	California	21.2777	1						
17	MNO	California	6.6460	6						
18	XYZ	New York	19.1082	2						
19	MNO	California	24.3649	7						
20	XYZ	California	24.1996	8						
21	MNO	California	59.8262	1						
22	ABC	New York	1.9608	8						
23	MNO	California	3.5087	1						
24	MNO	New York	9.6244	5						

Loss Data is in Variable:

VAR 3: Losses

☑ Fit Positive Losses Only
☑ Segment Risk Category by:

VAR 1: Risk Type

☑ Segment Business Lines by:

VAR 2: Biz Unit

○ Data is within one analysis period
◉ Data is from multiple periods:

Period Identifier: VAR 4: Date Index

Simulation Trials: 10,000

☐ Apply Seed Value: 123

Kolmogorov-Smirnov

Run Distribution Fitting

Save the data if desired:

Name: Bank Loss Data

List of Saved Analyses: Save As

Analysis
Bank Loss Data
Sample

New   Delete
Edit   Save

Figure 5.2: Operational Risk Data in Advanced Measurement Approach (AMA)

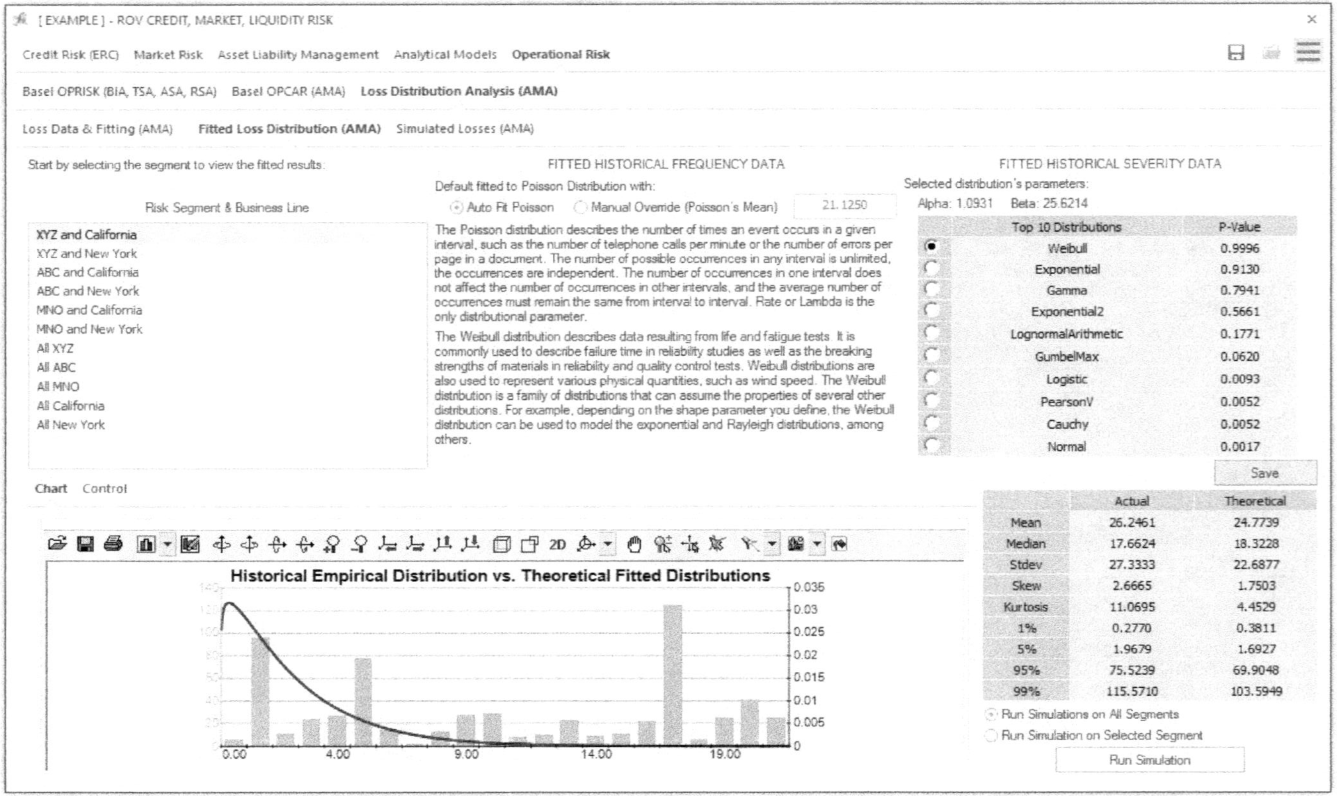

Credit Risk (ERC)   Market Risk   Asset Liability Management   Analytical Models   **Operational Risk**

Basel OPRISK (BIA, TSA, ASA, RSA)   Basel OPCAR (AMA)   **Loss Distribution Analysis (AMA)**

Loss Data & Fitting (AMA)   **Fitted Loss Distribution (AMA)**   Simulated Losses (AMA)

Start by selecting the segment to view the fitted results

Risk Segment & Business Line

XYZ and California
XYZ and New York
ABC and California
ABC and New York
MNO and California
MNO and New York
All XYZ
All ABC
All MNO
All California
All New York

FITTED HISTORICAL FREQUENCY DATA

Default fitted to Poisson Distribution with:

( ) Auto Fit Poisson   ( ) Manual Override (Poisson's Mean)   21.1250

The Poisson distribution describes the number of times an event occurs in a given interval, such as the number of telephone calls per minute or the number of errors per page in a document. The number of possible occurrences in any interval is unlimited, the occurrences are independent. The number of occurrences in one interval does not affect the number of occurrences in other intervals, and the average number of occurrences must remain the same from interval to interval. Rate or Lambda is the only distributional parameter.

The Weibull distribution describes data resulting from life and fatigue tests. It is commonly used to describe failure time in reliability studies as well as the breaking strengths of materials in reliability and quality control tests. Weibull distributions are also used to represent various physical quantities, such as wind speed. The Weibull distribution is a family of distributions that can assume the properties of several other distributions. For example, depending on the shape parameter you define, the Weibull distribution can be used to model the exponential and Rayleigh distributions, among others.

FITTED HISTORICAL SEVERITY DATA

Selected distribution's parameters:

Alpha 1.0931   Beta 25.6214

Top 10 Distributions	P-Value
Weibull	0.9996
Exponential	0.9130
Gamma	0.7941
Exponential2	0.5661
LognormalArithmetic	0.1771
GumbelMax	0.0620
Logistic	0.0093
PearsonV	0.0052
Cauchy	0.0052
Normal	0.0017

Save

	Actual	Theoretical
Mean	26.2461	24.7739
Median	17.6624	18.3228
Stdev	27.3333	22.6877
Skew	2.6665	1.7503
Kurtosis	11.0695	4.4529
1%	0.2770	0.3811
5%	1.9679	1.6927
95%	75.5239	69.9048
99%	115.5710	103.5949

( ) Run Simulations on All Segments
( ) Run Simulation on Selected Segment

Run Simulation

Chart   Control

Historical Empirical Distribution vs. Theoretical Fitted Distributions

0.036
0.03
0.025
0.02
0.015
0.01
0.005
0

0.00   4.00   9.00   14.00   19.00

Figure 5.3: Fitted Distributions on Operational Risk Data

[EXAMPLE] - ROV CREDIT, MARKET, LIQUIDITY RISK

Credit Risk (ERC)   Market Risk   Asset Liability Management   Analytical Models   **Operational Risk**

Basel OPRISK (BIA, TSA, ASA, RSA)   Basel OPCAR (AMA)   **Loss Distribution Analysis (AMA)**

Loss Data & Fitting (AMA)   Fitted Loss Distribution (AMA)   **Simulated Losses (AMA)**

Select simulated segment to view:
XYZ and California

Left Tail <=
Percentiles: 99.90   %

Mean of Loss Distribution Analysis (LDA): 522.8088
Economic Capital of Unexpected Losses (LDA): 3,250.3492
99.90% Economic Value at Risk (LDA): 3,773.1580

Simulated Frequency

Simulated Severity

Simulated Expected Loss Distribution

	Frequency	Severity	Loss Distribution
Mean	21.1737	24.7215	522.8088
Median	21.0000	18.3829	376.6986
Stdev	4.6047	22.6047	501.4317
Skew	0.2015	1.7628	2.0223
Kurtosis	-0.0159	4.4984	6.5344
0.1%	9.0000	0.0470	0.7053
0.5%	10.0000	0.2366	4.6221
1.0%	11.0000	0.4135	8.3095
99.0%	33.0000	102.0910	2,319.5030
99.5%	34.0000	117.1569	2,644.5911
99.9%	37.0000	157.2480	3,773.1580
Left Tail 99.90%	37.0000	157.2480	3,773.1580

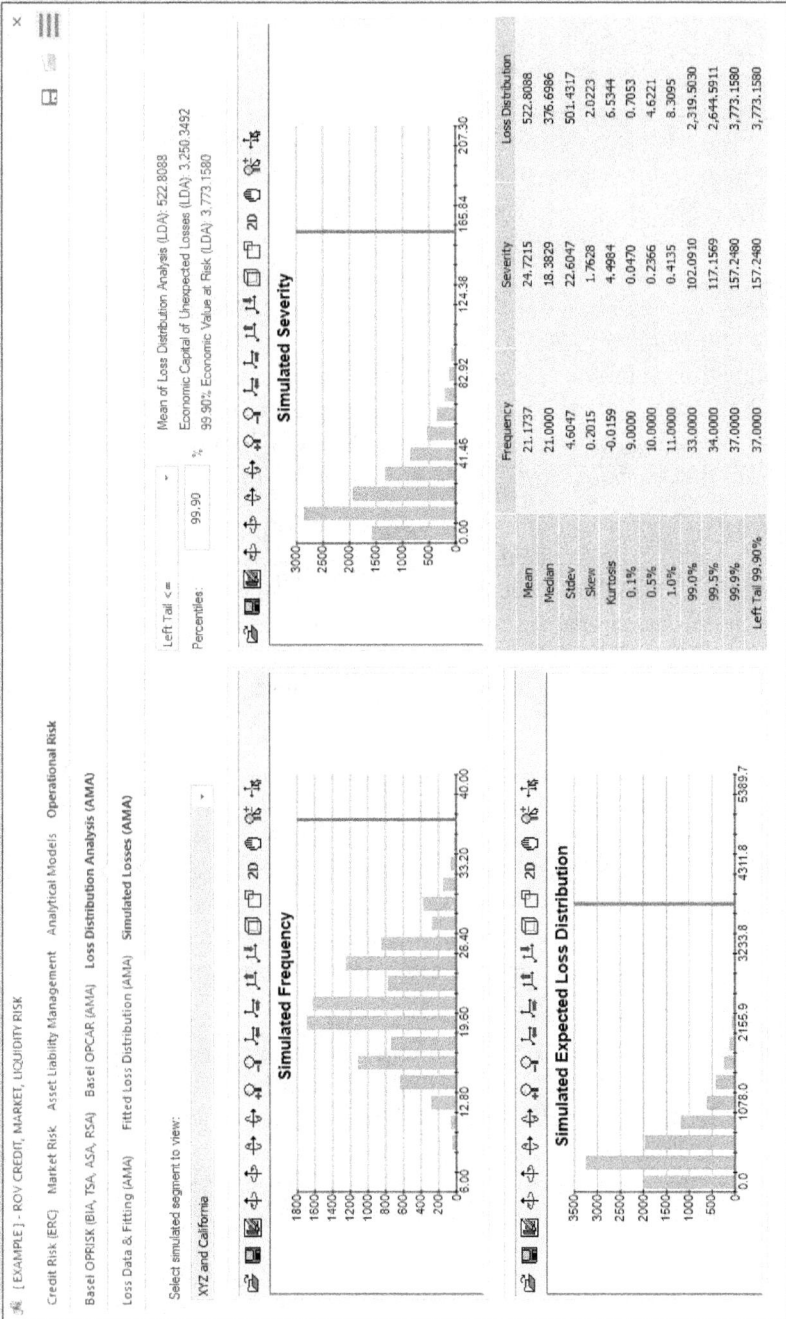

Figure 5.4: Monte Carlo Risk Simulated Operational Losses

Figure 5.5 shows the computations of Basel III/IV's OPCAR (Operational Capital at Risk) model where the probability distribution of risk event Frequency is multiplied by the probability distribution of Severity of operational losses, the approach where Frequency × Severity is termed the Single Loss Approximation (SLA) model. The SLA is computed using convolution methods of combining multiple probability distributions. SLA using convolution methods is complex and very difficult to compute and the results are only approximations, and valid only at the extreme tails of the distribution (e.g., 99.9%). However, Monte Carlo Risk simulation provides a simpler and more powerful alternative when convoluting and multiplying two distributions of random variables to obtain the combined distribution. Clearly the challenge is setting the relevant distributional input parameters. This is where the data-fitting and percentile-fitting tools come in handy. See Dr. Johnathan Mun's *Modeling Risk, Third Edition* (Thompson–Shore) for more details.

Figure 5.6 shows the convolution simulation results where the distribution of loss frequency, severity, and expected losses are displayed. The resulting Expected Losses (EL), Unexpected Losses (UL), and Total Operational Capital at Risk (OPCAR) are also computed and shown. EL is, of course, the mean value of the simulated results, OPCAR is the tail-end 99.90th percentile, and UL is the difference between OPCAR and EL.

Figure 5.7 shows the loss severity data fitting using historical loss data. Users can paste historical loss data, select the required fitting routines (Kolmogorov–Smirnov, Akaike Criterion, Bayes Information Criterion, Anderson–Darling, Kuiper's Statistic, etc.) and run the data-fitting routines. When in doubt, use the Kolmogorov–Smirnov routine. The best-fitting distributions, p-values, and their parameters will be listed, and the same interpretation applies as previously explained.

Figure 5.8 shows the loss severity percentile fitting instead, which is particularly helpful when there are no historical loss data and where there only exist high-level management assumptions of the probabilities certain events occur. In other words, by entering a few percentiles (%) and their corresponding values, one can obtain the entire distribution's parameters.

These modeling tools allow smaller banks to have a first approach at more advanced operational risk management techniques.

The use of internal models allows for a better calibration of regulatory capital that knowingly overestimated for operational risk. The use of different scenarios providing various results can allow smaller banks to have a much more efficient capital allocation for operational risk that, being a Pillar I risk, tends to be quite expensive in terms of capital, and quite dangerous at the same time if capital was severely underestimated. Together with the traditional operational risk management tools, such as self-assessment and KRIs, these basic models allow for a proper IMMM risk management structure, aligned with the latest international standards.

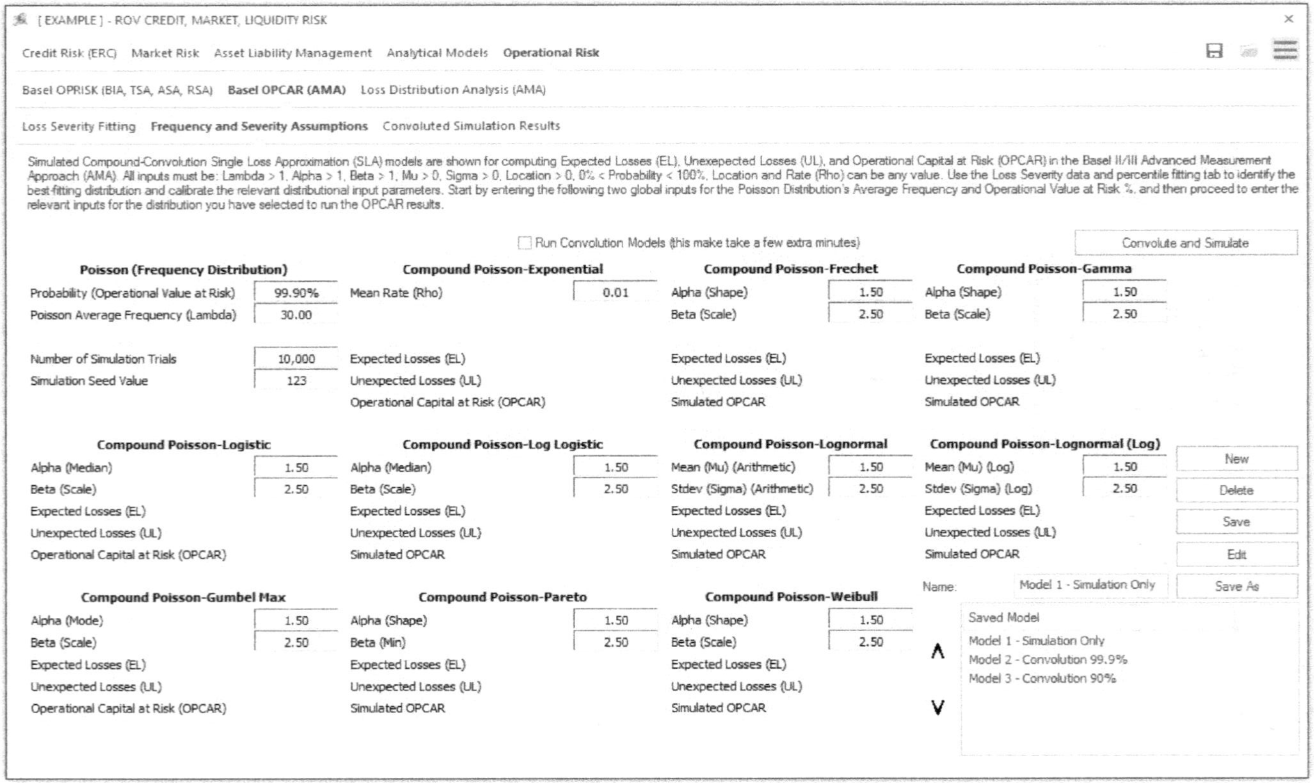

Credit Risk (ERC)　Market Risk　Asset Liability Management　Analytical Models　**Operational Risk**

Basel OPRISK (BIA, TSA, ASA, RSA)　**Basel OPCAR (AMA)**　Loss Distribution Analysis (AMA)

Loss Severity Fitting　**Frequency and Severity Assumptions**　Convoluted Simulation Results

Simulated Compound-Convolution Single Loss Approximation (SLA) models are shown for computing Expected Losses (EL), Unexpected Losses (UL), and Operational Capital at Risk (OPCAR) in the Basel II/III Advanced Measurement Approach (AMA). All inputs must be Lambda > 1. Alpha > 1. Beta > 1. Mu > 0. Sigma > 0. Location > 0. 0% < Probability < 100%, Location and Rate (Rho) can be any value. Use the Loss Severity data and percentile fitting tab to identify the best-fitting distribution and calibrate the relevant distributional input parameters. Start by entering the following two global inputs for the Poisson Distribution's Average Frequency and Operational Value at Risk %, and then proceed to enter the relevant inputs for the distribution you have selected to run the OPCAR results.

☐ Run Convolution Models (this make take a few extra minutes)　　　　　　　　　　　　Convolute and Simulate

Poisson (Frequency Distribution)

Probability (Operational Value at Risk)	99.90%
Poisson Average Frequency (Lambda)	30.00

Number of Simulation Trials	10,000
Simulation Seed Value	123

Compound Poisson-Exponential

Mean Rate (Rho)	0.01
Expected Losses (EL)	
Unexpected Losses (UL)	
Operational Capital at Risk (OPCAR)	

Compound Poisson-Frechet

Alpha (Shape)	1.50
Beta (Scale)	2.50
Expected Losses (EL)	
Unexpected Losses (UL)	
Simulated OPCAR	

Compound Poisson-Gamma

Alpha (Shape)	1.50
Beta (Scale)	2.50
Expected Losses (EL)	
Unexpected Losses (UL)	
Simulated OPCAR	

Compound Poisson-Logistic

Alpha (Median)	1.50
Beta (Scale)	2.50
Expected Losses (EL)	
Unexpected Losses (UL)	
Operational Capital at Risk (OPCAR)	

Compound Poisson-Log Logistic

Alpha (Median)	1.50
Beta (Scale)	2.50
Expected Losses (EL)	
Unexpected Losses (UL)	
Simulated OPCAR	

Compound Poisson-Lognormal

Mean (Mu) (Arithmetic)	1.50
Stdev (Sigma) (Arithmetic)	2.50
Expected Losses (EL)	
Unexpected Losses (UL)	
Simulated OPCAR	

Compound Poisson-Lognormal (Log)

Mean (Mu) (Log)	1.50
Stdev (Sigma) (Log)	2.50
Expected Losses (EL)	
Unexpected Losses (UL)	
Simulated OPCAR	

Compound Poisson-Gumbel Max

Alpha (Mode)	1.50
Beta (Scale)	2.50
Expected Losses (EL)	
Unexpected Losses (UL)	
Operational Capital at Risk (OPCAR)	

Compound Poisson-Pareto

Alpha (Shape)	1.50
Beta (Min)	2.50
Expected Losses (EL)	
Unexpected Losses (UL)	
Simulated OPCAR	

Compound Poisson-Weibull

Alpha (Shape)	1.50
Beta (Scale)	2.50
Expected Losses (EL)	
Unexpected Losses (UL)	
Simulated OPCAR	

New
Delete
Save
Edit
Save As

Name: 　Model 1 - Simulation Only

Saved Model
Model 1 - Simulation Only
Model 2 - Convolution 99.9%
Model 3 - Convolution 90%

< >

Figure 5.5: Basel OPCAR Frequency and Severity Assumptions

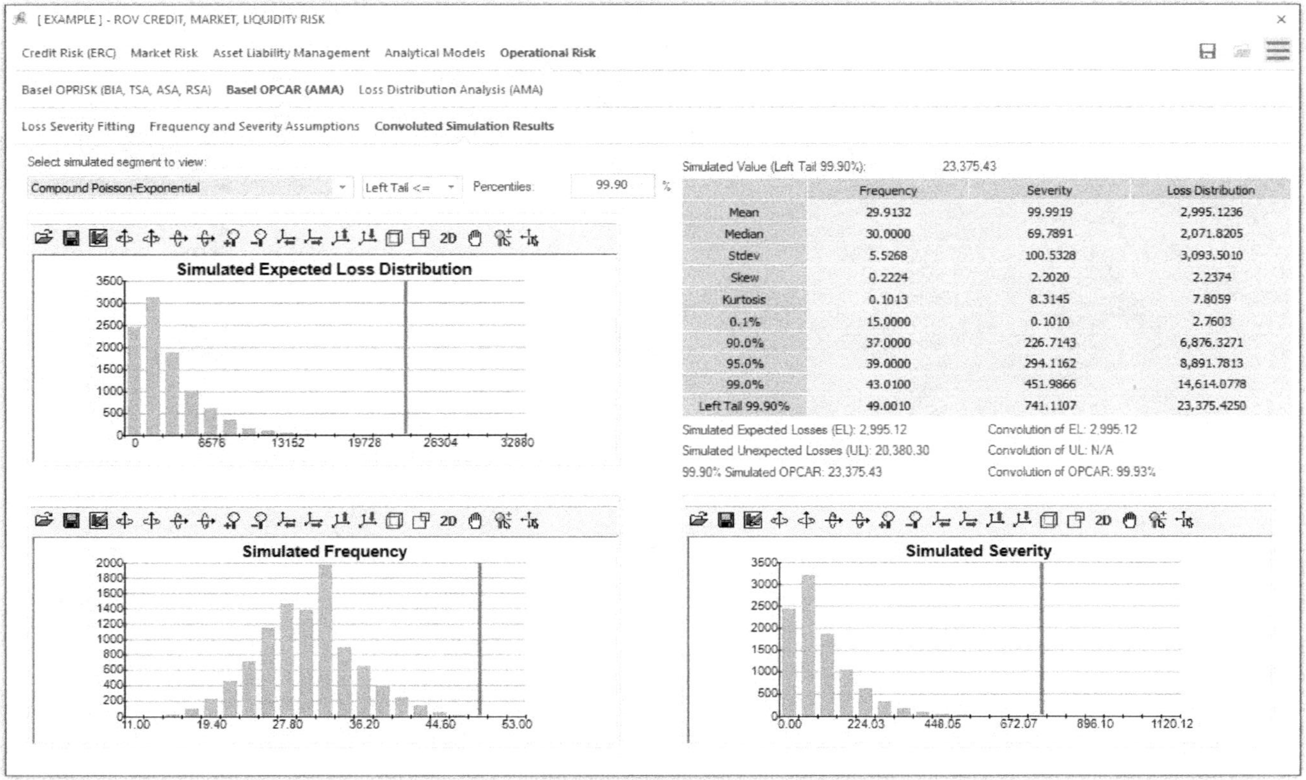

[EXAMPLE] - ROV CREDIT, MARKET, LIQUIDITY RISK

Credit Risk (ERC) Market Risk Asset Liability Management Analytical Models **Operational Risk**

Basel OPRISK (BIA, TSA, ASA, RSA) **Basel OPCAR (AMA)** Loss Distribution Analysis (AMA)

Loss Severity Fitting Frequency and Severity Assumptions **Convoluted Simulation Results**

Select simulated segment to view:

Compound Poisson-Exponential   Left Tail <=   Percentiles   99.90   %

Simulated Value (Left Tail 99.90%): 23,375.43

	Frequency	Severity	Loss Distribution
Mean	29.9132	99.9919	2,995.1236
Median	30.0000	69.7891	2,071.8205
Stdev	5.5268	100.5328	3,093.5010
Skew	0.2224	2.2020	2.2374
Kurtosis	0.1013	8.3145	7.8059
0.1%	15.0000	0.1010	2.7603
90.0%	37.0000	226.7243	6,876.3271
95.0%	39.0000	294.1162	8,891.7813
99.0%	43.0100	451.9866	14,614.0778
Left Tail 99.90%	49.0010	741.1107	23,375.4250

Simulated Expected Losses (EL) 2,995.12   Convolution of EL: 2,995.12
Simulated Unexpected Losses (UL) 20,380.30   Convolution of UL: N/A
99.90%: Simulated OPCAR 23,375.43   Convolution of OPCAR: 99.93%

Simulated Expected Loss Distribution

0   6676   13152   19728   26304   32880

Simulated Frequency

01.00   19.40   27.80   36.20   44.60   53.00

Simulated Severity

0.00   224.03   448.05   672.07   896.10   1120.12

Figure 5.6: Basel OPCAR Convoluted Simulation Results

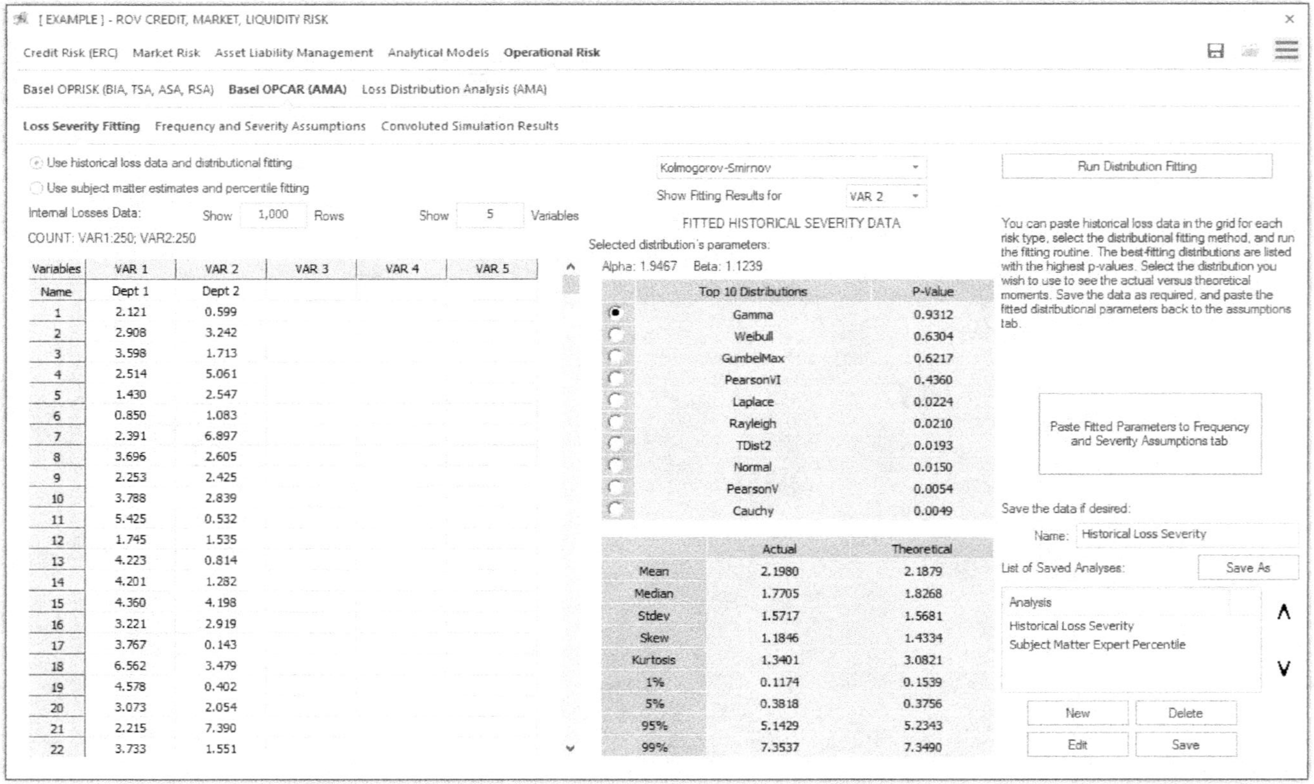

Credit Risk (ERC)   Market Risk   Asset Liability Management   Analytical Models   **Operational Risk**

Basel OPRISK (BIA, TSA, ASA, RSA)   **Basel OPCAR (AMA)**   Loss Distribution Analysis (AMA)

Loss Severity Fitting   Frequency and Severity Assumptions   Convoluted Simulation Results

○ Use historical loss data and distributional fitting
○ Use subject matter estimates and percentile fitting

Internal Losses Data: Show 1,000 Rows   Show 5 Variables
COUNT: VAR1:250; VAR2:250

Name	VAR 1	VAR 2	VAR 3	VAR 4	VAR 5
Variables	Dept 1	Dept 2			
1	2.121	0.599			
2	2.908	3.242			
3	3.598	1.713			
4	2.514	5.061			
5	1.430	2.547			
6	0.850	1.083			
7	2.391	6.897			
8	3.696	2.605			
9	2.253	2.425			
10	3.788	2.839			
11	5.425	0.532			
12	1.745	1.535			
13	4.223	0.814			
14	4.201	1.282			
15	4.360	4.198			
16	3.221	2.919			
17	3.767	0.143			
18	6.562	3.479			
19	4.578	0.402			
20	3.073	2.054			
21	2.215	7.390			
22	3.733	1.551			

Kolmogorov-Smirnov
Show Fitting Results for   VAR 2

Selected distribution's parameters.
Alpha: 1.9467   Beta: 1.1239

FITTED HISTORICAL SEVERITY DATA

Top 10 Distributions	P-Value
● Gamma	0.9312
○ Weibull	0.6304
○ GumbelMax	0.6217
○ PearsonVI	0.4360
○ Laplace	0.0224
○ Rayleigh	0.0210
○ TDist2	0.0193
○ Normal	0.0150
○ PearsonV	0.0054
○ Cauchy	0.0049

	Actual	Theoretical
Mean	2.1980	2.1879
Median	1.7705	1.8268
Stdev	1.5717	1.5681
Skew	1.1846	1.4334
Kurtosis	1.3401	3.0821
1%	0.1174	0.1539
5%	0.3818	0.3756
95%	5.1429	5.2343
99%	7.3537	7.3490

Run Distribution Fitting

You can paste historical loss data in the grid for each risk type, select the distributional fitting method, and run the fitting routine. The best-fitting distributions are listed with the highest p-values. Select the distribution you wish to use to see the actual versus theoretical moments. Save the data as required, and paste the fitted distributional parameters back to the assumptions tab.

Paste Fitted Parameters to Frequency and Severity Assumptions tab

Save the data if desired:
Name: Historical Loss Severity

List of Saved Analyses: Save As

Analysis
Historical Loss Severity
Subject Matter Expert Percentile

New   Delete
Edit   Save

Figure 5.7: Basel OPCAR Loss Severity Data Fitting

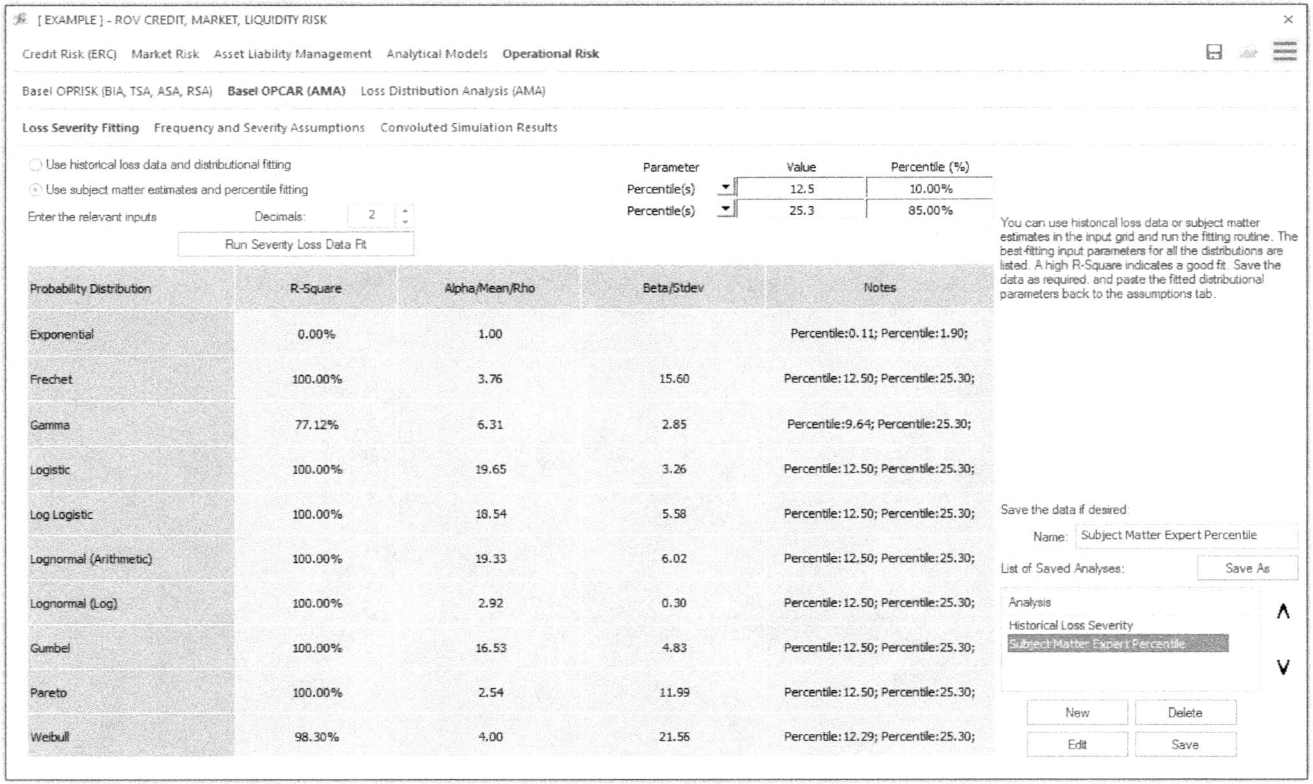

Figure 5.8: Basel OPCAR Loss Severity Percentile Fitting

SOFTWARE DOWNLOAD & INSTALL

As current versions of the software are continually updated, we highly recommend that you visit the Real Options Valuation, Inc., website and follow the instructions below to install the latest software applications.

- **Step 1**: Visit **www.realoptionsvaluation.com** and click on **Downloads** and **Download Software** (Figure A). You will be prompted to log in. Please first register if you are a first-time user (Figure B) and an automated e-mail will be sent to you within several minutes. (If you do not receive a registration e-mail after you register, then please send a note to support@realoptionsvaluation.com.) While waiting for the automated e-mail, browse this page and see the free getting started videos, case studies, and sample models you can download.

- **Step 2**: Return to this site and LOGIN using the login credentials you received via e-mail. Download and install the latest versions of **Risk Simulator** and **Real Options SLS** on this Web page. The download links, installation instructions, and Hardware ID information are also presented on this page (Figure C).

- **Step 3**: After installing the software, start Excel and you will see a Risk Simulator ribbon. Follow the instructions provided on the Web page to obtain and e-mail support@realoptionsvaluation.com your Hardware ID and mention the code "**MR3E 30 Days**" and you will be sent a free extended 30-day license to use both the Risk Simulator and Real Options SLS software.

Getting Started and Mo

www.realoptionsvaluation.com/getting started and modelling videos/

Testimonials | FAQ | Global Partners | Contact Us

English | Chinese (Simplified) | Chinese (Traditional) | French | German | Italian
Japanese | Korean | Portuguese (Brazil) | Russian | Spanish

0 items - $0.00

Real Options Valuation

CQRM CERTIFICATE | TRAINING | CONSULTING | SOFTWARE | BOOKS | DOWNLOADS | PURCHASE |

SOFTWARE DOWNLOADS

GETTING STARTED AND
MODELING VIDEOS

PRODUCT BROCHURES

SAMPLE MODELS

WHITEPAPERS AND CASE STUDIES

DOWNLOAD CENTER

You can also visit our mirror download site if you have problems downloading from this page.

Welcome to Real Options Valuation, Inc.'s download center. Here you will be able to download versions of the software you have purchased (license information required to install these full versions), product brochures, case ... ple training videos to help you get started in using our software, as well as sample Excel models to use with Risk Simulator and Re... ...ftware.

GETTING STARTED AND MODELING VIDEOS

The following are some live-motion and voice narrated videos which are playable on your computer using Windows Media Player or other video players capable of WMV playback. You can simply click on any of these links below to view the streaming videos.

ROV SOFTWARE GETTING STARTED VIDEOS

We also have some more detailed Risk Analysis and Risk Simulator software getting started videos that you can download and watch. These videos total about 2 hours. For even more detailed training, please check out our set of 12 Training DVDs (over 30 hours) or our hands-on Certified in Risk Management seminars (4 days). The following are updated detailed getting started videos on Risk Simulator, featuring all the new tools such as Auto ARIMA, GARCH, JS Curves, Cubic Spline, Maximum Likelihood, Data Diagnostics, Statistical Analysis, Modeling Toolkit, and more...

Figure A: Step 1 – Software download site

DOWNLOAD CENTER

You can also visit our mirror download site if you have problems downloading from this page.

Welcome to Real Options Valuation, Inc.'s download center. Here you will be able to download trial versions of our software, full versions of the software you have purchased (license information required to install these full versions), product brochures, case studies and white papers, and sample training videos to help you get started in using our software, as well as sample Excel models to use with Risk Simulator and Real Options Super Lattice Solver software.

YOU ARE REQUIRED TO LOGIN TO VIEW THIS PAGE.

Username

Password

LOG IN   REGISTER

Figure B: Register if you are a first-time visitor

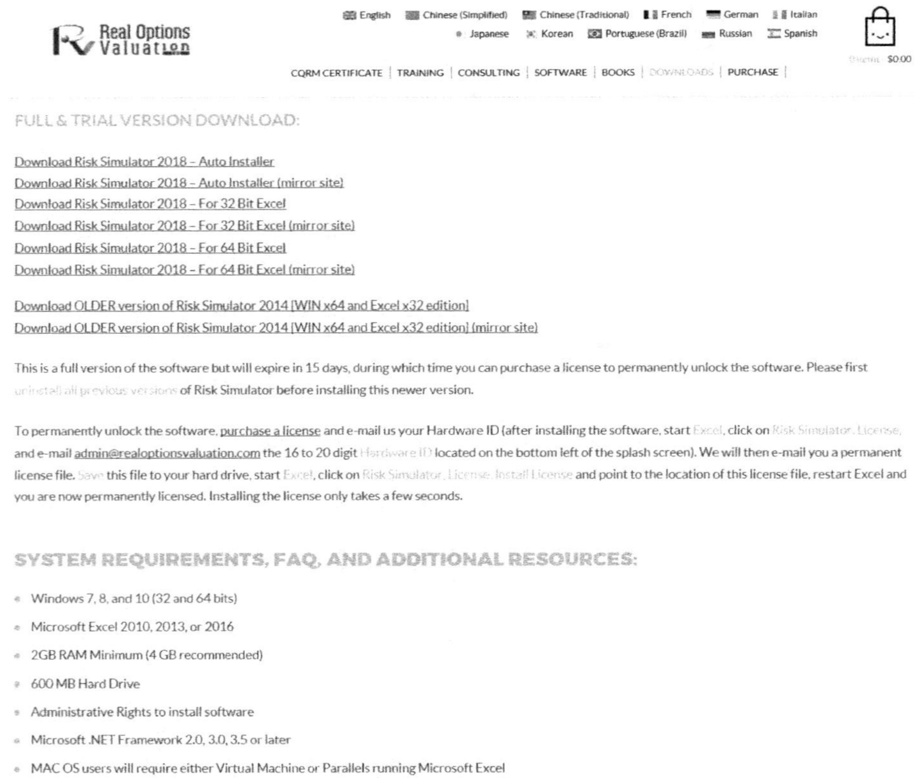
Real Options Valuation
English
Chinese (Simplified)
Chinese (Traditional)
French
German
Italian
Japanese
Korean
Portuguese (Brazil)
Russian
Spanish
$0.00
CQRM CERTIFICATE | TRAINING | CONSULTING | SOFTWARE | BOOKS | DOWNLOADS | PURCHASE |
FULL & TRIAL VERSION DOWNLOAD:
Download Risk Simulator 2018 – Auto Installer
Download Risk Simulator 2018 – Auto Installer (mirror site)
Download Risk Simulator 2018 – For 32 Bit Excel
Download Risk Simulator 2018 – For 32 Bit Excel (mirror site)
Download Risk Simulator 2018 – For 64 Bit Excel
Download Risk Simulator 2018 – For 64 Bit Excel (mirror site)
Download OLDER version of Risk Simulator 2014 [WIN x64 and Excel x32 edition]
Download OLDER version of Risk Simulator 2014 [WIN x64 and Excel x32 edition] (mirror site)
This is a full version of the software but will expire in 15 days, during which time you can purchase a license to permanently unlock the software. Please first uninstall all previous versions of Risk Simulator before installing this newer version.
To permanently unlock the software, purchase a license and e-mail us your Hardware ID (after installing the software, start Excel, click on Risk Simulator, License, and e-mail admin@realoptionsvaluation.com the 16 to 20 digit Hardware ID located on the bottom left of the splash screen). We will then e-mail you a permanent license file. Save this file to your hard drive, start Excel, click on Risk Simulator, License, Install License and point to the location of this license file, restart Excel and you are now permanently licensed. Installing the license only takes a few seconds.
SYSTEM REQUIREMENTS, FAQ, AND ADDITIONAL RESOURCES:
Windows 7, 8, and 10 (32 and 64 bits)
Microsoft Excel 2010, 2013, or 2016
2GB RAM Minimum (4 GB recommended)
600 MB Hard Drive
Administrative Rights to install software
Microsoft .NET Framework 2.0, 3.0, 3.5 or later
MAC OS users will require either Virtual Machine or Parallels running Microsoft Excel

Figure C: Download links and hardware ID instructions

INDEX

www.ingramcontent.com/pod-product-compliance
Lightning Source LLC
Chambersburg PA
CBHW060036210326
41520CB00009B/1146